Castles *of* G
and the Clyde

Gordon W. Mason

GOBLINSHEAD
Musselburgh

The Castles of Glasgow
and the Clyde

First Published 2000
© Gordon W. Mason

Published by GOBLINSHEAD
130B Inveresk Road, Musselburgh EH21 7AY, Scotland
Tel: 0131 665 2894 Fax: 0131 653 6566
Email: goblinshead@sol.co.uk

British Library Cataloguing in Publication Data
A catalogue record for this book is available from the British
Library.

ISBN 1 899874 18 6

Typeset by GOBLINSHEAD using Desktop Publishing

Other books on castles and related areas by Goblinshead
Castles of Scotland 3E (pbk) £15.95
Castles of Scotland 3E (hbk) £25.00
Wee Guide to Castles and Mansions of Scotland £3.95
Wee Guide to Haunted Castles of Scotland £3.95
Castle Touring Guide: West and Heart of Fife £4.95
Wee Guide to Old Churches and Abbeys of Scotland £3.95
Haunted Places of Scotland £7.50

Contents

Preface

As an eight-year-old, I became absorbed by stories of Robert the Bruce. One day I read in an old history book that he had died at Cardross. I was taken with this idea. My Gran lived at Craigendoran, and every Saturday my parents and I got on 'The Blue Train' to gran's and the penultimate stop was Cardross. Robert the Bruce died near my Gran's house, wow!

Thereafter my weekends down the Clyde took on new meaning, and from Dalreoch to Craigendoran my gaze, formerly fixed on the beautiful Firth, turned inland. I started taking my bike on the train, spending whole summer holidays searching for Bruce's Castle, finding others, but not his. Thirty years later, I've a pretty good idea where it was, and wasn't, but I've learned about a few others on the way. This book contains much of that, within the area described.

I would like to thank Martin Coventry for the invitation to expand the descriptions and material for this area from his own *The Castles of Scotland*, as well as Joyce Miller of Goblinshead. Also Mr and Mrs Gareth Edwards to whom thanks are due for allowing their property to be photographed.

Thanks also to my wife, Janette, for her patience and for allowing me to indulge in this second of my obsessions (the first is fishing), and my daughter Nicola, for her own special contributions.

Finally, as thanks for their encouragement and inspiration, may I dedicate this book to my late parents, Tom and Ina.

GWM, Drumsagard, January 2000

How to Use the Book

An introductory section describes the development of castle roles and architecture from the earliest times. It includes a historical perspective, relating the fashions and requirements of castle building in relation to national events.

A map shows the distribution of mottes within the area, the narrative describing the reasoning behind this, and including many place name origins.

Regional maps indicate the dispersal locations and quality of castle sites within each area. These areas are divided according to modern boundaries, ancient links, and cultural ties. The areas are:

- The City of Glasgow
- Renfrewshire
- North Lanarkshire
- South Lanarkshire
- The Lennox and East Dunbartonshire

If touring and exploring sites within a particular area, then this is the place to start. The gazetteer section can then be used to discover the history, architecture, ownership and legend associated with each. Each entry will provide a rough guide and directions to the site, and exact position when established, by Ordnance Survey sheet number and grid reference. An architectural description then follows, with historical narrative and legend completing the entry.

The 'star rating' system is as follows:

* = nothing or virtually nothing remains of the original castle.

** = part of the castle survives, although it is quite ruinous or what remains is incorporated into another building.

*** = substantial part of the castle survives, either as a ruin, or altered to form part of another building.

**** = most of the original castle survives and/or it is particularly large, interesting or representative.
The price rating for entry to properties is as follows:
£ = up to £3.50; ££ = £3.50-£5.00; £££ = more than £5.00.

Some family names (such as Semple rather than Sempill and Stewart instead of Stuart) have been standardised throughout the book because of the complexities of spelling.

The inclusion of a site does not authorise access, many are on private ground, others are still used as homes. For many sites access is denied. Please respect other people's property when going exploring: it only takes one visitor to upset a landowner and no one else will be allowed on the land. All the data has been checked as far as is possible, and visiting arrangements are described where they exist. However, many of these sites are not worth visiting because of the nature of the site. Either nothing remains, or because the defensive nature of castle sites makes access a risky business. Not all of these sites have been visited (it could take a lifetime to do that) but many are not developed as visitor attractions since any visit will be unexpected. It would not be the first time that the author was looked upon as an item of curiosity by a farmer who could not understand why an apparently rational man would want to roam over his wee bit rubble in the corner of his midden!
   It should be pointed out that because of the defensive nature of sites and the decaying nature of many structures, castle sites can be dangerous places. The author and publisher cannot be held responsible for any misplaced sense of adventure harboured by the reader. Finally a warning, particularly relevant to sites on farms: beware of the dog!!

Introduction

and

Development of

Castles

Newark Castle

Corehouse Castle

Introduction

This book is derived from *The Castles of Scotland* by Martin Coventry. Martin conceived the idea of writing a large book containing as much detail as was available on each site in his book. In the end this would not have proved viable, and so this is one in a series of smaller books covering different areas of Scotland. There is a similar aim, to list all known sites, and describing in greater detail – when possible – the history, the architecture, the ownership, and the legend associated with each castle or fortified house.

In this volume it is intended to describe all the castles which stand or stood within the watershed of the River Clyde and its tributaries. The castles appear within an alphabetical gazetteer, and on a series of maps covering the area described. This coverage consists of the entire shire of Renfrew, as it was during the castle construction period, and the castles of the City of Glasgow. To the north are covered fortified sites from Kilcreggan, around the coast to the River Leven and up to the shores of Loch Lomond. Then by Endrick, into the Campsie Fells and naturally to the south of the Fells through the Glazert valley, Kelvin valley, and the Cumbernauld/Kilsyth area. The castles of North Lanarkshire and lastly those of South Lanarkshire will complete the picture.

It is worth noting that in defining each area conventional boundaries have not necessarily been followed. A mixture of the ancient and the modern have been used, often providing variance where local contacts could not separate a group of sites. Local identity has also been taken into account, as well as ancient influence.

But what is a castle? Most people will think of Dumbarton in this area, a large fortress-like building with cannon guarding the approaches to foreboding walls. Then Crookston, a tall pile atop a steep hill surrounded by a ditch and overseeing what was once countryside stretching as far as the eye could see. It provided a view interrupted only by the ecclesiastical centres of Govan and its superior seat of Glasgow. But what of Provanhall, recognised easily as an ancient house, but as a castle?

A castle was any building designed to be defended by those living within and usually the seat of a landowner. A ditch is a defensive feature, as is a surrounding wall, a gunloop, a spiral stair, or turnpike, specifically designed to allow the defender upstairs a free swing with a sword, while the intruder was impeded by the central pillar. Other features include placing the main entrance on the first floor, and accessing it by way of a removable ladder, or having the door in the re-entrant of an L-plan building in order that covering fire could protect it from two sides. The presence of a single feature defines a castle, and as a result an enormous variety of defendable buildings are described as such. There must have been thousands of castles in Scotland, but to determine that a particular site had a defendable building can take many days or months of searching ancient books and records, hoping that some description of the nature of the building still exists. Often it does not, and although all the clues are there – long history, occupation by a reasonably wealthy family, a grant of land by the reigning monarch or feudal superior – it still cannot be said for certain. Some sites have been included since it is far more probable that the house was fortified than not, many possible sites are omitted because as yet there is not enough evidence to support an entry. There are many red herrings: the word castle in a name does not mean that it was.

The Victorians were particularly fond of romanticising their mansions by describing them as castles, as well as alluding to a grandeur that may have improved their lot socially. Sites such as Craigrownie or the second Balloch Castle can prove disappointing for those seeking true castles. For many the earthwork which represents the last vestige of the Balloch Castle of the great medieval Earls of Lennox is a much more rewarding find than the adjacent 'modern' house, giving a sense of history and atmosphere to the area.

The reverse situation may also mislead, a great pile such as Finlaystone House appears to all intents and purposes to be an altered Georgian mansion, but discounting this site would be to ignore hundreds of years of history, and confirmation that a castle once occupied the site. Indeed, the concentration of known sites is very uneven: North Lanarkshire has the least, and South Lanarkshire by far the most. There are several reasons for this. The first was the predominant ownership of land by the pre-Reformation church in Scotland. From Govan to the Gorbals, from Partick to Provan, and then neighbouring Monklands. These were all church lands.

In most areas of the country the Reformation meant a large increase in land ownership for those who had supported the Protestant cause. There was a resultant increase in castle building on former church land throughout the country in the second half of the 16th and early 17th centuries. Understandable, since the church had owned the greater share of the most fertile lands in the country, and the new owners sought to protect their newly won wealth from greedy and acquisitive neighbours.

The scene in Glasgow and North Lanarkshire differed though. Merchants from the city were discovering their own source of wealth via a developing trade with the Americas, due in part to the new fashion of smoking tobacco. These merchants, rather than feeling threatened by their neighbours, wanted to keep up with the Joneses, with security provided by the ongoing development of a standing army and local urban militia. The result, particularly on the south bank towards Govan, was a rash of large country mansions such as Ibrox, Ibroxholm, Plantation, Bellahouston and so on.

In the Monklands, a few similar properties began to appear, such as Drumpellier House. But the Monklands were ripe for other development, and in the centuries that followed entrepreneurs began to invest in the digging up of the countryside. Coal production, begun on a small scale by the clerics, was rapidly expanded to fire the furnaces of new iron works and to fuel the mansions of the city. This destroyed much of the surrounding countryside, as did the expansion of the city and towns, and as a result many sites have been lost. Numerous properties of possible interest were destroyed, and since most were of little historical importance, only names survive with no written record to verify the nature of the building.

Elsewhere patches of agricultural land survived the onslaught of industry. Renfrewshire, the Lennox, East Dunbartonshire, and South Lanarkshire had considerable mineral wealth, but retained importance as areas of farming activity. Hence the survival rate of the buildings was higher outside the industrial heartland. These differences have been deliberately maintained in the division of the maps, not simply to reflect the cultural and economic divisions between areas, but to impress the effect on the distribution of identifiable sites.

But what of the future: will these ancient buildings survive? As the most characteristic examples of our own brand of architecture their importance cannot be underestimated. The attractiveness of sites such as Edinburgh or Eilean Donan to the tourists who have become an enormously important part of our economy is obvious. However, the smaller houses and ruins around the country add the mystery and atmosphere which must, to these important guests, be a lure to return. They spread the interest across the land, adding character to scenery so often devastated by our industrial past.

The preservation of as many buildings as possible is extremely important, not simply economically, but culturally, as our national identity disappears in a sea of Tartan and Malt. The work of Historic Scotland, the Historic Monuments Department and The National Trust For Scotland is as essential as it is to be admired, but it would be impossible to create the revenue required to retain the number of buildings involved.

The alternative is private enterprise, and it has become an increasingly popular investment to restore an old tower house as a home, or even as a business premises. Such projects should be encouraged, and although the initial outlay must be tremendous, the returns in terms of self-satisfaction, pride and more practically resale price appear to be rewarding.

One consequence is that those of us with a lower income can still admire the work of these entrepreneurs as they enhance our environments, while wishing that there were more like them on our local councils.

Our elected representatives have in the last few decades ordered or condoned the demolition of many buildings, ignoring the investment potential of restoration or often simply to free land for development. Glasgow itself since 1960 has lost Drumry Peel, Garscadden House, and Castlemilk, while Cathcart is reduced to a stump. Rutherglen has lost Stonelaw and Farme, Coatbridge has lost Old Monkland and the list could go on. While acknowledging that such buildings are not always within the direct responsibility of a council, they should be implored to exercise their duty of care and a little more thought to get the best from these uniquely Scottish buildings.

The Development of Castles

The west central region of Scotland is peppered with the remains of hill forts and duns, which represent the earliest defendable sites. These generally consist of a series of ditches, banks and walls, which surrounded settlements. The earliest stone 'castles' in Scotland are the brochs which appear predominantly in the north and the Highland west. It is widely assumed that Celtic peoples were responsible for the construction of these stone towers, which most certainly date from pre-Roman times. Some survived in use until the 17th century.

The broch consisted of a double-shelled dry stone wall, up to 50 ft in height forming a circular tower. A single narrow entrance, wide enough to permit only single file passage, was controlled by a sturdy wooden door and a guard chamber just within. The internal structure was of wood, with a stair and several floors supporting a roof or platform from which projectiles could be thrown upon an attacking force. Rather than providing residences, brochs seem to have been built as bolt holes, possibly used when Roman slavers were raiding, where the local population and their animals would flee in times of attack. There would normally have been subsidiary buildings around the base, or within easy reach, where perhaps the inhabitants lived their daily lives. The broch appears to have been the central refuge of the community in times of strife. Another hypothesis argues that the internal space within the broch was inadequate to support the livestock, and that only the people themselves were sheltered within. The argument continues that, since the majority of the 500 or so identified sites are around the coast, the brochs were built by fisher folk, which seems to reinforce the seaborne raiders theory, though does not explain brochs with inland sites. Alternatively it has been suggested that they were constructed by a group of roving masons by way of promotional work, though the sheer number of structures involved appears to negate this idea. You may even have your own theory.

Whichever argument is preferred, the aura of mystery surrounding our ancient past is certainly enhanced by the surviving examples. There are few surviving brochs in the region of the Clyde, the peoples south of the Antonine Wall requiring less protection as they had come under the influence of the Roman Empire.

Following the period of Roman activity, these lands were ruled predominantly by the Britons of Strathclyde. Their kingdom stretched from the 'Clach nam Breatuinn' (stone of the Britons) in Glen Falloch at the head of Loch Lomond, past their capital at Dumbarton (fort of the Britons) and down the west coast as far as North Wales. The legendary King Arthur was one of their number. At Castlehill in Dumbarton a mound preserved by The National Trust as the site of the death place of Robert the Bruce (likely erroneously) is referred to as Arthur's Castle on old Ordnance Survey maps and in several ancient records. This ancient mound may in fact be one example of the earliest structures remaining which could be called castles: a motte.

In the 12th century it was a deliberate policy of the Scottish royal house to befriend the Normans of England, renowned as the most efficient and feared warriors of their day. This policy was most vehemently applied by David I, who was educated in England and raised at their court. There were two distinct waves of settlement as the Normans were brought north and granted lands to strengthen the military and administrative abilities of the nation. The first wave brought Flemish and Norman settlers to south west Scotland, mainly Galloway and Clydesdale, and in the second wave from about 1160 most settled north of the Forth. Obviously this first wave provides the interest for this book. It included families who in later years were to be identified by name as Scottish. The Stewarts, descended from Fitzallan, brought in as High Steward to David I and based at Renfrew, later becoming the royal house. De Brus further south being Scotticised to Bruce, settling Annandale though eventually having an enormous effect on the country as a whole when their most famous son became king. Comyn, the enemy of Bruce, later Cumming or Stirling. The Flemish families settled in Biggar and upper Clydesdale became the Flemings – and so the list goes on.

The administrative centre and main residence of each settling lord was the motte and bailey castle. This was a rapidly built and readily defended structure in the days when Norman knights on heavy horse, heavily armoured and armed with lances, were the most advanced and powerful tools of war available. It consisted of an earthen mound, often layered alternately with stones to provide stability, built steeply within the perimeter of a deep ditch. Atop this mound would have been a wooden tower as the main residence of the lord. The whole was surrounded by a larger area known as the bailey, containing a living area for the garrison and livestock, again surrounded by a ditch and supporting subsidiary buildings such as a chapel, brewery, and stables. The defences were supplemented by palisades, or wooden walls, surrounding both the motte and the bailey, the ditches filled with water creating a moat, or heavy spikes set into the ground so thickly as to provide an impenetrable barrier to charging heavy cavalry.

There were many variations to motte and bailey design. The motte of the Somervilles at Carnwath was excavated, revealing that the tower was entered via a radial tunnel through the base of the motte, and then by a central well and ladder to the centre of the block house. The motte of Sir James Graham's castle overlooking the Carron Valley Reservoir was sculpted from a natural spur of the hill, and had a dry moat 33 ft wide and 10 ft deep. The motte was a rough square of about 75 ft each side and would have been entered by a wooden drawbridge from the hillside. The size and shape of these structures also varied: Maiden Castle, at the foot of the Campsie Fells at Lennoxtown, was of the traditional Christmas pudding shape with a small summit area, while along the road at Kilsyth is Balcastle, a large motte shaped as an upturned frying pan, with a circular summit about 90 ft in diameter.

Nowadays the remains of these structures provide unusually contoured, though attractive, additions to our landscape, mellowed by the action of nature over the centuries. But in their heyday their appearance would have been a blight, appearing as mounds of raw black earth against a gentle green countryside. Add to this a foreboding array of spikes, aimed to threaten those outside from every angle, and the stench of rotten corpses from the nearby Gallowhill: all presenting a fierce and sinister symbol of the power of the lord within.

Mottes were built in regions which had traditionally provided unrest and rebellion for the nation, and this is why David I had made these areas prime settlement targets for his new Norman aristocracy. These men had to earn their lands. They were held of the Crown in return for military service in the national cause, but they were also to provide stability within the country itself. Galloway, particularly, had persistently been a thorn in the side of Scottish rule, having their own lords who reigned as kings, and so as a priority was settled in the first phase. Lanarkshire, its close neighbour, must have been influenced by the Lords of Galloway, the hilly country in the Upper Clyde region acting as its north eastern border, and so there was prolific settlement in and around the upper reaches. The names of some of these men remain as those of villages: Roberton from Robert the Fleming, Thankerton and Symington from the brothers Tancard and Simon Loccard, while other settlers took their names from the lands, the Coulters and the Carmichaels as example. A note of caution though: there is evidence that, at least in the Clydesdale area, mottes were built as temporary residences at least until the 14th century. A motte at Moat, two miles south of Roberton, has been shown to have been built in the 14th century. When excavated it gave up pottery of this period from the ground below the moat, and cannot be attributed as the work of Robert the Fleming. It is thought to have been built by Mary of Stirling, who had supported the anti-Bruce faction throughout the reign of Robert I and David II, and who had been compelled to provide herself and her retinue with safe lodgings in the area.

As the river moves toward the Firth we come into a region traditionally threatened by the Western Isles (another once independent lordship), harried by Highlanders from north of the great fault line, and assailed from the sea by Vikings. They, until the Battle of Largs a century later, ruled much of the western seaboard from Ireland, the Isle of Man, and through the west Highlands and isles to Caithness and Sutherland, their very own south land, now the northern part of the Scottish mainland, as well as Orkney and Shetland.

And so David's policy of settlement extended, with a defensive line of mottes stretching from the royal fortress at Dumbarton, to that at Stirling. This medieval Maginot Line included Catter, Balfron, Fintry, Maiden Castle, Colzium and Balcastle. These guarded the natural travel ways from north to south, routes later used as drove roads by the cattlemen of the Highlands. The Firth itself was guarded by his loyal Steward, with properties at Inverkip, Dunoon, Rothesay, and Renfrew. The great Somerled, recognised as King of the Isles by Norway, had met his death in treacherous circumstances close to the last of these sites while threatening the peace of the area.

Compare this to the rich fertile regions of the Lothians where evidence of mottes is rare. Eventually to become the main killing field in the wars between Scotland and England, in David's day there was peace. David's sister was married to Henry I, the men had been reared and educated at the English Court, and David had been one of Henry's Earls, that of Huntingdon. Prior to his acceding to the throne he had been based in Carlisle, under Henry's authority, with a remit to quell his troublesome northern lands. The two then were understandably close, and no threat would have been perceived in the settled counties, with little need for demonstrations of military power at least until Henry's death in 1135. Indeed, after the Battle of the Standard in 1138, the border was considerably further south of Lothian than its modern counterpart: Cumbria and Northumberland becoming part of the Scottish kingdom.

But Norman settlement was only part of his master plan to redesign the administration of the land. At the same time he devised the parish system of local government, and built many of the abbeys and priories of the country, making generous grants of land, in Lanarkshire and elsewhere, to various sects of the Roman Church, which had been introduced by his mother Saint Margaret to replace the traditional Celtic form of worship. And so David I set the scene for Scotland and its administration, and it was one that was to last for 450 years, barring a few enforced English incursions. It is not then until the closing days of the 12th century that the first stone castles of the medieval age began to appear.

One of the earliest confirmed datings of a surviving stone castle is Castle Sween, built around 1200, give or take a decade. These early castles consisted simply of a high thick curtain wall or enceinte, which supported a parapet from which the entry and walls could be defended. In these earliest castles the enclosed courtyard would initially have supported lean-to wooden buildings, the largest functioning as the main hall and lord's residence. These simple structures evolved as new defensive features were developed and incorporated in response to the increasing sophistication of assault weapons and tactics, a process continuing even today in modern warfare. Initially corner towers would have been added, gatehouses, and then stone keeps, with the result that the remaining castles from this period require close study to reveal how the surviving structure came about over the centuries. These additional features became part and parcel of the design of each new castle, individual buildings reflecting the wealth and social standing of its lord.

Bothwell Castle is an excellent example of this, despite having never been completed to its original plan. Castles took a great many man hours to build, accumulating in years of construction time. A period of peace was therefore required in order that the structure could be completed without the threat of attack in the interim. It would have been a great investment for a lord to contemplate, peace allowing him to accrue the necessary funds. The actual work force would have included a number of expensive and highly skilled tradesmen, masons, carpenters, armourers, not to mention a multitude of labourers. In its original planned form Bothwell would have become one of the grandest residences in the land.

The great keep, or donjon, displays stonework of great quality, and its sheer size is a statement of the status of the de Moravia (Moray or Murray) family. If the Wars of Independence had not interceded, the intended internal area would have exceeded any contemporary Scottish castle. Much of it had reached only foundation level at the time of Edward I's invasion in 1296. By then all that had been completed was the donjon and adjacent prison tower, with interceding wall. Even in this incomplete condition it took a siege of 14 months for the Scots to regain Bothwell from English hands in 1298.

The Wars of Independence resulted in the deliberate policy of rendering indefensible all castles which could be held by an invader against the Scots. This policy was conceived by Robert the Bruce. Dumbarton and Berwick were to be the only exceptions among royal castles, although Bruce also built or strengthened castles such as at Tarbert in Kintyre. The consequence is that only the sections of buildings which were left in a repairable state survive as testament to the skill of the early medieval tradesmen.

Following the death of 'Good King Robert' in 1329 and the subsequent attempt to re-establish a Balliol monarchy, the Scots appear to have relearned the value of fortified residences. Simple keeps were the order of the day in the 14th century. These consisted of a tall square block normally within a courtyard, with exceptionally thick walls and battlements. There were as a rule three storeys, the basement having no communication with the other floors. The main entrance was by removable stair from the courtyard to the main hall on the first floor, the private quarters on the floor above entered by a narrow stair built within the structure of the wall. Often additional rooms were created within the walling, these mural chambers serving as smaller guest rooms or as a garderobe (toilet). The roofs were of stone, a parapet providing a fighting platform around the wall tops, and slabbing the remainder to protect against attack with fire.

As always, the grander the house the greater its lord, with later additions masking the original building. Mearns, Duntreath and the original keep at Murdostoun represent three excellent examples within this area, while Crookston is an exception, illustrating aptly – that as symbols of power – the lord's castle tended to reflect the wealth available to him.

It is worth mentioning at this point that wealth was not necessarily a monetary commodity in these early days, but a direct reflection of political influence, and the fighting manpower available under the lord's superiority. Crookston is unusual among the castles of this period, having had a massive main central block of at least three storeys, further strengthened by four corner towers, providing a rough X-plan. It does not appear to have had a courtyard as such, subsidiary buildings being within the perimeter of the deep and wide ditch which protected its predecessor: the ring work of Robert Croc of Neilston.

Until 1400 the expense of building stone castles limited their construction and ownership to the upper echelons of society. However, as part of a systematic reduction of the power of the great lords, the crown passed an act of parliament in 1401 which took the baronies directly, though independently, under royal control whenever the superior earldom fell to the Crown. This division of these great properties allowed the granting of smaller, though substantial, parcels of land to lesser lords, and heralded an explosion of activity in the construction of lesser houses. These new lords were eager to display their new found status and as a result the traditional Scottish tower house was born.

Later, in 1535, another act of parliament demanded that each land holder 'on the borders or inland' was obliged to build a barmkin, a small courtyard, with a tower within if required as residence. The result was a two year flurry of activity on the building front.

Finance and the standing of the resident lord determined the complexity and size of the tower house. Initially a single tower, then more commonly an L-plan in the 16th century, later developing added protection and extra living space by additional towers to create the Z-plan, T-plan and E-plan. The tower house is the most frequently occurring variety of Scottish castle. Each was surrounded by a barmkin, which supported lesser buildings such as stables and stores. Usually of three or four storeys, early access was to a basement with vaulted ceiling, often with no access to the floors above. The main entrance to the simple tower would, like the stockier keeps of previous years, have been to the first floor by a removable stair. The standard arrangement provided one room per floor, the first floor as the hall, and private quarters above. A good example was Drumry Peel, now sadly demolished.

L-plan castles provided better defensive ability and improved domestic planning. They began to appear from the early 16th century, either as new buildings, or extended single towers. The position of the main entrance within the re-entrant made it possible to place the door at ground floor level, covering fire being given from gunloops at strategic positions on the adjacent walls. Additional defensive features were various caphouses, bartizans, parapets and open rounds. An iron gate or yett protected the door. The hall would have remained on the first floor, though a more complex arrangement of numerous rooms to each storey was now possible. The increasing sophistication and tastes of the gentry now demanded wine cellars, numerous bedrooms, kitchens, food stores, and separate stair towers. There are many superb examples within the area, such as Jerviston, Jerviswood and Haggs. As these tastes developed into the latter part of the 16th century, extensions were added to create the more complex structures of E-, Z- and T-plan, each geometrically enhancing the defensive capability of the building.

Following the Union of the Crowns in 1603, defensive features should have become less necessary. Wisely, the Scots were slow to give up the fortified design of their homes. It proved a sensible precaution as religious war, civil war, and the various Jacobite rebellions were to show. By the latter part of the 17th century, fortifications were gradually omitted as comfort and spaciousness became the main driving force. Many castles were extended until they eventually became the lesser part of grand mansions, such as at Finlaystone.

A development of the 15th and 16th centuries was the arrival and widespread use of gunpowder. Financially the viability of defending against artillery was limited. For the vast majority to reflect this new destructive power in the nature of their buildings meant defence by use of small arms, muskets, and small cannon or mortars. A few wealthy individuals were able to afford defence against larger cannon, creating a new challenge in castle design.

Craignethan stands out as a local example. The defensive works of Sir James Hamilton ('the Bastard of Finnart') were built as a showpiece. In his role as Master of Works to King James V he was in a position of considerable influence and power, and his name will crop up frequently. Sir James designed and built Craignethan, from the old castle of Draffane, to create a state of the art fortress with many unique design features, curiously in a position where all of these defences could be outflanked by artillery. The ridge opposite would have provided a perfect platform from which the bombards of the day could have strafed the entire site. But then it was built to display what could be done, as this entrepreneurial character endeavoured to amass a personal fortune.

The period 1560-1650 brought the bastle house, a simple fortified farmhouse which defended stock and inhabitants against the reivers of the borderland and Clydesdale. These structures varied in character a great deal, and so any description is bound to be a generalisation. Their purpose was as that of the brochs, while also used as a main residence of the land holder, and as a barn.

The ground floor was the animal shed entered by a single door, usually wooden, which could be defended from the floor above. In some there was a vaulted ceiling. The upper floor consisted of the living quarters, reached by an internal stair. A garret was standard. There was not normally a courtyard, though a collection of outbuildings clustered around would have formed a yard of sorts. Often there were earthworks or dykes around the whole. The bastle house was the best building in the farmstead, and represented the working core and main residence. Most have disappeared, though ruins survive in some of the far-flung corners of the upper ward of Clydesdale. Glendorch is one of the more substantial ruins, and had a vaulted ground floor. An example was uncovered at Thorril during the M74 fieldwork project in 1990. Others stood at Snar,

Nemphlar, Glenochar and Windgate among many.

As the period of the fortified house closed, the creation of fortresses built to sustain a full time garrison from the standing army became necessary. The example of Dumbarton stands out, losing much of its ancient stonework and character in favour of a more martial design. Gun batteries, barracks, and cell blocks replaced the personal touch of the Governor who had on occasion to provide lodging for his royal patron. In short, it became less of a home, and more a military installation.

The lands surrounding Glasgow and the Clyde have a huge variety of castles, which are now covered on an individual basis.

Maps

Map 1 – City of Glasgow

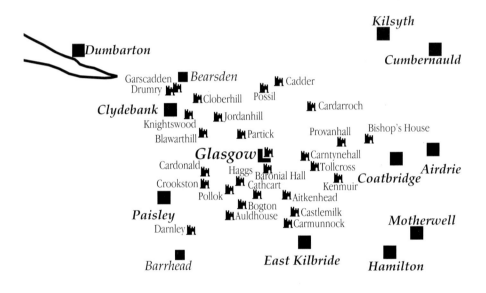

Locations are approximate.

City of Glasgow

Map 2 – Renfrewshire

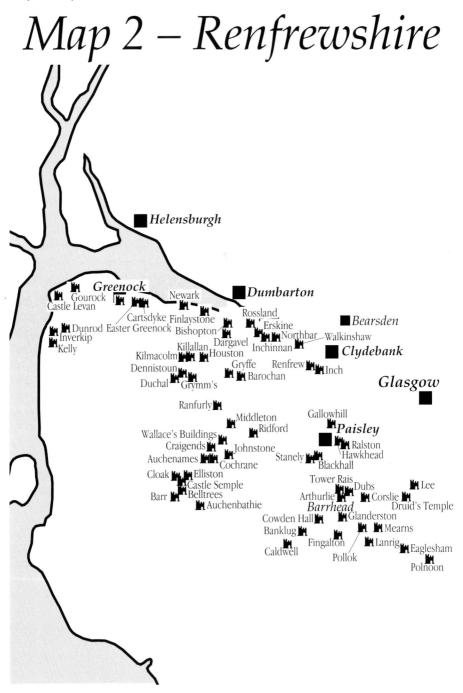

Locations are approximate.

Renfrewshire

Map 3 – North Lanarkshire

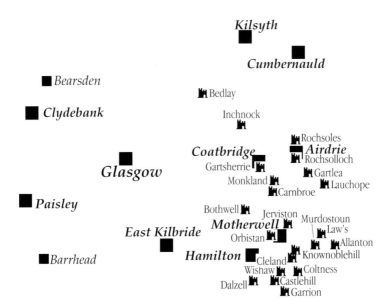

Kilsyth

Cumbernauld

■ *Bearsden*

Bedlay

■ *Clydebank*

Inchnock

Rochsoles

Coatbridge   *Airdrie*

Gartsherrie   Rochsolloch

Glasgow   Gartlea

Monkland   Lauchope

Carnbroe

■ *Paisley*

Bothwell   Jerviston   Murdostoun

East Kilbride   *Motherwell*   Law's

Orbistan   Allanton

■ *Barrhead*   *Hamilton*   Cleland   Knownoblehill

Wishaw   Coltness

Dalzell   Castlehill

Garrion

Locations are approximate.

North Lanarkshire

Map 4 – South Lanarkshire

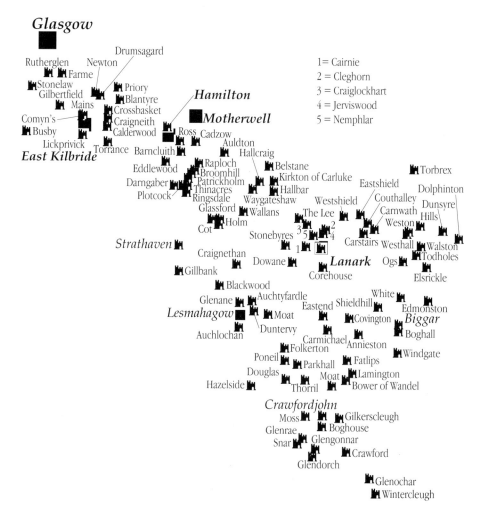

Glasgow

Drumsagard

Rutherglen Newton

Stonelaw Farme

Gilbertfield Priory

Mains Blantyre

Comyn's Crossbasket

Busby Craigneith

Lickprivick Calderwood

East Kilbride Torrance Barncluith

Hamilton

Motherwell

Ross Cadzow

Auldton

Hallcraig

1 = Cairnie
2 = Cleghorn
3 = Craiglockhart
4 = Jerviswood
5 = Nemphlar

Eddlewood Raploch Belstane Torbrex
Broomhill Kirkton of Carluke
Darngaber Patrickholm Hallbar Eastshield Dolphinton
Plotcock Thinacres Westshield Couthalley Dunsyre
Ringsdale Waygateshaw Carnwath Hills
Glassford Wallans The Lee Weston
Cot Holm 3 2 Carstairs Westhall Walston
Strathaven Stonebyres 5 4 Todholes
Craignethan 1 *Lanark* Ogs Elsrickle
Gillbank Dowane Corehouse
Blackwood White
Glenane Auchtyfardle Eastend Shieldhill Edmonston
Lesmahagow Moat Covington *Biggar*
Auchlochan Duntervy Boghall
Carmichael Annieston Windgate
Poneil Folkerton
Douglas Parkhall Fatlips
Hazelside Moat Lamington
Thorril Bower of Wandel
Crawfordjohn
Moss Gilkerscleugh
Glenrae Boghouse
Snar Glengonnar
Glendorch Crawford
Glenochar
Wintercleugh

Locations are approximate.

South Lanark-shire

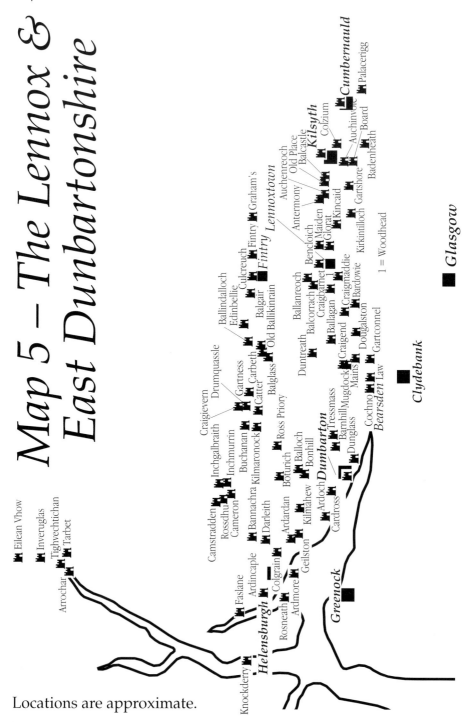

Map 5 – The Lennox & East Dunbartonshire

Eilean Vhow

Inveruglas

Tighwechtichan

Tarbet

Arrochar

Faslane

Ardincaple

Colgrain

Rosneath

Ardmore

Knockderry

Helensburgh

Camstradden

Rossdhu

Cameron

Bannachra

Kilmaronock

Darleith

Inchgalbraith

Inchmurrin

Buchanan

Ardardan

Geilston

Kilmahew

Cardross

Ardoch

Boturich

Balloch

Bonhill

Dumbarton

Craigievern

Drumquassle

Gartness

Catter

Carbeth

Balglass

Ross Priory

Ballindalloch

Edinbellie

Balgair

Old Ballikinrain

Culcreuch

Fintry Lennoxtown

Fintry, Graham's

Duntreath

Ballanreoch

Balcorrach

Craigparnet

Craigend

Ballagan

Craigmaddie

Mains

Dougalston

Bardowie

Gartconnel

Barnhill

Mugdock

Dunglass

Tressmass

Cochno

Bearsden Law

Auchenreoch

Antermony

Bencloich

Maiden

Kincaid

Glorat

Kirkintilloch

Gartshore

Old Place

Balcastle

Kilsyth

Colzium

Auchinvole

Board

Badenheath

Cumbernauld

Palacerigg

1 = Woodhead

Clydebank

Glasgow

Greenock

Locations are approximate.

28

The Lennox & East Dunbartonshire

Map 6 – Mottes

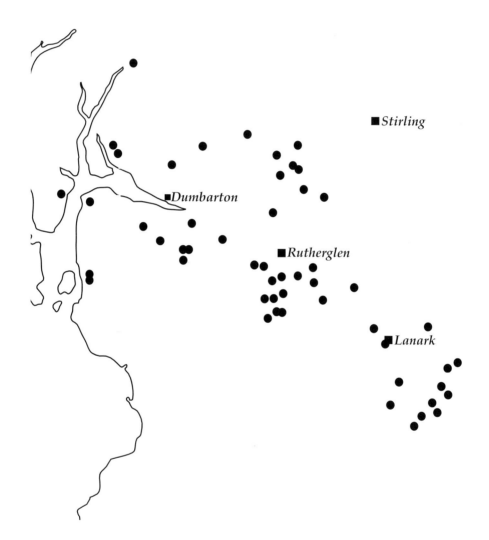

Locations are approximate.

Alphabetical Guide to the Castles A–Z

A

Aitkenhead Castle (*)

City Of Glasgow
Ruin or site   OS 64   NS 596603
In King's Park, Glasgow, 0.5 miles east of B766, at Aitkenhead House.
Site of a fortified house, replaced by a mansion.

Two properties existed carrying the name, one a straw-thatched cottage known as Meikle Aitkenhead, and this more substantial house of Aitkenhead.

Anciently part of Walter the Steward's great Renfrewshire estate, Robert II granted this portion to the Maxwells. At some point the estate was divided, though Meikle Aitkenhead was sold to the Hamiltons in 1611, then to the Gordons. A tower house appears on Bleau's Atlas of the 17th century.

Airdrie House (*)

North Lanarkshire
Ruin or site   OS 64   NS 749654
North of A89, at Monklands General Hospital, Airdrie.
Site of a house originally owned by the Cleland family, and from 1490 by the Hamiltons. Airdrie House, a Scots baronial mansion was built on the site, possibly incorporating part of an earlier structure.

One of the earliest stories, emanating from local legend, asserts that a Cleland (Keuland) of Airdrie was brother-in-law to William Wallace. While marshalling his forces the night before the disastrous Battle of Falkirk, Wallace and his army camped beside the house.

John Hamilton of the Torrance family gained Airdrie in 1490, and died at the Battle of Flodden in 1513. His son Methusalem was a foremost reformer and cousin to Patrick Hepburn, 'the first Scottish martyr', burned at the stake for heresy at St Andrews 1528. Gavin Hamilton of Airdrie was among the party involved in the attempted capture of the young James VI from Stirling Castle in 1571. Robert Hamilton of Airdrie supported the Covenant, and fought at the Battle of Drumclog. After the battle, Airdrie House was captured and used as a barracks for Claverhouse's dragoons. Hamilton had fled into exile, and on his return was imprisoned in the tollbooth of Edinburgh. On his release in 1693 Hamilton planned the town as a weaving centre. The estate passed to Lord Elphinstone, then to an American named Aitchson in 1769. Later it was owned by Sir John Wilson, until used as the local maternity hospital. It was demolished in 1964 when the new Monklands General Hospital was to be built.

Alcuith *see* **Dumbarton**

Allanton House (*)
North Lanarkshire
Ruin or site   OS 72   NS 838572
1.5 miles north east of
Newmains, by A71, at or
near Allanton.
Site of a castle which had
been incorporated into a
large mansion designed
by Gillespie Graham.
There was an extensive
garden with a picturesque
lake. The mansion was
completely demolished in
the 20th century.

Allanton House (1916) – demolished

Originally an estate of
Arbroath Abbey, Allanton came to the Stewarts. This family was descended
from Alexander the 4th High Steward. It was visited by Cromwell in 1650.

Alt Clut *see* **Dumbarton**

Annieston Castle (*)
South Lanarkshire
Ruin or site   OS 72   NS 997366
3 miles south west of Biggar, south of the Clyde, on minor road north of A72, 1 mile
north of Symington.
Site of a tower house.

Antermony Castle (*)
The Lennox & East Dunbartonshire
Ruin or site   OS 64   NS 668770
1 mile north of Kirkintilloch and 1 mile east of Milton of Campsie, on minor roads
north of A891, on north shore of Antermony Loch, at Antermony.
Site of a tower house of the Flemings, who had held the estate from 1424. It
passed to the Lennox family, but the castle was demolished in the 18th century
to clear the site for a new mansion, itself now demolished. The property had
passed to the Bell family.

Ardardan Castle (*)
The Lennox & East Dunbartonshire
Ruin or site   OS 63   NS 331785
1 mile west of Cardross and 2 miles south east of Helensburgh, south of A814, by
track and minor road, at the neck of Ardmore Point, at Ardardan.
Site of a tower house of the Nobles.
Other references: Ferme

Ardencaple Castle *see* Ardincaple

Ardincaple Castle (*)
The Lennox & East Dunbartonshire
Ruin or site   OS 56   NS 283830
West of Helensburgh, on minor roads north of A814, at or near Ardencaple Farm.
Ardincaple Castle, once a large castellated mansion, incorporated an early castle of the MacAuleys. Some of the work was from as early as the 12th century,
but the whole building was pulled down in 1957.
   The MacAuleys had held the estate from the 13th century and were vassals of
the Campbells of Argyll. The castle was abandoned as a roofless ruin, then sold
to the Campbells in 1767. It was remodelled and extended in 1764 and 1772. It
had passed to the Colquhouns of Luss by 1890, but was demolished to allow
development of the site for Naval housing.
Other references: Ardencaple

Ardmore Castle (**)
The Lennox & East Dunbartonshire
Private   OS 63   NS 317785
2 miles west of Cardross, 2 miles south of Helensburgh, south of A814, by track and
minor roads, on Ardmore Point, on the north shore of the Firth of Clyde.
A castle here was rebuilt or replaced in 1654. It was then remodelled and extended as a mansion with a central battlemented tower in 1806. Three towers of
the 16th to 17th centuries survive, one with gunloops.
   It was a property of the Geils family until the 18th century, and is now managed by the Scottish Wildlife Trust. There is a nature trail. Ardmore was originally an island.
Other references: Hill of Ardmore

Ardoch Castle (*)
The Lennox & East Dunbartonshire
Ruin or site   OS 63   NS 364768
1.5 miles south east of Cardross, 2 miles west of Dumbarton, on minor road north of
A814, north of Ardoch, at Ardochmore Farm.
Site of the tower house of the Bontines. It passed by marriage to the Grahams of

Gartmore. They built Ardoch House to the south, a small mansion of 1840 with a round stair tower at one corner. One of its occupants was Robert Bontine Cunninghame Graham, first president of the Scottish Labour Party in 1888, and President of the National Party of Scotland in 1928.

Arrochar Castle (*)
The Lennox & East Dunbartonshire
Ruin or site   OS 56   NN 297044
In Arrochar, just east of Loch Long and A814, and south of A83, at the Cobbler Hotel.
The Cobbler Hotel has a date stone of 1697, the last remnant of the castle of the MacFarlanes which had previously occupied the site.

 MacFarlane of Arrochar sacked Boturich Castle in the early 16th century.

Arthurlie House (*)
Renfrewshire
Private   OS 64   NS 504588
Arthurlie Street, off A736, Barrhead.
The 19th century mansion was successor to a series of earlier structures. In 1372 Robert II granted the estate to a son of Pollok of that Ilk. He lost the estate, and in 1439 the lands were divided into West Arthurlie and Arthurlie. They were given to Ross of Hawkhead and Stewart of Castlemilk respectively. The Stewarts retained their lands until the 18th century. There may also have been a castle at West Arthurlie.
Other references: Nether Arthurlie, East Arthurlie

Auchenbathie Castle (*)
Renfrewshire
Ruin or site, OS 63 NS 397565
3.5 miles north east of Beith, near the junction of the B776 and a minor road, just west of Barcraig Reservoir.
A little rubble remains of this tower house of the Wallaces. Blind Harry states that the property was held by Sir Malcolm Wallace, father to Sir William. It is likely though that the motte to the north at NS 337713 was his seat, and that the family re-sited when deciding to build in stone.

 Near Barcraig is Auchenbothie House, a rambling harled castellated mansion of 1898 with towers, corbiesteps, turrets and dormer windows.
Other references: Barcraig

Auchenames Castle (*)
Renfrewshire
Ruin or site   OS 63   NS 395625
2 miles south of Bridge of Weir, on minor roads to the south of the A761, 0.5 miles

south west of Kilbarchan, at Auchenames.
Site of a much altered 14th century castle of the Crawfords.
   The family were granted the lands in 1320 by Robert II, and retained them until they sold the property in the 20th century.

Auchenreoch Castle (*)
The Lennox & East Dunbartonshire
Ruin or site   OS 64   NS 678767
3 miles south west of Kilsyth, just east and south of the junction of the A803, and A891, at or near Auchenreoch Mains.
Site of a 16th century tower house of the Kincaid family, which later passed to the Buchanans.

Auchenvole Castle *see* Auchinvole Castle

Auchenvoil Castle *see* Auchinvole Castle

Auchinbathie Castle *see* Auchenbathie Castle

Auchinames Castle *see* Auchenames Castle

Auchinreoch Castle *see* Auchenreoch Castle

Auchinvole Castle (**)
The Lennox & East Dunbartonshire
Private   OS 64   NS 714769
On south bank of River Kelvin, 0.5 miles south of Kilsyth, north of B8023, west of B802.
Much altered and extended, Auchinvole was a late 16th or early 17th century L-plan building with a vaulted basement. There was a very small stair turret corbelled out above third floor level, leading to a watch tower in the re-entrant. The basement contained a wide arched fireplace recessed into the gable. From there a wide turnpike stairway led to the second floor, and the upper floors via the stair wing. A bartizan topped one corner.

Auchinvole Castle

This entire structure was demolished a few years ago. There remains only three sides of a wall enclosing a large rectangular yard, possibly the remains of a walled garden. This reaches no great thickness, maximum 3 ft, though on the southern wall there remains a roofless round doocot tower, possibly of later date than the original house. On the eastern and thickest portion of wall there is a bricked up postern gate guarded by an arrow slot. This section of wall appears intact to its original height of about 10 ft

Auchinvole was evidently haunted by a lady whose lover was murdered. He was reputedly buried by a tree stump on the river bank, a spot at which her spectre stares. The castle was built by the Stark family under the superiority of the Flemings at Cumbernauld. It may later have passed to a family of Wallaces.

In recent decades the yard has been owned and utilised by a haulage contractor. Permission should be sought from the office before approaching the site. Parts of the wall are in a dangerously dilapidated state, and risk of injury enhanced by poor ground conditions and debris.

Beware of a temperamental German shepherd!

Other references: Auchenvole, Auchenvoil

Auchlochan Castle (*)
South Lanarkshire
Ruin or site   OS 71   NS 806375
1 mile south of Lesmahagow, south of New Trows, on minor roads south of B7078, at or near Auchlochan.
The family of Broun, or Brown, were church vassals from an early date, though the present mansion replaced their castle in about 1814.

Auchtyfardle Castle (*)
South Lanarkshire
Ruin or site   OS 71   NS 826409
1 mile east of M74 at Lesmahagow, off minor road off B7018, at or near Bogside.
Between 1180 and 1203 the lands of Dowane were granted by the Abbot of Kelso, Superior of Lesmahagow, to one Constantine, who took the name De Dowane and was son of a priest at Lesmahagow named Gilbert. In 1294 the estate was divided into two, Dowane and Auchtyfardle, and each apparently supported its own 'tenement', or tower house. Both properties came to the Weir, family, as did much of the area. However, Auchtyfardle became a Kennedy holding in 1546.

Auldhouse (**)
City of Glasgow
Private OS 64   NS 556605
West of B769, 3 miles east of Barrhead, 2 miles north of A726, at Auldhouse Court.
Originally part of the Steward's Renfrewshire estates, Auldhouse was granted

to the Maxwells with other local properties in 1344. There was probably some sort of residence here from an early date, either fortified or otherwise.

Normally described as a mansion, but also a 'castle', Auldhouse has been greatly altered over the years having been used as a children's home. Recently it was converted to flats, and the extensions removed to reveal the nature of the building.

On an L-plan, this three storey house has a stair tower in the re-entrant, at the top of which is a watchroom. It has corbiestepped gables, and is fairly compact when compared to similar houses. All the windows have been altered, those to the front giving a Georgian

Auldhouse

feel to the building. Those to the rear have been blocked up, with the exception of two tiny ones in the watchroom. Stonework above the second floor appears to be of a slightly different date to that below, though later alterations may be partly responsible. Many original features may have disappeared, but a fireplace apparently retains a lintel inscription of 1631:

THE BODIE FOR THE SAUL WAS FRAMED; THIS
HOUS THE BODIE FOR; IN HEAVNE FOR BOTH
MY PLACE IS NAMD IN BLISS MY GOD T'ADOR.

George Maxwell, minister of Mearns, or his son John, minister of Eastwood and the High Church of Glasgow built it. The next Auldhouse Maxwell, George, inherited the lordship of Pollok. He zealously pursued witches, and was involved in a witch trial at Gourock in 1676. A little later he believed himself bewitched when he suffered 'a hot and fiery distemper'. Later his effigies were found stuck with pins in the home of a local widow. She and her family were burned at Paisley with their effigies. Sir George recovered, only to die later that year. His son died childless, and the Maxwells of Blawarthill succeeded.

Auld Machans Castle *see* Broomhill Castle

Auldton Castle (**)
South Lanarkshire
Private   OS 64   NS 795502
2 miles east of Wishaw by the A72, then south by minor roads to the east of Ashgill.
This ancient house has been adapted, and retains none of its defensive features.

Avondale Castle *see* Strathaven Castle

B

Badenheath Castle (*)

The Lennox & East Dunbartonshire
Ruin or site   OS 64   NS 716722
*4 miles south west of Cumbernauld, Mollinsburn, just north east of A80/M73
Mollinsburn Intersection, at Sewerage Treatment Work.*

All that remains of this 15th century keep is a carved stone set
upon a plinth within the precincts
of the sewerage works. The stone
carries the date 1661 and the initials E. W. K. and I. C. K. (Earl William of Kilmarnock, and I. Countess of Kilmarnock, probably com-
memorating the 1661 award of the
Earldom). The Lords Boyd built
the castle before they gained the
neighbouring lands of Bedlay at
the Reformation. Robert Boyd of
Badenheath was a member of
Queen Mary's bodyguard at Langside, and was exiled by the Regent
Moray for his trouble.

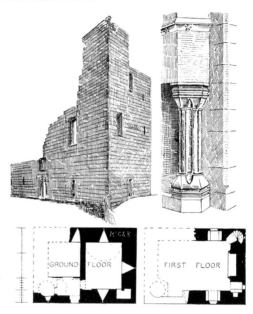

Badenheath Castle (McGibbon and Ross) c. 1875

The castle consisted of a rectangular keep 42 ft by 30.5 ft of fine
ashlar blocks, later pillaged by local builders. There were four stor-
eys, over walls between 6 and 7 ft thick, with two vaulted rooms on the ground
floor. A turnpike stair led from the entrance to the hall on the first floor. The
quality of the fine mouldings around the main entrance, hall fireplace, remaining windows, and the corbelling for corner turrets caused McGibbon and Ross
to conclude in 1887 that it had been 'a superior tower of its class', although by
their time only about half of the building remained. In its original state there
was a moat.

By 1900 parts of the remains were still habitable, and appear to have been
used to house farm workers. It was still owned by a family of Boyds, though in
the late 17th century may have been occupied by a family named Couper and
from 1708 by Keiths. In 1953 this picturesque local landmark was demolished
to make way for the current, less attractive occupant of the site.

Balcastle (*)

The Lennox & East Dunbartonshire
Ruin or site   OS 64   NS 702782.
0.75 miles west of Kilsyth, off minor roads north of A803, just west by foot from Balcastle farm.
Balcastle stands within the confluence of two streams which descend the hills to the north. It is protected on this side by a deep ditch adjoining the two gorges.

This was one of a series of 12th century strongholds of the Earls of Lennox, who also built the nearby motte at Colzium. Later the de Callendar family gained Balcastle. Their vast central Scotland estates passed by marriage to the Livingstones, who continued to use Balcastle along with numerous other local strongholds for several centuries. Its original name was Kelvesith, later Kilsyth, a name which they transferred to their 15th century castle at Allanfauld Farm.

The original name of the parish and village was Moniebroch, the name Kilsyth not being used for other than the castle until 1620 when Sir William Livingstone of Kilsyth acquired the status of burgh for his newly planned town.

Balcorrach Castle (*)

The Lennox & East Dunbartonshire
Ruin or site   OS 64   NS 614789
1 mile west of Lennoxtown, 0.5 miles south east of Clachan of Campsie, on north side of A891, at Balcorrach.
Site of a 15th century castle of the Lennox family, which was occupied in 1421. The family moved to Woodhead in 1570. They were descended from Donald, son of Duncan, 8th Earl of Lennox.

Balgair Castle (*)

The Lennox & East Dunbartonshire
Ruin or site   OS 57   NS 607884
1 mile west of Fintry, by minor road west of B822, north of Endrick water, south of Overglinns Farm.
A few pieces of masonry and rubble remain of this 15th century tower built by Cunningham of Glengarnock. He gained the property in 1467, before his family passed it to a cadet line of the Galbraiths of Culcreuch in 1563. It was granted to the Buchanans in 1605 by James VI.
Other references: Old Place of Balgair, Overglinns

Balglass Castle (*)

The Lennox & East Dunbartonshire
Ruin or site   OS 57   NS 585876
4 miles east of Killearn, on minor roads south of A818, at or near Place of Balglass.
Only earthworks remain of this once strong 13th century castle. It was granted to the Stirlings of Craigbarnet in 1486. A dated stone of 1602 bearing the initials

41

of Michael Stirling was taken to the farmhouse.

William Wallace is said to have sheltered here during the Wars of Independence. It later passed to the Bontines, one of whom murdered the Reverend John Collins on his way home from a presbytery meeting in his parish of Campsie in 1648.

The ruins on the site are of a later farm steading.

Other references: Baron's Place.

Ballagan Castle (*)

The Lennox & East Dunbartonshire
Ruin or site   OS 64   NS 573795
Just north of A891, 0.5 miles east of junction with A81 at Strathblane, 3.5 miles north of Milngavie, at Ballagan House.

Site of a large 12th century castle of the Stirlings, later held by the Earls of Lennox. In about 1760 the castle provided building materials for Ballagan House, which then replaced it. Excavation late in the 19th century revealed the plan and dimensions of the old castle.

The main building had a total perimeter of 140 ft within an internal courtyard measuring 82 ft by 72 ft The external walls of this building were 5 ft thick, and the internal walls 3 ft thick. The main entrance to the internal courtyard was centrally placed on the west wall, with entry to the larger outer courtyard placed on the north side. There was a moat around it all, 14 ft wide and 11 ft deep, traversed by two drawbridges, one at this main entrance, and a larger second for horse and cart to one side.

The site is picturesque, set at the south western base of the Campsie Fells, with a glorious waterfall known as the 'Spout of Ballagan' providing a backdrop as it falls from the precipitous hill behind.

Other references: Campsie Castle, Strathblane Castle

Ballanreoch Castle (*)

The Lennox & East Dunbarton-shire
Private   OS 64
NS 610794
1.5 miles north west of Lennox-town, just north of A891 at Haughead, at Clachan of Campsie.

Ballanreoch Castle

Site of a tower house built by the Brisbanes, who were granted the lands by the Grahams in 1423. In 1652 it was sold to MacFarlane of Keithton, a son of the Arrochar-based chief.

The former Campsie Glen Hotel now occupies the site, and probably incorporates part of the old house. The hotel was burnt out in the 1980s, but has recently been renovated for another use.

Ballikinrain Castle *see* Old Ballikinrain

Ballindalloch Castle (*)
The Lennox & East Dunbartonshire
Private   OS 57   NS 540885
On minor roads north of A875/south of A81, 1 mile west of Balfron, at Ballindalloch.
Only a sundial of the early 17th century survives from Ballindalloch Castle, which appears on Bleau's Atlas Novus. A large Victorian mansion now occupies the site.

Balloch Castle (*)
The Lennox & East Dunbartonshire
Ruin or site   OS 56   NS 386826
North of Balloch, 3 miles north of Dumbarton, east of A82 and north of A811, in Balloch Castle Country Park, on east shore of Loch Lomond.
Only earthworks and a ditch remain of this 13th century castle of the Earls of Lennox. It was a property of the Lennox family by the 15th century.

A castellated mansion of 1808, which carries the name, stands on the hill above. This contains a visitor centre, and there are gardens.
Park open all year, visitor centre Apr-Oct. Tel: 01389 578216 – see page 215.

Banklug Castle (*)
Renfrewshire
Site Only   OS 64   NS 446564
1 mile north of Shillford on A736, 1 mile east of Uplawmoor, and 5 miles south west of Barrhead, at or near Banklug.
Site of a tower house which appears on Bleau's Atlas Novus of the 17th century as Lugbank.

Bannachra Castle (**)
The Lennox & East Dunbartonshire
Ruin or site   OS 56   NS 343843
3 miles east and north of Helensburgh, on minor roads south of the B831, 1 mile west of A82 at Arden, just south of Fruin Water, at Bannachra.
A ruined rectangular tower house of the 16th century, measuring about 45 ft by 23 ft, Bannachra had three storeys, corbiestepped gables and shot holes below

43

the windows.

Bannachra was a property of the Galbraiths until gained by the Colquhouns. They built the castle in about 1512. Sir Humphrey Colquhoun was murdered here by the MacFarlanes in 1592. A servant illuminated him by holding up a lamp as he retired to bed, allowing a MacFarlane bowman to shoot him through a window.

The MacGregors and Colquhouns battled in Glen Fruin ('glen of weeping') in 1602. Less of a battle and more of a massacre, the MacGregors killed 200 of the people of Luss in this infamous meeting – which subsequently led to

Bannachra Castle (McGibbon and Ross)

35 of their own number being hanged with their chief, and partly contributed to the proscription of the clan.

Bardowie Castle (***)

The Lennox & East Dunbartonshire
Private   OS 64   NS 580738
1.5 miles east and south of Milngavie, on minor roads north of A807, on north bank of Bardowie Loch, at Bardowie.

Bardowie consists of a simple rectangular tower house of the early 16th century, extended in the late 17th century by the addition of a two storey block. Further additions and remodelling of the 18th and 19th centuries have created a mansion from the extensions.

The original tower is 33 ft by 27.5 ft, with three storeys and a garret. The corners are rounded. There is string coursing at second-floor level on the southern wall. The gables are corbiestepped at the eastern and western ends. The entrance stands centrally in the thicker south wall facing the loch. This leads to a vaulted basement, and

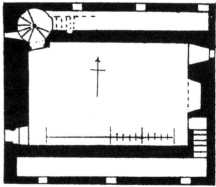

Bardowie Castle – plan top floor (M&R)

straight stair to the first floor. This stair continues within the thickness of the north wall to the second floor. Thereafter a turnpike stair leads to the northern battlements. From the southern side of the second floor a mural stair leads to the battlements on that side.

The first floor consisted of a vaulted main hall with plain fireplace, and the second of a large single room. Unusually, the garret space has been filled with another hall, covered by the wide sloping roof which extends to cover the battlements on both sides. This extra hall and extended roof may be a later alteration allowed by heightening of the gables. There are three openings in the southern wall at this level which would correspond with an original parapet. Additional small windows in the end walls provide illumination. The roof is of open timber over this hall – there is no ceiling. It has no fireplace. Part of the building carries an initialled stone of John Hamilton and his wife Marion Colquhoun, and the date 1566, which may signify early alterations, or simply their marriage.

Bardowie Castle

Bardowie was originally a seat of the Galbraiths of Baldernock, who had other local castles at Gartconnel and Craigmaddie. They were chiefs of their clan: however, they died out. Janet Keith was heiress, having inherited through her mother, and took the property by marriage to David Hamilton of Cadzow. Craigmaddie was the main seat until the family moved to newly built Bardowie, leaving the old house to fall into ruin.

The Hamiltons of Bardowie were an argumentative lot, and had more than their share of feuds with neighbours. In 1526 John Hamilton of Bardowie was killed at nearby Blairskaith fighting with the Logans of Balvie. His son Alan was killed by another neighbour, Colin Campbell of Auchenbowie and Dowan, and then in 1591 another laird had a serious quarrel with Walter Graham of Dougalston.

In 1707 Mary Hamilton, sister of the laird, married Gregor 'Black Knee' Mac-

Gregor. He was nephew and chief to Rob Roy and is renowned for having driven the White Bull of Gallangad through the Pass of Balmaha. This animal had a fierce reputation, and it is possible that in reality the roles were reversed – and that the bull drove MacGregor.

The 16th Hamilton laird died, and the estate passed through his sister to Thomas Buchanan of Spittal and Leny.

Barncluith Castle (***)
South Lanarkshire
Private   OS 64   NS 730545
Above west bank of River Avon gorge, 1.5 miles south east of Hamilton, on minor road south of A72, at Barncluith.
The name Barncluith is from 'baron's cleugh'. Barncluith is a small rectangular 16th century tower house of three storeys and a garret. Due to its site on a steep slope, the basement is subterranean. There are twin doors on the northern wall: one leads down a stair to the basement; the other upwards by a turnpike stair to the first floor.

While the upper storeys remain in their original state, the two lower floors were restructured internally to house a heating system for a neighbouring mansion. The original small windows remain unaltered. There was an extension to the north which has been demolished.

The house was built in 1583 by the ancestor of the Lords Belhaven, John Hamilton. John Graham of Claverhouse allegedly spent the eve of the Battle of Bothwell Brig in the house in 1679. He awoke to see the Covenanters defeated by the Duke of Monmouth.

Barnhill House (*)
The Lennox & East Dunbartonshire
Private   OS 64   NS 425756
1 mile north of Milton, 1.5 miles east of Dumbarton, off A82, to the north of Loch Bowie, Dumbarton.
Since 1543 this has been the home of the Colquhouns of Milton. Part of the old castle may be incorporated into the present house.

Barochan House (*)
Renfrewshire
Private   OS 64   NS 415686
2 miles north east of Bridge of Weir, on minor roads east of B789, at Barochan.
The earliest defendable building at Barochan was on nearby castlehill. This structure burned down, and the castle was built in the 16th century.

Barochan House is a mansion of the 19th century, which incorporated a corbiestepped tower of the old castle. The visible older parts of the house were pulled down in 1947, and at some earlier stage may also have been burned.

Alexander III granted the lands to the Flemings, who passed them to the Semples in the 16th century. The spinster heiress died in 1863, and the lands – being lost to the Semples – appear to have been divided.

Baronial Hall (*)

City of Glasgow.
Ruin or site   OS 64   NS 590643
100 yards south of Gorbals Cross, on Gorbals Street, at or near The Citizens' Theatre, Gorbals, south of Glasgow.
Nothing remains of this tower extended to form a C-plan mansion of the 16th century.

In the early years the Gorbals constituted part of the Govan ward of the barony of Glasgow, and as such belonged to the church. At this time the village was known as Bridgend, and became world famous as a manufacturing centre for quality swords and small firearms.

By 1512 the lands had been leased by George Elphinstone, and were subsequently passed through his family. The third of his name had dropped the 'e' from the surname by 1563, when he acquired the lands of Blythswood in the west of the city. His lease was then granted as a feu holding by Bishop Boyd in 1579.

A leper hospital serving the city stood close to the site, but had fallen into disuse by this time, and Elphinston converted its chapel into a place of worship for his family. He began construction of a C-plan mansion with a courtyard, incorporating a castellated tower, effectively a keep, which faced on to the main street.

James VI knighted Elphinston in 1594, and granted the status of free barony to the lands, hence the barony of Blythswood. Elphinston was elected as Provost of Glasgow in 1600, and later sat in the Scottish parliament. He fell into debt, and in 1634 sold the estate to Viscount Belhaven, who extended the house.

Baronial Hall, Gorbals (McGibbon and Ross) – demolished

In 1661 the city purchased the estate, and the tower was subsequently used as a gaol and town hall. It survived the remainder of the mansion by many years, as did the chapel, which was demolished before 1870.
Other reference: Elphinston Tower

Baron's Place *see* Balglass Castle

Barr Castle (***)
Renfrewshire
Ruin or site   OS 63   NS 347582
0.5 miles south west of Lochwinnoch, 0.25 miles west of the Barr Loch, just south of the A760.
Barr is a well preserved, rectangular tower of the early 16th century. Little now survives of the courtyard drawn by McGibbon and Ross, and since their time a gable has collapsed. No internal access can be gained due to the damage caused.

The courtyard was entered via a round arched gateway in the northern wall guarded by gunloops in the adjacent wall. The courtyard supported various subsidiary buildings, including a wing attached to the southern wall of the tower, all long gone.

The main building itself measures 35.5 ft by 26 ft, and was of four storeys and a garret. The wing was probably added later in the 16th century.

Entrance was via a porch of later date from the courtyard at the north western corner of the house. Above this the original entrance at first floor level is closed up. The ground floor contained a corridor accessing two vaulted chambers. One of these functioned as the kitchen and has an arched fireplace 11 ft wide and 4.5 ft deep. From the north end of the corridor a turnpike stair leads to the floors above.

The first floor consisted of a hall of 24 ft by 17 ft. Illumination was by four windows, one to each wall. There is a large fireplace in the western wall. In the north eastern corner there is a small mural chamber with ventilation slots.

There were various cupboards and a sink within the wall. A con-

Barr Castle

48

tinuous corbel supported the floor above. A small stair ascends from the south western corner to the floors above.

Subsequent floors consisted of two rooms to each, with garderobes and a variety of mural chambers.

The battlement was continuous around the roof, interrupted by roofed corner turrets. A series of continuous corbels project from the walls to support it. There are various water spouts around the circumference. Little now remains of the garret.

Various initialled and dated stones are incorporated into the structure, possibly indicating dates of renovation or alteration. These are I. W. & M. H. over the porch, L. H. I. C. 1680, over the lintel at the stair foot, and W. O. 1699 on the battlements.

Barr is believed to have been built by the Glen family, who retained it until it was acquired by the Hamiltons of Ferguslie at the close of the 16th century. It was abandoned for a new mansion in the 18th century, itself likewise abandoned for a successor in the 19th century.

Bedlay Castle (***)

North Lanarkshire
Private   OS 64   NS 692701
0.25 miles east of Chryston, 3 miles south east of Kirkintilloch, and 0.5 miles west of Moodiesburn, on the north side of the A80 at Bedlay.
Bedlay sits on the end of a long ridge, and prior to the construction of terraces around the house, was protected by steep escarpments on three sides. At the foot of these slopes, on the north and west sides, the Bothlyn Burn and a tributary provided added protection.

The castle is of two periods, the older section at the eastern end being of the late 16th century. This consisted of a rectangular keep with offset square stair tower at the north eastern corner. The tower is of two storeys and an attic, with two vaulted chambers on the ground floor. One of these acted as the kitchen, the other as a store later adapted as a bedroom. Along the northern side of these a vaulted corridor runs the

Bedlay Castle

full length of the building, providing a link from the entrance at the base of the stair tower to the later western portion. Above this on the first floor are two rooms, created from what was once the hall. One of these contained the old fireplace, now altered. A link corridor has also been created, similar to that on the ground floor. The north eastern stair tower has an additional storey, and provides the entrance on its south face. A turnpike stair which formerly gave access to attic level, now reaches only the first floor, a later stair tower having been corbelled out in the re-entrant from first floor level. The space within the stair tower released by this adaptation has provided additional rooms, that at the head of the stair acting as a vestibule. Each of these towers has corbiestepped gables, at the eastern and western ends of the main block, and northern and southern ends of the stair tower. The stair tower widens at corbelling above the first floor.

The western portion of the house was added about 100 years after the initial construction. It consists of a square block of two storeys and an attic, with round towers at the north western and south western corners. These provide additional space as a storey below the ground floor level of the main building, since they were constructed down the escarpment.

Bedlay Castle (McGibbon and Ross)

Each floor of this block consists of a single room, entered from the link corridors of the old block. The extra cellar spaces of the round towers are entered by floor hatches from the rooms above.

At the junction of these two main blocks, another square stair tower is built out from the north face. This may represent part of the original building, since it has fittings similar to that in the older section. It provides access to all floors at the western end of the link corridors.

Between this and the north eastern stair, the space has been filled by a two storey block of the 18th century, giving the existing structure a continuous facade.

Various portions of the building have been altered to provide more modern amenities. However, features such as a garderobe chute have been utilised to carry water pipes, and so survive. The windows have been enlarged, and one sign of modern convenience is the satellite TV dish on the roof. There were a few interesting features remaining when McGibbon and Ross surveyed it, such as the garderobe within the north wall, the 16th century fireplace, and Tranter noted the 'squinch arch' upon which the corbelling for the stair turret is built.

Bedlay (or Ballayn) was a property of the diocese of Glasgow from early times, and it is recorded that Bishop Cameron had a castle here. David I restored the lands to the church in his 'Inquisition' following their despoliation. In 1180, William the Lion confirmed the grant to Bishop Jocelyn. In 1580 James Boyd, titular bishop, granted them to his kinsman Robert Boyd of Kilmarnock. Boyd built the original portions of the castle, and in 1642 sold the property to the advocate James Robertson, later Lord Bedlay. About this time the western extension was added. The Boyds retained superiority of the estate, though sold it to Robertson's successors in 1740. The then Lord Boyd and Earl of Kilmarnock was subsequently beheaded for his part in the Jacobite Rising of 1745.

Bedlay was sold in 1786 and passed through various periods of ownership until bought by James Campbell of Petershill in 1805. It passed by marriage through a grand daughter to the Christies.

To the rear of the property a remnant of the old Glasgow to Stirling coach roads survives as a lane following the Bothlyn Burn from Chryston to Bedlay Cemetery. A gate from the garden opens on to this, and it is said that on a summer's evening a coach and horses can be heard. The spectre of a young girl follows, then a scream, and complete silence deadens even the rustling of the trees in the wind.

In the 1970s the apparition of a large bearded man was reported moving around the castle. Another spooky visitor is believed to represent Bishop Cameron, who died in suspicious circumstances in 1350 – possibly the same ghost.

When the Campbells moved in, they built themselves a mausoleum in the gardens. Spectral apparitions were reported and associated with the hooting of owls. The ghosts apparently left when the family had the mausoleum relocated to Lambhill Cemetery.

The house is privately owned and still occupied.

Belltrees Peel (**)

Renfrewshire
Ruin or site   OS 63   NS 363587
0.5 miles east of Lochwinnoch, west of A737, on peninsula in Castle Semple Loch.
On what was once an island, Belltrees Peel is an unusual low tower, being of an irregular hexagonal plan. It was built between 1547 and 1572.

It was a Semple property, and was occupied by Sir James Semple of Belltrees. He was educated with James VI, and acted as Ambassador to France in 1601. The Semples later used the Belltrees Peel as a shelter when sailing on Castle Semple Loch.
Other references: Beltrees, The Peel

Beltrees *see* Belltrees Peel

Belstane Castle (*)
South Lanarkshire
Ruin or site   OS 72   NS 850525
About 1.5 miles north of Carluke, on minor roads east of A73, at Belstane.
Site of a 16th century tower house of the Livingstones. It later passed to the
Lindsays, Maxwells, then the Douglases.

Bencloich Castle (*)
The Lennox & East Dunbartonshire
Ruin or site   OS 64   NS 635785
Just north of Lennoxtown, 3 miles north and west of Kirkintilloch, on minor roads
north of A891, at or near Bencloich Mains.
Site of a 15th century castle of the Lennox family, who held the estate from
1421. It was gained by the Livingstones of Kilsyth, who replaced the castle with
a mansion in 1659.

Biggar Castle (*)
South Lanarkshire
Ruin or site   OS 72   NT 041378
In Biggar, just south of junction of A702 and B7016, in garden of manse.
Only a mound remains of Biggar Castle, first settled around 1150 by Baldwin
the Fleming, who had a large motte and bailey castle here. He was the leader of
a group of Flemish immigrants granted estates in this region by David I.
Abington was held by his stepson John. His followers also built mottes at
Wolfclyde, Roberton, and possibly the site now occupied by the remains of the
Bower of Wandel.

Later Biggar was developed into a more substantial and impressive stronghold by his descendants, the Fleming family. In the 14th century they finally
abandoned the site in favour of their castle at Boghall.

William Wallace defeated the English nearby in 1297, though Blind Harry's
estimate of 60,000 men in the vanquished force seems a typical exaggeration.
Biggar, like the other Fleming village at Cumbernauld, retains its medieval plan,
with a wide main street and narrow strips of land behind each property.

Bishop's Castle, Glasgow *see* Glasgow Castle

Bishop's House, Lochwood (*)
City of Glasgow.
Ruin or site   OS 64   NS 692667
3.5 miles north west of Coatbridge, and 1 mile north east of Easterhouse, off minor

roads west of A752, south of Bishop Loch.
Site of a hunting lodge of the Bishops of Glasgow, the Bishop Loch always having been noted for its population of wildfowl.

The bishops are reputed to have dug a narrow canal linking the Molendinar Burn, Hogganfield Loch and Frankfield Loch to the Bishop Loch in order that they could sail by barge from Glasgow. This would explain the remarkably straight waterways hereabouts, although similar work was carried out to supply water to the Monkland Canal from various lochs. Perhaps not so ancient work after all.

Lochwood passed to the Main family at the reformation. Its foundations were still visible in the field between the present house and the loch until about 100 years ago.

Bishopton House (**)

Renfrewshire
Private OS 64 NS 422717
3.5 miles north east of Bridge of Weir, 0.5 miles west of Bishopton, on minor roads south of the A8.
Bishopton House consists of a tall 17th century tower house with corbiestepped gables, built around an earlier L-plan structure which was extended at each end, and upwards. The older block has three storeys and a garret.

The core of the building is a plain L-plan tower with two vaulted chambers with arrow slots on the ground floor. One of these rooms functioned as the original kitchen, and has a wide fireplace.

The entrance is guarded by one of the arrow slots and lies at the base of the stair wing. It gives access to the vaulted chambers of the main block, and to a wide scale and platt stair to the upper floors. The

Bishopton House (McGibbon and Ross)

lower part of this building appears to be earlier, and has been extended upwards by additional floors. The main block has also been extended to the west by a two storey building containing the kitchen at ground floor level. Similarly a two storey extension has been added to the north of the stair wing. An extensive early 20th century extension has been added to the south.

The property belonged to the Brisbane family from at least 1332 and they built the house. They moved to Kelsoland in North Ayrshire at the close of the 17th century, renaming it Brisbane House. Bishopton then came to the Walkinshaws of that Ilk, and subsequently to the Dunlops, Semples, and Maxwells of Pollok. In the 19th century it passed to the Stewart Lords Blantyre. It

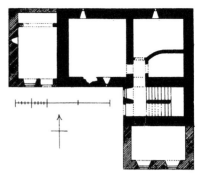

Bishopton House – plan (M&R)

came into use as a farmhouse, until converted and altered to work as the Convent of the Good Shepherd, which it remains.

Other references: Old Bishopton

Blackhall Manor (**)

Renfrewshire

Private   OS 64   NS 490630

0.25 miles south of Paisley Abbey, just south of Cart water, and north of A726, at Blackhall.

Blackhall is a restored 16th century house of two storeys and an attic. It is roughly T-plan, with a small projecting wing on the southern wall making the little leg of the T. It holds a turnpike stair. The gables are corbiestepped, as are those of the stair tower. There are numerous small windows on each floor. Three shot holes are evident, one guards the door, another is on the stair tower. Close to this is a carved stone bearing three hearts. A worn armorial stone is fixed to the gable wall.

The original round arched doorway is adjacent to the stair tower, and entered a lobby. From this three vaulted chambers can be entered. One of these is the kitchen. There was a slop drain. A later door had been opened from here through the eastern gable. There was a garderobe on this floor.

Blackhall Manor (M&R) – since restored

The first floor contained the hall and a private room, each entered from the stair head. There was a separate connecting door to the north. The hall had a large fireplace, and an inverted heart carved into the west wall. The garret had its own windows, and provided sleeping quarters.

Robert III granted this part of the ancient Steward's estate of Renfrew to Sir John Stewart in 1396. It passed to the Stewarts of Ardgowan in the 16th century, and they built this house. It came into use as a farmhouse by 1710, and was roofless by the 19th century. It was restored with great care by its present inhabitants in the 1980s, a process which involved rebuilding the roof, upper storeys complete with windows, and replacing the kitchen chimney.

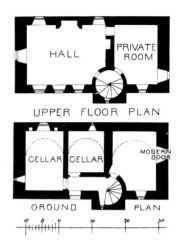

Blackhall Manor – plan (M&R)

Blackwood Castle (*)

South Lanarkshire
Ruin or site OS 71 NS 773433
4 miles east of Strathaven, at or near Blackwood House, off minor roads off A726 or west of B7078, 2 miles west of B7078/M74 junction, at Blackwood.
The Weirs appear to have had a house here from an early date, which later passed to the Lawries. In 1400 Rotaldus Were, the 'well beloved and faithful' baillie of Lesmahagow, had the lands of 'Blackwodd and Dermoundyston with the whole of Mossmynyne' granted to him and his male heirs by the abbot. In 1572 James Weir of Blackwood is recorded as one of Queen Mary's supporters, and was indicted as an accessory in the murder of Darnley. The Weirs of Blackwood appear to have been chiefs of their line – in the early 17th century at least.

Blantyre Castle (*)

South Lanarkshire
Ruin or site OS 64 NS 679566?
2 miles east of East Kilbride, off B7012, near Blantyre Old Parish Church, High Blantyre.
Patrick, Earl of Dunbar, and his wife dedicated Blantyre Priory to the Holy Rood in 1239. The Dunbars retained feudal superiority over the lands and very probably had a castle near High Blantyre. They lost the property in the years after Bannockburn when Robert the Bruce granted them to his nephew Thomas Randolph. In 1368 they passed to the Earl of March, then at the Reformation to the Stewarts of Minto. They subsequently gained the title Lords Blantyre, and adopted the priory as their home.

Blantyre Priory (*)
South Lanarkshire
Ruin or site   OS 64   NS 687594
1 mile south west of Uddingston, 1 mile north of A724, by B758, at Priory Playing Fields, 0.5 miles east of car park by foot.
Little remains of the building. It consisted of a perimeter wall of 115 ft by 150 ft, up to 10 ft high and 3 ft thick. This was surrounded by a ditch on three sides, the fourth being the precipitous drop of the ravine to the River Clyde. Within the wall were a series of buildings, including the prior's house and a further structure at one time thought to be the chapel. There was evidence that at least one of these structures had vaulted chambers.

The Augustinian Priory of Blantyre was an outpost of Jedburgh Abbey. Its founders, Patrick, Earl of Dunbar, and his wife dedicated it to the Holy Rood in 1239. Superiority of the barony passed via the Randolphs to the Earl of March.

At the Reformation the estate passed to the Stewarts of Minto. They subsequently gained the title Lords Blantyre, and adopted the priory as their home. The first Lady Blantyre, however, could not tolerate the strange noises and eerie goings on in the priory, and left her husband to live here alone. Meantime she and her daughters moved into another recently acquired property at Cardonald.

One of their grandchildren was Francis Stewart, 'La Belle Stewart' who so infatuated the courtiers at London that King Charles insisted that she model as Britannia. Her image appeared on many coins of the realm until decimalization in 1970.

Blawarthill Castle (*)
City of Glasgow
Ruin or site   OS 64   NS 520687
At or near Blawarthill Hospital, 2.5 miles east of Clydebank, north of A814, Glasgow.
Site of a 15th century castle, which appears on Bleau's Atlas. In the 17th century it was a Maxwell property.

Board Castle (*)
The Lennox & East Dunbartonshire
Ruin or site   OS 64   NS 713750?
2 miles north east of Kirkintilloch, 1 mile south east of Twechar, off minor roads south of B8023 and north of A80 and B8048, near Wester Board and Easter Board.
Probable site of a castle. The lands of Board were a property of the Erskine family until 1339. They were exchanged with Patrick Fleming, the second son of Sir Malcolm of Biggar and Cumbernauld, for Garscadden.

The exact site is not known, though Over Croy cottage contained sculpted stone fragments which had obviously been taken from a superior medieval structure. Close by is a subterranean vaulted chamber, built into the side of a bank. The entrance is low, and there is a hatch in the ceiling. This may simply be an ice house built about the same time as the cottage, but was probably part of, or belonged to, a much larger residence. Over Croy farmhouse carries dates of 1618 and 1728 on its door lintels. The village was built in the 19th century to house quarriers. The name Croy is from the Gaelic 'cruaidh', a hillside.

Boghall Castle (**)

South Lanarkshire
Ruin or site   OS 72   NT 041370
0.25 miles south of Biggar on minor roads and foot south of A702, south east of Boghall Farm.
Scraps of one square and two almost circular corner towers survive of this 14th century courtyard castle of the Flemings. The scant remains are of 15th and 17th century origin.

McGibbon and Ross pieced together a fair picture of Boghall, the ruins being only a little more substantial in their day. From archive material they describe a very large courtyard within a ditch set in the midst of a marsh, hence the name. It was an irregular hexagon shape, of uneven sides, the entrance being at an angle of the northern wall. This was a large gatehouse of the 15th century, with guardrooms either side, a battle-mented parapet and corner turrets.

At either end of this wall were the two round towers about 17 ft in diameter of which something survives. Gunloops show that they were later additions to the structure. Against the southern wall was a later mansion block with square stair tower placed in the centre of one wall. Part of this remains. Just below the eaves of this stair tower was inscribed the date 1670.

Excavations at various times have been carried out by teachers and pupils of Biggar High

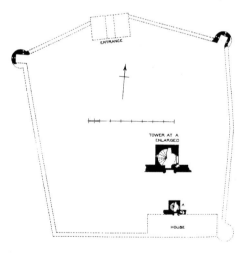

Boghall Castle – plan (M&R)

School. This revealed the foundations of a 15th century L-plan tower house in the western section of the courtyard.

The property passed to the Flemings of Biggar by marriage in the late 13th century. They were descended from Baldwin of Biggar who, in addition to his estate here, held lands at Houston and Inverkip in Renfrewshire. He became Sheriff of Lanarkshire.

Edward II of England stayed at Boghall in 1310. In 1458 the family were made Lords Fleming of Cumbernauld, and more of their history can be read in that entry. James V visited, as did Mary Queen of Scots in 1565. In 1568 during the aftermath of the Battle of Langside, the castle was surrendered after a siege to the Regent Moray.

In 1605 the family became Earls of Wigtown, and in 1650 the castle was again besieged, then occupied by Cromwell. The 6th and last Earl died in 1747, and the castle fell into ruin. Over the years it has been used as a useful supply of stone and so has deteriorated to its present poor state.

Boghouse Castle (*)
South Lanarkshire
Ruin or site   OS 71   NS 877236
Just south of Crawfordjohn, just east of the B740, 3 miles south west of its junction with the A74.
Site of a 16th century castle, probably built by Sir James Hamilton, 'the Bastard of Finnart'. Sir James was granted a licence to build towers within the barony in 1528. It is thought that he built Boghouse so that James V could liaise with his mistress Catherine Carmichael, daughter of the keeper of Crawford Castle. Sir James was known to have encouraged the young king in all 'manly pursuits'. Perhaps he supervised developments in the relationship from his property at Crawfordjohn nearby? Sir James had exchanged this estate and another at Kilbirnie with Lawrence Crawford for his own property at Drumry in the Lennox. This was in 1528, but in 1535 he exchanged Crawfordjohn with the king for the barony of Kilmarnock. Deft dealings or utmost generosity toward his liege? Either way the king's opinion was shown in 1540 when Sir James was beheaded for treason.

Bogton Castle (*)
City of Glasgow
Ruin or site   OS 64
NS 575596
2 miles west of Ruther-glen, just west of B767, and east of Muirend railway station, at Bogton Avenue.
Site of a tower house of the Blairs, who obtained the estate and built the castle in 1543. It was pulled down

Bogton Castle – site

and probably replaced by a mansion, itself now also demolished.

Bonhill (*)

The Lennox & East Dunbartonshire
Ruin or site   OS 63   NS 395795
About 3 miles north of Dumbarton, east of River Leven, off A813, at or near Bonhill.
Site of a house of the Smolletts, burgesses of Dumbarton, which may have been fortified. It is said to have dated from the 14th century, but was demolished in 1950. From as early as 1546 it was a Lindsay property, and in 1622 one Quentin Lindsay of Bonhill obtained a grant of Pillanflat. Bonhill was a ferry point across the Leven anciently used by cattle drovers as it provided a more economic toll than payment to the garrison at Dumbarton. A dispute raged through the later 17th century as the Duke of Lennox attempted to extend the levy due to the castle governor from the town to the Boat of Bonhill. The case went as far as the Privy Council, before being settled a year after the Duke's death in 1673. The house was said to have had a ghostly piper, the spectre of a man sent to search a tunnel beneath the building.

Bothwell Castle (****)

North Lanarkshire,
Ruin   OS 64   NS 688594
200 yards west of Castle Avenue, off B7071, 0.5 miles south of Main Street, Uddingston.
Set spectacularly above a gorge on a bend in the Clyde, and protected on the landward sides by a deep ditch, Bothwell guards what was once a critically important crossing point of the river. Bothwell's bridge was the point at which any invading army from the south using the west coast route would meet the Clyde. The ruins at Bothwell reflect the importance of the site.

A massive though partly demolished donjon or great keep of the 13th century – 90 ft to the parapet, 65 ft in diameter and with walls 15 ft thick – domin-

Valence Tower, Bothwell Castle

ates the western end of this large courtyard castle. Most of the remaining structure is of 14th and 15th century origin. This consists of a massive wall of enceinte, interrupted at various intervals by strong corner towers.

Bothwell Castle – courtyard

The donjon provided the living quarters of the lord, and despite having been partially demolished in the early 14th century was repaired to provide an impressive residence. It has its own, now dry, moat within the courtyard, crossed by drawbridge. Sluices for draining the moat can still be seen through the base of the tower, even these have a defensive element to the stonework preventing surreptitious entry. The keep consists of three floors plus basement and fighting platform at parapet level. It has a finely moulded pointed arched entrance. Despite its circular exterior, the rooms within were octagonal, and a central stone pillar rose from the basement to support the floors at the first and second storeys. This may have been continued to the other floors in wood. The basement contained the well, and a recess adjacent in the wall housed the winding gear and bucket. A mural stair leads to the first floor, where a twisting rib-vaulted corridor entered the lord's hall, mural stair to the second floor, main entrance, and a vaulted room which housed the lifting gear for the drawbridge and portcullis. The entrance is guarded from this room by impressive arrow slots. A second or 'common hall' was on the floor above, both halls having a latrine within the thickness of the walls. The third floor is thought to have been the lord's private chamber, and provided a separate door leading to the wall-walk providing a means of escape for the lord. The battlemented parapet had machiolations, or slots, through which fluids or objects could be dropped on attackers at the base of the wall 90 ft below.

During the Wars of Independence, Bothwell consisted of only this tower, and the prison tower. It was nevertheless a formidable building, and was occupied by Sir Aymer De Valence, an English lord, for much of this period. The tower therefore earned the by-name of the Valence Tower. In the south wall, just east of the donjon, stands the lower section to wall height of the prison tower, with its pit prison. At its eastern base, some 15 ft below the level of the yard, is the postern gate. A steep bending slope carries up from the gate to the interior, the embankment to the side allowing defence from above. A further steep slope descends from the exterior of the gate, along a narrow causeway below the walls with a similar purpose. The postern originally had a portcullis. High above the exterior of the gate the arms of Douglas can still be made out carved into the wall.

The southern wall continues to complete the perimeter at this side with the south eastern tower, and is interrupted by a series of windows. The largest, again a pointed arch, gave light to the chapel dais at the south eastern corner of the yard. The wall at the chapel site shows sockets for flooring at first floor level, with stone window seats, fonts for Holy Water, basins within the walling, and the remains of the vaulted ceiling.

The south east tower is another impressive and decoratively structured building, again machiolated, with hexagonal rooms within a circular exterior. Each floor had a single room, each with an ornate fireplace.

The eastern end of the courtyard is occupied by a large tenement block of two storeys, the upper storey being the hall. There was a dais and large ornate pointed arch windows, the largest illuminating the dais. There are three vaulted storage rooms at ground level. The eastern wall runs to almost full height to terminate at the fragmentary remains of the rectangular north east tower. This was once loftier than even the great donjon. It represented the main residence of the Douglas lords until superseded by the hall block. Little now remains, but it had its own portcullis, and the massive proportions of the foundations impress.

The wall continues to form the northern perimeter, turning back to meet the donjon at the north western corner. Midway along this wall the modern entrance was built in 1987, filling a gap where

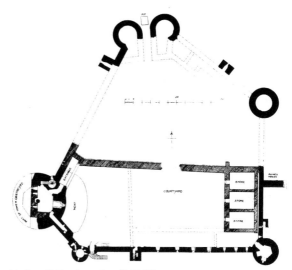

Bothwell Castle – plan (M&R)

61

once stood a huge gatehouse. This would have contained the quarters of the Constable, who was responsible for the administration of the castle. The position of the modern shop, just west of the hall in the northern wall, with a fireplace and oven built into the wall above it, indicate the site of the original kitchenblock. A buttress on the exterior of this section of the enceinte supports an impressive example of corbelling, which presumably was once surmounted by a turret. There are latrine chutes at various points on the external wall.

Outwith the surviving structure, foundations were uncovered a little more than a century ago. These were those of a latrine tower and a massive gatehouse. It is believed that these structures were never completed. However, their distance outwith the existing walls, and just within the deep ditch which marks the original perimeter, illustrate the original intended scale of the castle, about double its present area.

The barony of Bothwell originally consisted of the lands bounded by the two Calders, that is the North and South Calder Waters. It was granted to David Olifard (Oliphant) in the time of David I. His son and grandson, both Walter, succeeded in inheriting the estate and the position of Justiciar of Lothian. The daughter of Walter jnr married Walter de Moravia (Moray), and he inherited in 1242. The site of the original caput of the barony is not known, but was probably close to St Bride's Kirk in the town. He also gained the other neighbouring Olifard barony of Drumsagard with its motte at Greenlees, though in time the estates were divided, and the inheritors of Drumsagard went their own way.

Walter of Moray lost little time in showing off his new found position, and began construction of his new castle. However, by the time of the Wars of Independence it was not complete. Only the donjon and prison tower represented the defendable structure, the other towers reaching only foundation level. A palisade and the ditch probably defended the rest of the site.

During the invasion of 1296, Edward I of England captured William Moray of Bothwell, and took his castle. His nephew, Andrew took revenge at the Battle of Stirling Bridge a year later, but was fatally wounded. In 1298 the Scots commenced a 14 month siege before successfully recovering Bothwell. Edward I, or 'Longshanks', returned in 1301, and used specially constructed siege engines to retake Bothwell. One particularly successful siege engine was given the name 'Bothwell', and was subsequently used against Stirling Castle. This may have been the tower, or 'belfry' built at Glasgow, for which the woods of the city were plundered for material. The castle was left under the control of the Earl of Pembroke, and Governor of Scotland, Aymer de Valence.

The castle remained in English hands until in 1314 and in the aftermath of Bannockburn several English lords sought refuge within its walls. However, on the arrival of their Scots pursuers, the constable, Fitzgilbert opened the gates and surrendered the castle and his compatriots. This 'gentleman' was from Homildon in the North of England, and as reward was given a grant of land at Cadzow. His motte stands behind the mausoleum of his descendants, in the town which took his name: Hamilton.

Bothwell Castle

However, the English retook Bothwell in October 1336, Edward III making it his headquarters in the invasion to support Edward Balliol's claim to the throne. The Scots by this time had laid it waste, and a master mason by the name of John de Kilbourn was charged with repairing the damage. Some of the 14th century work is his.

By March 1337 the posthumously born son of Sir Andrew Moray, another of the same name, arrived with a siege engine called 'Bowstoure' and quickly retook his ancestral home. In accordance with Bruce's policy he pulled down the western side of the donjon, which fell into the river. The damage caused by his action remains to this day.

The castle remained in a ruinous state until 1362, when Joanna of Bothwell married Archibald 'The Grim', or Black Archibald, later Lord of Galloway and Earl of Douglas. He undertook to rebuild, his work being completed by his son following his death in 1400. The result is substantially what we see today.

The Black Douglasses were forfeited in 1455, and the crown took possession. Bothwell was given in turn to Lord Crichton, then to Sir John Ramsay, who were both forfeited. James IV granted the barony and its castle to Patrick Hepburn of Dunsyre, the 2nd Lord Hailes, in 1489. He was created Earl of Bothwell, a title borne by his more infamous descendant in the reign of Mary Queen of Scots. The castle did not stay with the Hepburns as the title did. With the permission of the king, Hepburn exchanged it for Hermitage in Liddesdale, with another Archibald Douglas, Earl of Angus, this time of the Red Douglasses. James IV visited in 1503 and 1504. The crown incurred expenses for the castle in 1544, but it seems still to have belonged to the family, since in 1584 Dame Margaret Maxwell, Countess of Angus, was in residence with her husband, William Baillie of Lamington. Ten years later the couple were accused of conducting a catholic mass in the chapel, a practice much denounced in those post-

Reformation years.

Another Archibald Douglas, the 1st Earl of Forfar, gained possession in 1669 and began to take stone to construct his new mansion. The second Bothwell Castle stood in the park behind the original castle. This mansion survived until 1926, when it was demolished due to the effect of coal mining. There are a few uninspiring remnants of this unfortified house as you approach Bothwell from the castle. After a lawsuit in the 18th century it went to the Stewarts of Grandtully, then by descent to the Earl of Home. In 1935 the castle was taken into state care and is now managed by Historic Scotland.

Bothwell Castle – courtyard

Historic Scotland: open Apr-Sep, daily except closed Thu PM and Fri Oct -Mar. Tel: 01698 816894 – see page 215.

Other references: Valence Tower

Boturich Castle (*)

The Lennox & East Dunbartonshire
Ruin or site   OS 56   NS 387845
1.5 miles north of Balloch, 4 miles north of Dumbarton, by minor roads north of the A811, on the southern shore of Loch Lomond.

Site of a 15th century castle now occupied by a castellated mansion of the same name built by John Buchanan to a design by Robert Lugar in 1830.

The estate was owned by the Haldanes of Gleneagles, who obtained it on the forfeiture of the Earls of Lennox in 1425. John Haldane of that family died at Flodden in 1513. The castle was sacked by the MacFarlanes of Arrochar. It later passed to the Buchanans of Ardoch, then in the 1850s to the Findlays.

Bower of Wandel (*)

South Lanarkshire
Ruin or site   OS 72   NS 952228
About 3.5 miles north of Abington, just west of A73, 1.5 miles north of junction with M74, on east bank of River Clyde, at Bower of Wandel.

On a rocky eminence that may once have been a motte, and surrounded on three sides by the Clyde, part of a basement with gunloops survives of a 15th century tower house. It was a property of the Jardines from the 12th to 17th centuries, and was popular with James V as a hunting lodge.

Broken Tower *see* Cadder

Broomhill Castle (*)
South Lanarkshire
Ruin or site   OS 64   NS 758508
0.5 miles south of Larkhall, on minor roads west of the B7078, east of Avon Water, south of Millheugh, at Broomhill.
The parish of Dalserf (then Machanshire) was granted to Walter Fitzgilbert by Robert I in 1312. On his death it was divided between his descendants, and this portion came to the Hamiltons of Broomhill. They built the castle.

The family supported Mary Queen of Scots, Sir John Hamilton dying of his wounds after the Battle of Langside in 1568. His son Claud fled to France. On the orders of the Regent Moray, the castle was torched in the 1572 by Sir William Durie, Governor of Berwick. Claud Hamilton returned from his exile, building Broomhill House upon the foundations of the old castle in 1585. It was remodelled and extended in later centuries.

At the Reformation an angry reformist crowd approached intent on burning the nearby chapel. Lady Elizabeth Hamilton shouted to the mob: 'If ye dinna burn it doon, I'll mak a guid barn o' it'. This promise was apparently kept, and a barn it remained until it fell into disrepair in 1724. The chapel site is given as just beyond a railway bridge, off Broomhill Avenue.

The estate passed to the Birnies, but the house was demolished after a fire in 1943, leaving only the cellars.

There was apparently a spectral 'Black Lady', a ghost of more recent years, believed to have been the wife or serving women of one of the lairds. She may have been murdered, and her apparition is said to have been seen at the site. Other references: Castle of Auld Machan, Auld Machan Castle

Buchanan Castle (**)
The Lennox & East Dunbartonshire
Private   OS 57   NS 463886
0.5 miles west of Drymen, off minor roads south of B807, and west of A809, at Buchanan Castle Golf Club.
An early castle near here to the south and known as Buchanan Peel was abandoned in favour of an L-plan tower house. This was later incorporated into the present castellated mansion, itself now ruined though consolidated.

The old castles were the seats of the Buchanans who allegedly ran into financial difficulty, and were bought out by the acquisitive Grahams.

The tower burnt out in 1850, and a new mansion built designed by William

Burn. The gardens were designed by Capability Brown, but have been suppressed by the creation of a golf course.

In 1940 Hitler's deputy Rudolf Hess flew a solo mission in an attempt to create peace between

Buchanan Castle (1914) – now ruinous

the Germans and Britain. He crash landed at Floors Farm near Busby, and was brought to Buchanan Castle as a prisoner.

Busby Peel (**)

South Lanarkshire

Private   OS 64   NS 594561

2.5 miles west of East Kilbride, 1 mile south of Carmunnock, east of Busby, at the north side of the junction of the A726 and B766.

On a defensive knoll above the Kittoch Water, Busby Peel consists of an altered 16th century L-plan tower house of four storeys, with numerous later extensions. There is a complicated corbelling pattern supporting an ashlar parapet. The remainder of the old tower is harled. The stair tower extends from the north eastern corner and contains a very wide turnpike. It appears to be of the 17th century and is believed to have replaced a smaller original stair tower in a similar position. The roof has been altered in style and is not original.

More modern extensions of the 18th century extend to the west and south.

The Hamiltons of Rossavon gained Carmunnock parish on the forfeiture of the Douglases in 1455. They settled here and built The Peel. The estate passed through several owners, such as the Semples, and was acquired by the Houstons of Jordanhill in 1793. It remains occupied as a private dwelling.

Other references: The Peel, The Peill

C

Cadder Castle (*)

The Lennox & East Dunbartonshire
Private   OS 64   NS 605728
3 miles west and south of Kirkintilloch, off minor roads 0.75 miles north of A803,
Cadder House (Cadder Golf Course), Bishopbriggs, on south bank of River Kelvin.
Cadder House, now a golf club house, dates in part from 1624, standing both
on the site of the earlier castle and close to the line of the Antonine Wall. The
house apparently contains some fine Roman carved stone relics from the wall.

Cadder House

A motte of the Stirlings stands close to Cadder Kirk to the south east.
   The Stirlings of Cadder were made a grant of the parish of Cadder in the 12th
century by the Bishop of Glasgow. Allegedly originally Comyns, this branch of
the family became hereditary Sheriffs of Stirling and adopted the surname.
Cadder was the chiefly line and the family first recorded in 1147. Later senior-
ity passed to the Stirlings of Craigbarnet, then to those of Glorat.
Other references: Broken Tower, Calder Castle, Cawder Castle

Cadzow Castle (***)

South Lanarkshire
Ruin or site   OS 64   NS 734538
1.5 miles south east of Hamilton, on minor roads south of the A72, in Hamilton High Parks, on southern side of Avon gorge, opposite Chatelherault.

An early castle in Cadzow was used as a hunting lodge by David I and his successors in the 12th century. Royal charters by him were issued here from as early as 1139. The present tower house and courtyard with subsidiary buildings dates from 1540. It represents an early example of a castle built to withstand artillery.

Cadzow was the original name of the estate and parish of Hamilton. The site of the early castle was considered by most local historians of the 19th century to have been on an eminence above the Coven Burn, just west of the Avon and south of the Old Avon bridge. This site was known as Castlehill, and a house of that name was built on the site. By the beginning of the 20th century, the site had been developed for housing.

The present Cadzow Castle may be built upon the foundations of another predecessor. The ruins are being consolidated, though view-

Cadzow Castle (1913)

ing is restricted to outside the perimeter due to their crumbling and dangerous nature. Of what remains interpretation is difficult. There are remains of a dry ditch to the west, and there are comparisons to be drawn with the plan at Craignethan, a weaker outer courtyard having been added later.

The royal estate was divided in 1222, and Alexander II granted the portion at Rossavon to the monks of Kelso Abbey, while at some point Cadzow came to the Comyns. Following their forfeiture, Robert I granted the estate to Walter Fitzgilbert. He hailed from Homildon in Northumberland, and his motte remains close to the mausoleum. The family name developed as Hamilton, and from 1455 the name of Hamilton was formally adopted for the town and district. This honoured the award of a lordship of parliament to Sir James Hamilton. He married Princess Mary Stewart, sister to James III, emphasising the importance that the family had established on the national scene. The family gained the title Earls of Arran, and in the reign of Mary Queen of Scots the 2nd Earl was appointed Governor of the Realm. James Hamilton was then awarded the title Duke of Chatelherault by Henry II of France. Queen Mary stayed in

Cadzow after escaping from Lochleven Castle.

In 1570 the Earl of Lennox besieged the castle during his fight with the Hamiltons, and it capitulated within two days. In 1579 forces under the direction of the Regent Morton captured and dismantled it.

The grounds of Chatelherault and the High Parks are open to the public all year except Christmas and New Year..

Consolidation of the castle is being conducted by Historic Scotland.

Tel. 01698 426213 – see page 215.

Cairnie Castle (*)

South Lanarkshire

Ruin or site   OS 71   NS 855436

1.5 miles west of Lanark, on A72, above south bank of Clyde near Stonebyres Falls, at or near Linmill

The Old Statistical Account of 1794 describes the last remains of Cairnie Castle as 'a series of narrow archways, which probably represents a vaulted basement'.

Calder Castle *see* Cadder Castle

Calderwood Castle (*)

South Lanarkshire

Ruin or site   OS 64   NS 658560

1 mile north east of East Kilbride, on minor roads south of A725, east of River Calder.

Calderwood was a massive keep of 69 ft by 40 ft, and 87.5 ft high. There appear to be no records of the construction of the castle, though it may have been of an early date. The structure collapsed in 1773. The remaining outbuildings were later enclosed within a mansion, which was extended in 1840.

It was a property of the Maxwells of Calderwood for 500 years. They were a branch of the Pollok family, descended from Sir Robert Maxwell, 1st of Calderwood, who died in 1363.

Some sources credit Sir James Hamilton of Finnart with the building of Calderwood, though there was certainly some structure on site before his time.

Other references: East Kilbride

Caldwell Tower (**)

Renfrewshire

Ruin or site   OS 64   NS 422551

2 miles north of Lugton, 1 mile west of Uplawmoor, and 4 miles south west of Neilston, on north side of B776, 0.5 miles west of its junction with A736.

Caldwell Tower overlooks the valley of the Lugton Water from a lofty position at the end of a ridge. It consists of a small square 16th century tower of three storeys, and probably had a garret in its original form. There is a parapet supported by two layers of chequered corbelling, though the parapet itself may have been replaced.

The basement is entered from its own door in the west front. It consists of a single vaulted chamber with fireplace and slit windows. There is no access to the upper floors.

The main entrance is at first floor level in the north wall, now reached by a stairway built against the walling, though originally there would have been a removable stair. This stair continues within the wall to the floor above. The hall on the first floor is also vaulted, and has a fireplace and garderobe. There are small windows illuminating each of the floors above basement level. These have sealed up gunloops below and simple roll mouldings above. The floor above is greatly altered.

The tower was renovated on several occasions, possibly as a folly or as a riding shelter. It may contain elements of an older structure, though is very probably the only remnant of a much larger castle.

It was a property of the Mures of Caldwell, being a cadet branch of the chiefly line of Mure of Rowallan. The family were involved in a dispute with the Pollok Maxwells over ownership of Glanderston in the 15th century. In the 17th century William Mure was involved in the Pentland Rising of the Covenanters which ended in defeat at Rullion Green in 1666. He went into self imposed exile, and his forfeited estate was given to Dalziel of The Binns. The family returned in 1698 to reclaim their estate, though did not appear to reoccupy the tower. They built a new house at Caldwell Hall to the west early in the 18th century, and in 1773 moved to their new mansion at Caldwell House, designed by James and Robert Adam. Both of these later houses survive.
Other references: Tower of Caldwell

Cameron House (*)
The Lennox & East Dunbartonshire
Private   OS 56   NS 377831
On the west bank of Loch Lomond, east of the A82, 3.5 miles north of Dumbarton.
The Scots baronial mansion of the Smolletts stands on the site of previous houses dating back to the 14th century, which may have been fortified. The building is now a well known hotel (see page 216), and said to be haunted.

Campsie Castle *see* Ballagan Castle

Camstradden Castle (*)
The Lennox & East Dunbartonshire
Private   OS 56   NS 359952
On west bank of Loch Lomond, 7 miles north east of Helensburgh, 0.5 miles south of Luss, east of A82, near Camstradden House.
Once sited on an island in the bay, Camstradden was owned by the Colquhouns

of Luss from 1395. The 6th Laird of Camstradden fought at the Battle of Pinkie in 1547.

Other references: Castle of Camstradden

Carbeth Castle (*)

The Lennox & East Dunbartonshire
Private   OS 57   NS 524876
At Carbeth House, 1 mile north of Killearn, on minor roads north of A875/B818 junction.
Carbeth is derived from 'Caer Beath', the fort of life. A 15th century tower house of the Buchanans previously occupied the site. They held the lands by grant of the Grahams from 1476.

The present mansion dates in part from the 17th century, and may incorporate part of the old castle. It was remodelled as a castellated mansion in 1840, and was subsequently altered in 1879. It remains occupied.

Cardarroch House (*)

City of Glasgow
Ruin or Site   OS 64   NS 638695
1 mile east of Bishopbriggs, and 3 miles south west of Kirkintilloch, just south of B812, 0.5 miles east of Robroyston Mains, near Wallace's Well.
Nothing remains of this transitional, two storey house with attic, which was dated 1625. Originally an L-plan, a small stair tower extended from the north west corner. It had comparatively thick exterior walls, and the gables were corbiestepped. The wide staircase went to the first floor, then a steep stair led to an attic.

In 1718 an extension was added to the west of the main

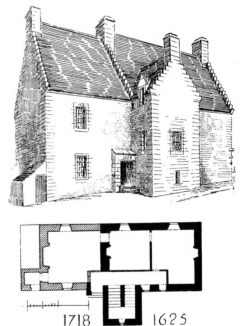

Cardarroch House and plan (M&R)

block, making a T-plan. The interior of the old block was adapted in the modernisation at that time, altering the appearance of the house from that of a small tower to that of a comfortable, 18th century house. This included window enlargement and the construction of a porch.

A building to the north was originally a carriage house with doocot on the upper floor, though this building was converted to provide another house.

Cardonald Place (*)

City of Glasgow
Ruin or site   OS 64   NS 526645
On minor roads south of A8, in Cardonald, at end of Cardonald Place Road, on north bank of White Cart Water, 0.75 miles north of Crookston Castle, at former Cardonald Place Farm.

Place means Palace or Palis, an old Scots word for hallhouse. Cardonald Place was a large two storey hallhouse of 1565. It was demolished in 1848 to make way for the present 19th century farmhouse, which contains an armorial stone dated 1565 from the original building.

The lands of Cardonald belonged to Johannes Norwald and his descendants until obtained in 1487 by the Stewarts of Darnley. The first laird was Alan Stewart, a son of the 1st Stewart Earl of Lennox, though their remains some doubt as to his legitimacy. His descendant James Stewart built the castle in 1565, and his initials adorn the armorial stone mentioned. This also bears the arms of Stewart, crossed by a black diagonal bar signifying illegitimacy, though this may have been added in error at some restoration.

James Stewart died in 1584, and is buried in Paisley

Cardonald Place farm – now a private home

Abbey. His epitaph indicates that he was once Captain of the Scots Guard to the French royal house. On his death the estate passed to his nephew Walter Stewart of Minto, commendator of Blantyre Priory. He became Lord Blantyre in 1606. He had been a childhood companion of James VI. His wife was unhappy living at the priory, and moved with her daughters to the palace.

One of Walter's grand daughters was Frances Theresa ,'La Belle Stewart' who so infatuated the courtiers at London that Charles II had her model as Britannia. She was willing to marry 'any gentleman of £1500 a year who would have her in honour'. She eventually married the Duke of Richmond and Lennox, and is associated with Lennoxlove in Lothian, currently home to the Duke of Hamilton.

The family eventually purchased the Erskine estates and moved to Erskine House, now the renowned hospital for ex-servicemen. The 12th and last Lord Blantyre died in 1909, the estate passing to the Laird family of Erskine and Lennoxlove.

Cardonald Place Farm came into the ownership of the city, and for many years the house and farm functioned as a nursery for the City Parks Department. It was sold and renovated, and is occupied as a family home.

Cardross Castle *see* Cardross Manor House

Cardross Manor House (*)

The Lennox & East Dunbartonshire
Site or ruin   OS 63   NS 384758
In Dumbarton, 0.5 miles west of River Leven, just north of A814, north of Brucehill, adjacent to Notre Dame School, at Castlehill.

A large mound within a small area of parkland held by The National Trust for Scotland commemorates the death place of King Robert the Bruce. The parish of Cardross once extended as far as the River Leven, and the medieval church remains as a ruin within Levengrove Park.

About 1326 Robert the Bruce decided to build himself a comfortable home, after his years of warring with the English, and looked for a new site. He chose the parish of Cardross and obtained it by exchanging royal estates with local landowners, principally Sir David Graham. This gained the Grahams the estate of Old Montrose, with which the family are normally associated.

Argument has raged over the years as to whether this was a castle or not. Ancient documentation describes it as a 'manororium', or manor house. However, the presence of a single feature built to aid defence qualifies it for inclusion in this book, and there are good reasons for including it.

No evidence exists to suggest that the structure was fortified. Documentation reveals that it had a single stone wall bordering the king's apartment. It had thatched roofs and some of the windows were glazed. It was a large building, with a separate chamber for the queen, a chapel, a hall, and from 1328 a 'new chamber'.

There was a garden and a hunting park with a specially built falcon house surrounded by hedging. The king was known to have kept galleys here to sail the western seas, including one he called his 'great ship'.

Argument also surrounds the actual site. That given above indicates the site used by the NTS, and it is only fitting that they should commemorate the death place of Scotland's greatest king in some way. However, evidence suggests that the actual site was nearer the Leven, and various sites are suggested. These include the vicinity of Mains of Cardross Farm ('mains' meant demesne in old terminology indicating a home farm). Some other suggestions are more fanciful, such as at Tullichewan. Only archaeological evidence could indicate the true site, and similarly establish the nature of the mound at Castlehill. It is likely that Castlehill was a

Castlehill, Cardross

motte, possibly the Graham's seat in the estate.

There are records showing that the king's great ship was pulled up for repairs into a burn which ran beside the house. This illustrates that the actual site must have been very close to the Leven. Since most of that bank was industrialised, and over the years the course of the river altered, then it is very unlikely that any trace will ever be found.

Bruce died here in 1329, his heart was cut out as he requested, and taken on crusade. It was carried in a silver casket by Sir James Douglas. Douglas and many of his entourage died in battle against the Moors in Grenada, though Bruce's heart was returned and interred in Melrose Abbey. His body was buried at the Abbey of Dunfermline. The manor does not appear to have been used after his death. The estate was absorbed within the castle lands of Dumbarton, remaining royal property and providing revenues used to maintain the castle.

Carluke Castle *see* Kirkton of Carluke

Carmichael House (*)

South Lanarkshire
Private   OS 72   NS 938391.
5 miles south of Lanark, on minor roads west of A73, north of Cleuch Burn, at Carmichael.
Site of a 14th century castle. The present ruinous house was never completed, and consists of two wings and a linking corridor.

The Carmichaels descend from Richard of Karemigel. He took his name in 1259 from Kirkmychael, the ancient church of the parish. John Carmichael slew the Duke of Clarence, brother of Henry V of England, at the Battle of Bauge in

1421, and the family crest of a broken spear commemorates this. Another Carmichael chief fought against Charles I at Marston Moor in 1644, then against Montrose at Philiphaugh in 1645, despite two of his brothers supporting the Royalists. The family were created Earls of Hyndford in 1701, and were Hanovarians in the Jacobite years. John Carmichael, 3rd Earl, was a British Envoy to the courts of Prussia and Russia in the 1740s. It was he who built the present house on the site of the old castle. The remains of ornamental gardens contain many fine examples of decorative stonework, and host regular clan gatherings. The estate passed to the Anstruthers, who changed their name to Carmichael-Anstruther, and have reverted to Carmichael. They still own the estate, which operates a deer farm and sawmill.

Carmunnock Castle (*)

City of Glasgow
Ruin or site   OS 64   NS 600570
2 miles north west of East Kilbride, at or near Carmunnock village, 1 mile east of Busby and north of A726, by B759 or B766.
Carmunnock is derived from 'Caer Mynnock', the monk's fort. The Exchequer Rolls confirm that the Douglasses had two castles in this parish: the sites are now lost. There are some indicators though. It may be that they occupied the sites latterly occupied by Busby Peel and Castlemilk, though it is more likely that other sites were used.

When describing Busby Peel, Rev. D. Ure in *The History of Rutherglen and East Kilbride* of 1793 stated that the last vestiges of an older castle stood about a quarter of a mile to the west. This corresponds with the motte known as Castlehill. Of twin mottes astride the Kittoch water, east of Busby, he names that to the north as Castlehill, though there was no evidence of a building. This site is described as being the end portion of a ridge, which has been separated from the main section by a ditch, 57 ft wide and 11 ft deep.

That to the south known as Roughhill supported remains of a rubble built building measuring 73 ft by 63 ft, which was being used as a source of stone for local dyke building. During stone collection, workers exposed a subterranean vault, which they cleared of rubbish in the hope of finding something of value. They were disappointed, and filled in the vault when finished. The mounds stand 200 yards apart, the area between is known as Castleflat.

Ure could not give any of the history of these sites, though it does shed a little light on possible sites of the two Douglas castles with definite evidence of two of the three having supported stone buildings. It could be that the second Castlehill site, with no stonework, is what remains of one home of the original Norman lord, Anselm. The estate was then held by the Comyns, until dispossessed by Robert I who granted it to the Douglasses. They were forfeited in 1455, and the Hamiltons of Rossavon acquired the property. They divided the estate, and feud the Cassiltoun portion to the Stewarts of Castlemilk, Dumfriesshire. The Hamiltons later built Busby Peel.

Carnbroe House (*)

North Lanarkshire
Ruin or site   OS 64   NS 735623
2 miles south of Coatbridge, off east of junction of B7070 and A725, above south bank of North Calder Water, just to the west of Carnbroe Mains Farm.
Carnbroe House was a much altered 16th century L-plan tower house of three storeys and a garret. It was demolished in the mid 20th century. Two round towers projected from the main block. There were three vaulted chambers in the basement, and a hall on the first floor.

It was a property of the Baillies, but later passed to the Hamiltons.

Carntynehall (*)

City of Glasgow
Ruin or site   OS 64   NS 635654
Just south of Carntynehall Road, at Carntyne Square, just south of A8, 1 mile east of junction with A80, Glasgow.
The hall or house of the Grays of Carntyne stood here from the Reformation until Carntyne House was built in 1802. The hall was partly demolished, then came into use as farm buildings and as a residence for the estate factor. It is likely that the hall was fortified.

Carnwath House (*)

South Lanarkshire
In or near Carnwath, close to junction of A70 with A721, and B7016.
Private   OS 72   NS 982464?
Carnwath House may contain elements of an earlier structure, possibly a medieval castle. The earliest fortification here is represented by the motte of Sir John Somerville, on the golf course at the west end of the village.

The Somervilles owned Carnwath from 1140, but it passed to Lockhart of The Lee in the 17th century. In 1739 Robert Dalziel was created Earl of Carnwath. This was a Jacobite family, and they were forfeited following the rising of 1715.

Carnwath motte

Carstairs Castle (*)

South Lanarkshire
Ruin or site   OS 72   NS 938461
Near A70, in Carstairs.
Nothing survives to give a clue as to the exact site of this stone castle of the Bishops of Glasgow.

In 1535 the castle was rented to Sir James Hamilton of Finnart. It later passed to the Stewarts, then the Lockharts. The castle was dismantled to provide material for the parish church which was built in 1794 to replace the earlier St Mary's. Carstairs was created a Burgh of Barony in 1765, and planned and rebuilt by Henry Monteith, who purchased the estate in 1819. He built himself a Tudor-Gothic mansion, designed by William Burn, which survives as St Charles Hospital. With the exception of the State Hospital and railways, the village is essentially as Monteith planned.
Other references: Casselterras

Cartsdyke Castle (*)

Renfrewshire
Ruin or site   OS 63   NS 287756
1 mile east of Greenock on minor roads south of A8, 0.5 miles south of Firth of Clyde, at Cartsdyke.
Near the Cartsburn stood a 16th century tower of the Crawfords. Sir Patrick Crawford of Cartsburn was denounced as a rebel after fighting for Mary Queen of Scots at Langside in 1568.

The castle was probably destroyed with the development of Port Glasgow, in which Sir Thomas Crawford invested heavily. He lost heavily in the Darien Scheme.

Casselterras *see* Carstairs

Cassiltoun *see* Castlemilk

Castle Crawford *see* Crawford Castle

Castlehill (*)

North Lanarkshire
Ruin or site   OS 64   NS 788534
1 mile south of A721, at or close to Castlehill Farm, Gowkthrapple Road, south of Wishaw.
The Lockharts of Castlehill built Cambusnethan House in 1820 to replace their 17th century tower at Castlehill. The old house had burnt down in 1810.

Castle Levan (***)

Renfrewshire
Private   OS 63   NS 216764
1.5 miles south west of Gourock, on minor roads south of A70, just south of Firth of Clyde, at Levan.

Castle Levan stands high above a ravine in a strongly defensive position over-looking the Firth of Clyde. At variance with the L-plan, it consists of two blocks of separate dates, linked at one corner. The older main block dates from the late 14th or early 15th century and has been altered when the extension was added. The other is a little smaller, and dates from the 16th century. Each is of three storeys and a garret, with parapet, wall walk, and open rounds at the corners, all supported on chequered corbelling. The walls reach 5 ft in thickness and have many arrow slots and small windows. The corbelling and parapet of the older block was altered to match the style of the extension.

Castle Levan (McGibbon and Ross)

There are three entrances, all on the north in the re-entrant. One is more recent and enters the extension at the ground floor. Two are original and are in the main block. The first at ground level would originally have only entered the ground floor. It now leads to a mural stair and then to the first floor of the main block. Two vaulted cellar rooms can be entered from a linking corridor between the stair and door. The original main entrance was at first floor level, giving access to the hall, and has been enlarged. The recessed windows of the hall have stone seating. Mural stairways lead to the floors above.

The smaller block has been added to provide additional amenities, the vaulted basement providing storage, and the first floor a kitchen with a large fireplace. A mural turnpike has been carved out within the adjoining wall between the two blocks, and provides access to both the basement and kitchen.

Levan was a property of the Morton family, and was sold to the Semples by Adam Morton 'of Levane' before 1539. At this time Semple had the property absorbed into his own barony. James Morton, son of the vendor, was not happy and took out an interdict forbidding Semple from collecting his revenues from the estate. Semple eventually won a prolonged legal battle. In 1649 the Schaw-Stewarts of Inverkip gained the estate.

Parts of the upper floors collapsed as the structure fell into ruin. It has been restored and is occupied. It stands close to a 19th century mansion now used as a hotel.

There is apparently a 'White Lady' who haunts Levan. She is said to represent one Lady Montgomery who mistreated the peasantry. As punishment she was starved to death by her husband.

Castlemilk (*)

City of Glasgow
Ruin or site   OS 64   NS 608596
1.5 miles south and east of Rutherglen, in Castlemilk, just east of Machrie Drive.
Located on a knoll above a pond, nothing now remains of Castlemilk, a much-altered 15th century keep, extended to form a grand mansion. The original keep latterly formed the entrance block to the 19th century castellated structure, and was of three storeys with an added parapet and garret. The knoll was once separated from the top of the ridge by a deep ditch, filled in the 19th century.

Originally these lands were known, as 'Cassiltoun', being the castle town of the parish of Carmunnock, and an ancient motte in the woodland to the east at the head of a waterfall is one of several fortified sites within the old parish.

One Anselm owned the parish, then his son Henricus de Cormannock, then the Comyns, passing to the Douglasses after the Wars of Independence. They were forfeited in 1455, and the estate passed to the Hamiltons of Rossavon, who feud the Cassiltoun portion to the Stewarts of Castlemilk, in Dumfriesshire. They built the castle later in the 15th century, selling their Dumfriesshire estate in 1579 to Lord Maxwell, and transferring the name to their new home. It was the 18th century before Castlemilk was used confidently in local records as the name of the estate, and by this time the Stewarts had acquired the remainder of the parish, so that the church at Carmunnock was now regarded as being dependant on the goodwill and financial support of the family. They also held lands at Finnart (Greenock), Torrance (East Kilbride), and in 1706 inherited the large estate of Milton on the north of the city. This inheritance was dependant on them including the name Crawfurd in their own, and since by this time they had adopted the French style of their surname, and had married into the family of Stirling of Keir,

Castlemilk (1901) – now demolished

their name had become Crawfurd Stirling Stuart.

The Milton estate was large, including the modern areas of Balornock, Barmulloch, Milton, Hyndland, and Cowcaddens. This estate was particularly rich in coal and was feud to the city, much increasing the wealth of the family.

In 1938 the last laird died. The estate was sold to the city and from 1948 the castle was used as a children's home. This closed in the early 1960s, and – despite much public and media protest – the castle was demolished in 1969. Lady Helen, a surviving daughter of the last laird, died in a nursing home in Carmunnock in the 1970s. Castlemilk was one of the houses which claims to have provided lodging for Mary Queen of Scots the night before the Battle of Langside in 1568, which she lost and then fled to England. A room in the house was named Queen Mary's Room to commemorate the alleged event.

The woodlands, which remain in the area, are the remnants of the park surrounding the house, and abound in spooky tales. There were reported sightings of a 'White Lady' near a bridge over the burn, a 'Green Lady', and an ancient Scottish soldier who allegedly fired a ghostly arrow into the back of the head of a local, causing stitches to be inserted!

There was also 'the Mad Major' who used to ride by moonlight and at speed up to the doors of the house, and was believed to represent the return of Captain William Stirling Stuart from Waterloo. It is reported that the Major's horse was buried in the grounds.

Other references: Cassiltoun

Castle of Auld Machans *see* Broomhill Castle

Castle of Camstradden *see* Camstradden Castle

Castle of Glasgow *see* Glasgow Castle

Castle Qua *see* Craiglockhart

Castle Ru' *see* Rutherglen

Castle Semple
Renfrewshire
Ruin or site   OS 63   NS 377602
2 miles north east of Lochwinnoch, on minor roads west of A737 and Howwood, just east of Castle Semple Collegiate Church, and just west of Low Semple.
Site of a medieval castle, 'Castle Semple, the principal messwage of a fair lordship of the same denomination'. The castle was demolished about 1730 to clear the site for Castle Semple House, a classical mansion, itself mostly demolished in the 1960s. What remains are of the mansion's stable block and peripheral

walling with gates and lodge.

The Semple or Sempill family owned the estate from at least as early as the 14th century. John, 1st Lord Semple, was killed at Flodden in 1513, and William, Lord Semple, was captured after the Battle of Pinkie in 1547. In 1560 the castle was seized because of the opposition of the Semples to the Reformation. The family opposed the Jacobites, and fought with the Hanoverians in the risings of 1715 and 1745, and were at Culloden in 1746.

By 1727 the castle had passed to the MacDowall family. Colonel William MacDowall ordered the demolition of the old castle to clear the site for his new mansion, and in 1791 obtained plans from Robert Adam to remodel it. This plan was never executed as the family ran into financial difficulties. The estate was gradually broken up, and the house fell into disrepair. Park: see page 216.

Cat Castle *see* Cot Castle

Cathcart Castle (**)

City of Glasgow
Ruin or site   OS 64   NS 586599
1 mile south west of Rutherglen, off minor roads south of B767, west of Old Castle Road, and east of White Cart Water, at head of Linn Park.
Sited on a hilltop precipice above the White Cart, Cathcart Castle survives only to a height of about 4 ft The castle originally consisted of a simple oblong keep of 51 ft by 30.75 ft within a courtyard which extended a further 10 ft on each side. There were four round corner towers on the perimeter wall.

The original entrance to the courtyard was in the east, opposite the main entrance to the keep. This was of four storeys and probably a garret, the basement being vaulted. The main door at ground floor level entered a small

Cathcart Castle

corridor. Opposite was the entrance to the basement, to the north was a turnpike stair within the walls accessing all floors above, and to the south was a small chamber of 5 ft by 6 ft which may have acted as a prison since there was access from above. The main chamber at this level was illuminated by three slot windows.

The hall on the first floor measured 32.5 ft by 17 ft and had several larger windows one of which had stone seats. There was a large open fireplace in the south wall. In

Cathcart Castle (1907?) – before demolition

common with the floors above there were various mural chambers within the walls.

The floors above had originally consisted of large single rooms, though those on the second floor had been subdivided to provide two disproportionately sized rooms and a linking corridor.

The castle was demolished to its present height by Glasgow City Council around 1980 due to its deteriorating and dangerous condition. It is now overgrown, and daubed with graffiti.

The Cathcarts held the estate from the 12th century, though the site of their original caput is not known. Some suggest the ancient earthworks at Camphill within Queens Park, others identify the site of the present ruin.

The Cathcarts were made Lords Cathcart in 1447, and built the castle in 1450. The property passed to the Semples in 1546. They opposed Queen Mary at nearby Langside in

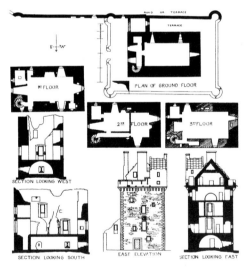

Cathcart Castle – plans and elevations (M&R)

1568, but despite this she reputedly watched proceedings from a knoll known as 'the Court Knowe' immediately west of the castle. It is also alleged that she may have stayed the night before in the castle, although both legends are unlikely. The Semples built Cathcart House just to the south, and abandoned the castle to move there in 1740. The house has long since been demolished. A descendant of the Cathcarts bought the estate back, and became Earl of Cathcart in 1814. Remains situated in Linn Park – see page 216.

Catter Castle (*)
The Lennox & East Dunbartonshire
Private   OS 57   NS 473871
0.5 miles south of Drymen, just south west of junction of A811 and A809, in garden of Catter House.
An impressive motte remains of an early castle of the Earls of Lennox. Catter guarded the ferry point over the Endrick which gave access the lands to the east of Loch Lomond from the south. It was also of strategic importance since it stood at the meeting of the main routes through the area to Glasgow, Dumbarton and Stirling. The castle was abandoned in the 14th century and replaced by Inchmurrin Castle.

Catter House is a three storey Georgian mansion, now owned by the Grahams, but once part of the Buchanan's estate from which they took their name.

Cawder Castle *see* Cadder

Claddach Castle *see* Tarbet Castle

Cleghorn Castle (*)
South Lanarkshire
Ruin or site   OS 72   NS 898461?
2 miles north of Lanark, on minor roads west of A706, just south of railway, and north of Mouse Water.
Cleghorn House was a mansion which incorporated part of a castle. It latterly belonged to the Lockharts, but was demolished in the 20th century.

Cleland Castle (*)
North Lanarkshire
Ruin or site   OS 64   NS 784577
1 mile north west of Wishaw, 2 miles east of Carfin, off minor roads, south of B7079, at or near Cleland House.
Site of a castle of the Cleland family. The family had other castles at Airdrie and Knownoblehill.

Cloak (*)
Renfrewshire
Ruin or site   OS 63   NS 346605?
1.5 miles north of Lochwinnoch, off minor roads west of B786, at or near Meikle Cloak.
Site of a castle.

Cloberhill Tower (*)
City of Glasgow
Ruin or site   OS 64   NS 703532
2 miles east of Clydebank, off Towerhill Road, off A82, Knightswood.
Site of a tower, owned from 1567 by the Crawfords. In 1612 Hew Crawford of
Cloberhill assisted a kinsman of Possil to assail Corslie Castle.

Clyde Rock *see* Dumbarton

Cochno Castle (*)
The Lennox & East Dunbartonshire
Private   OS 64   NS 497532
2.5 miles north of Clydebank, off minor roads, north of Duntocher and A810.
Site of a tower house with 16th century origins. The Hamiltons had gained the
property at the Reformation, the lands of Paisley Abbey, of which this was part,
having been settled on Lord Claud Hamilton. At least two Hamiltons of Cochno
were keepers of Dumbarton Castle.
    The present Cochno House was built in 1797 for the Hamiltons of Barns. It
replaced the 16th century tower. Since 1956 it has been owned the University of
Glasgow, and is used for animal husbandry and astronomy.

Cochrane Castle (*)
Renfrewshire
Ruin or site   OS 64   NS 418616
*1 mile south west of Johnstone, 1 mile east of Black Cart Water, on minor roads south
of A737, east of Auchengreoch Road, in the grounds of the 'Red House'.*
Cochrane Castle was ruinous by the time the Houstons rebuilt Johnstone Castle in 1771. In 1886 George Ludovick Houston built a small tower to commemorate the site, and incorporated an armorial stone with the Cochrane arms, dated
1592. Nothing else remains.
    The Cochrane family held the lands from the 14th century. They became bar-
ons of Dundonald in 1647, then Earls of Dundonald from 1669. The estate was
sold in 1760 to the Johnstones of Cochrane. The Cochranes had another stronghold nearby, once called Easter Cochrane, now Johnstone.

Colgrain Castle (*)
The Lennox & East Dunbartonshire
Private   OS 63   NS 324801
On A814, 2.5 miles west of Cardross, and 3 miles east of Helensburgh, at Colgrain.
The present house, which is known as Colgrain, may incorporate parts of, or
stonework from, the old fortified house of the Dennistouns of Colgrain.

The Dennistouns originally hailed from a place of that name near Kilmacolm in Renfrewshire, where they held an early castle. Later heads of the family became keepers of Dumbarton Castle for the Stewart kings.

The Dennistouns held the proud boast that
'Kings have come of us, not we of kings.'

This referred to the fact that Sir John Dennistoun was uncle to Elizabeth Mure of Rowallan, queen to Robert II.

They also owned the nearby property of Camis Eskan, though early buildings there were unlikely to have been fortified. The later mansion seems to have become their main residence prior to its use as a hospital.

Coltness House (**)

North Lanarkshire
Private   OS 64   NS 797564
Off minor roads, 1.5 miles north of A721, at Wishaw.
Purchased in 1653 by Sir Walter Stewart of Allanton for his younger brother James, it was described at that time as, 'a convenient little tower house consisting only of a vault and two rooms, one above the other, with a small room on top of the turnpike stair and a garret'. Sir James added 'a good kitchen, cellar, meat room or low parlour, a large hall or dyning room, with a small bedchamber and a closet over these, and above that two bedchambers with closets, and yet higher in the fourth storey, two finished roof rooms.'
It was remodelled and extended in 1800.

Colzium Castle (**)

The Lennox & East Dunbartonshire
Ruin or site   OS 64   NS 729788
*0.5 miles east of Kilsyth, north of the A803, by driveway through Colzium Lennox Country Park,
just north east of
Colzium House.*
A section of wall
(47.5 ft long by
16 ft high by 3.5
ft thick) is now
integrated as a
gable for a cot-
tage and its gar-
den wall. This is
all that remains
of this 16th cen-
tury   L-plan
tower and its ex-

Colzium Castle

tension. The outline of a vaulted roof is evident on the wall, as is an arched recess and a walled up entrance. There is an ice house of 1680 within the gorge to the east. It is essentially intact.

A motte at the western end of Banton Loch is the earliest fortification on this site. The motte was built in the 12th century by the Earls of Lennox as one of a series strung across the waist of Scotland from Dumbarton to Stirling.

These lands passed to the de Callendar family, and then by marriage to the Livingstones. Colzium was built by the Callendar branch of that family to replace the motte. It was erected upon a platform at the edge of the ravine of the Colzium Burn. Constructed in the mid 15th century, a large hallhouse was added in 1575, and it is a scrap of this which remains. The foundations of the original tower were excavated in 1977 prior to being covered in tarmac to create additional car parking. An inscribed stone from the castle is on display in the courtyard of the house, while a larger collection of stones from both Colzium and Kilsyth are displayed inside.

The 3rd Viscount Kilsyth ordered the demolition of the castle in 1703, just prior to inheriting the title and estate. In 1783 the Edmonstones acquired the estate on their return from Ireland, and built Colzium House. The family later restored their ancestral home at Duntreath, and on returning there granted Colzium and the estate to the burgh. Their walled garden is well maintained and very attractive and is open to the public – see page 216.

Banton Loch is a man-made reservoir used to supply water to the Forth and Clyde canal. The waters of the reservoir drowned the battlefield of Kilsyth, where in 1645 Montrose scored an important victory over a Covenanting army led by General Baillie. The names of a variety of hills around commemorate the event: Slaughter Knowe, Baggage Knowe, etc. Following the battle Baillie's army fled. Some sank trying to escape through Dullatur bog to the south, which is rich in preserving peat. On the digging of the Forth and Clyde Canal around 1770 several bodies of the Covenanting army were uncovered in remarkably good state of preservation: one apparently still mounted on his horse.

This is not a comfortable stretch of water to fish – especially at night – after hearing this tale!

Comyn's Castle (*)
South Lanarkshire
Ruin or site   OS 64   NS 628563
1 mile north of East Kilbride, west of Stewartfield, 100 yards north of Mains Castle, off minor roads north of B783.
Situated on a hilltop above its successor at Mains, a motte represents the only remains of the 12th century castle of John 'The Red' Comyn. Comyn was Robert the Bruce's main adversary in the scramble for the Scottish throne. However, the two men had made a pact, and when Bruce gained the throne, he was to give up his estates to the Comyn. Bruce was betrayed by Comyn, and in a

rage Bruce stabbed him before the high altar of Dumfries Kirk, the deed being done on 10 February 1306. Bruce's companions entered the church when his deed had become apparent, Roger Kirkpatrick of Closeburn uttering 'I mak' sikkar' (make sure), and Fleming of Cumbernauld is quoted as saying 'Let the deed shaw', both becoming the mottoes of their respective families. The Fleming's motto was later adopted for the town of Cumbernauld.

Bruce was crowned King on 25 March the same year. The Lindsays were granted this portion of the Comyn estates and used the castle until the 15th century when they built Mains.

Corehouse Castle (**)
South Lanarkshire
Ruin or site   OS 72   NS 882414
1.5 miles south of Lanark, on minor roads south of A72, on west bank of River Clyde above Corra Linn waterfall.
Standing on a promontory and protected on three sides by precipitous drops to the River Clyde below, Corehouse is a ruined 16th century tower house of the Bannatynes.

The main building stands on the promontory protected by a 100 ft drop to the river, then on the fourth and northern side by a deep ditch, 15-20 ft wide, cut into the rock. This originally would have been crossed by drawbridge, though now a road crosses a stone walled bridge. There is a large courtyard across the ravine to the west, though this is of later date.

A 6 ft thick wall with arched gateway protects the approach once across the ditch. At the end of the bridge, this angles off to the south east terminating in the remains of a round tower which may have housed a stair. On the interior

Corehouse Castle

and within the original courtyard, it can be seen that this also was one end of a secondary block with oven and drain.

The western end of the perimeter wall also acted as the gable of the main block. This block runs the length of the western ravine, and contains four vaulted chambers, two of which are linked and entered by one doorway. Both of the other chambers have their own doors from the courtyard. Above this the hall utilised two thirds of the floor space, while a private room occupied the northernmost third. Above this third, as shown in a painting of Corra Linn by Paul Sandby dated around 1753, was a further floor surmounted by a garret. This additional floor housed a bedroom. There do not appear to have been other floors above the hall. At the southern end of this block are the remains of a small square stair tower. Nothing now remains above the floor level of the hall.

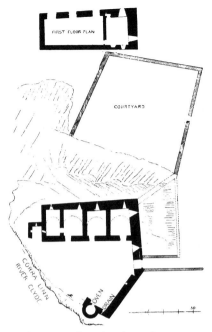

Corehouse Castle – plan (M&R)

The estate belonged to Kelso Abbey, superior of Lesmahagow, which priory owned the parish. It was granted to William Bannatyne in 1400, and they in turn sold it to the Somervilles of Cambusnethan in 1695. By the 19th century it had passed to the Cranstoun family, one of whom was raised to the bench as Lord Corehouse in 1826. The modern mansion can be visited – see page 217.

Also known as Corra Castle, the house and Corra Linn (a waterfall, one of the famous 'Falls of Clyde') are said to be named after 'Cora', a princess who allegedly leapt the fall on horseback.

Other references: Corra Castle, Corrocks

Corra Castle *see* Corehouse Castle

Corrocks *see* Corehouse Castle

Corslie Castle (*)
Renfrewshire
Ruin or site   OS 64   NS 545593?
2.5 miles east of Barrhead by the A726, just north east of junction with B769, at Crosslees House. Alternative site, on knoll in Woodhead Park, 1 mile to the east.
Corslie Castle had a walled courtyard, and probably stood on the first of the

sites given above. The second site may have been that of an earlier structure.

Corslie was a property of the Montgomery Earls of Eglinton. On the death of the Earl in 1612, he left an outstanding debt payable to Crawford of Possil. Crawford became frustrated at a lack of payment from the Earl's executors due to a dispute over the succession. He elected to take the law into his own hands.

On the cloudy night of 5 September, he attacked Corslie, scaling the walls using ladders. Assisted by Hew Crawford of Cloberhill, Crawford evicted Gabriel Montgomery, the caretaker, at gunpoint. Montgomery was grievously wounded. Tried and imprisoned, Possil spent the following two years in Edinburgh Castle. Corslie was last occupied at the end of the 17th century.

Cot Castle (*)

South Lanarkshire
Ruin or site   OS 64   NS 740458
2 miles north east of Strathaven, and 1 mile south west of Stonehouse, 0.25 miles north east of Bridgeholm Farm, just north of A71, and south of Avon Water.
Nothing remains of Cot Castle, occupied in about 1500 by the Hamiltons. The castle stood above the precipitous Avon Gorge, and the site was used for lime-kilns in the 19th century. Two arched draw holes with projecting buttresses set into a bank remain of these. Cot Farm was built on the site, but was abandoned in the 1970s and fell into disrepair.
Other references: Cat Castle, Kat Castle, Kot Castle, Kemp Castle

Cothally Castle *see* Couthalley Castle

Couthalley Castle (**)

South Lanarkshire
Ruin or site   OS 72   NS 972482
1.5 miles north west of Carnwath, east of B7016, south of Woodend, east of main Edinburgh-Carstairs railway.
Fragments remain of this castle of enceinte of the Somervilles. It probably originally consisted of a triangular courtyard castle within a moat, and was entered by drawbridge. Excavations in 1913 showed that the moat was in fact a series of three concentric ditches of little more than 1.5 ft deep, but 16 to 23 ft wide. These have become waterlogged due to the surrounding boggy ground, and at such a shallow depth could not be considered a true moat, but would nevertheless have presented an obstruction to would-be assailants.

The walls varied in thickness from 5 to 6.5 ft. There was an L-plan tower, a rectangular gatehouse, and other towers at the main points along the wall. These later structures took up almost all of the available wall space, giving the remaining enceinte the proportions of a barmkin wall. The entire structure measures 25 ft by 66 ft approx.

The castle was first recorded in the mid 12th century. The family had moved here from their motte and bailey castle at Carnwath. It was burnt by the English in 1320, and rebuilt in 1375. The structure was enlarged in 1415. Extensive additions and alterations were made in 1524, when William the second baron built the third tower.

The castle then consisted of a square tower to the north, a round tower to the east, and the new tower to the south. This latter is described as 'square, twice walled, and double battlemented'. The towers were quite separate, linked only by sections of the old enceinte of about 9 ft high. Each tower was of four storeys, with one room to each floor.

Besieged in 1557, it was again rebuilt in 1586, though the year previously the family had made their main residence at Drum in Midlothian. There were still substantial remnants of the towers in 1815.

James V visited, as did Queen Mary in 1563, and then James VI. James, 13th Lord, was a Hanoverian, and aide-de-campe to General Cope at Prestonpans, and Hawley at Falkirk during the 1715 Jacobite rebellion. The family died out in 1870.

Other references: Couthally, Cowthalley

Covington Castle (**)

South Lanarkshire
Ruin or Site   OS 72   NS 975399
6 miles east and south of Lanark, 2 miles north of Thankerton, on minor roads north of A73, just north of Covington.

Set on dry ground within what was once marshland, and surrounded by the complex and extensive ditches of its timber predecessor, Covington Castle or Tower is a ruinous 15th century tower house. There is a ruined 16th century circular doocot of 500 boxes a few yards away. This probably stood at one corner of a courtyard with gardens. A short section of the linking wall

Covington Castle (McGibbon and Ross)

remains. The village retains the classic medieval grouping of castle and church.

The upper floors and parapet of the tower have long since gone, though it was probably a four storey structure and measured about 47 ft by 38 ft. Built upon walls 11 ft thick, there were numerous slot windows, with slightly larger windows lighting the upper apartments.

The ground floor was vaulted and had a loft. There remains a stone sink and conduit drain within an aumbry in the west wall. There was probably a well, long since blocked. Entry from the courtyard was via a door centrally placed in the north side, and from this a short straight stair led to a turnpike and the floor above.

The hall utilised the whole of the first floor, and had large window recesses with stone seats and dressed ashlar arches. The fireplace was in the east wall, with mural chambers either side. Above these, additional long slot windows improved the lighting. A pit prison is built within the walls.

The ditches may represent the remains of the 'villa Colbani', the early moated manor house of the Flemish-Norman lord Colbin and his son Merevin.

Covington was granted by Robert the Bruce to the Keiths, Earls Marischal. The Lindsays gained the estate in 1368, and built the tower in 1442. In 1679 they sold it to Sir George Lockhart, President of the Court of Session.

Cowden Hall (*)
Renfrewshire
Ruin or site   OS 64   NS 468572
East of Lochlibo Road, off A736, Neilston, Renfrewshire.
Now a ruin, Cowden Hall has been in existence since the early 14th century, though in the 19th century had been extended in Georgian fashion.

The estate was granted to Walter Spreull in 1306, and was retained by his descendants until James Spreull sold it to Alexander Blair of that Ilk in 1622. He married the Cochrane heiress and adopted her name, their descendants becoming the Earls of Dundonald. It passed to the Marquis of Clydesdale in 1725, then to the 6th Duke of Hamilton. The Mures of Caldwell obtained it in 1766.

Sir Robert Croc had an early castle in Neilston, and there may have been a successor belonging to the Stewarts.

Cowthalley Castle *see* Couthalley Castle

Craigbernard Castle *see* Craigbarnet

Craigbarnet Castle (*)
The Lennox & East Dunbartonshire
Ruin or site   OS 64   NS 594790
2 miles west of Lennoxtown, just north of the A891, at Craigbarnet.
Once a large and important castle of the Stirlings, nothing remains of Craigbarnet Castle. It was replaced by a mansion, of which the walled garden and an ornate

barn remain. The mansion site is now occupied by a modern farm, and the adjacent castle site was cleared and planted as woodland by other developers.

Descended from the Cadder family of the same name, the Stirlings of Craig-barnet established their own importance on the national scene, becoming hereditary keepers of Dumbarton Castle.

James IV stayed here, and is recorded as having received 24 shillings from the treasurer to play cards 'that nicht in Craigbernard', 9 February 1507.

Sir John Stirling was a close friend and comrade in arms of the Marquis of Montrose, his near neighbour at Mugdock. Sir John was nicknamed 'Burrie' due to a speech impediment. In 1660 he decided to replace the old castle with a new mansion.

The now chiefly line of the Stirlings of Glorat are descended from a second son of Sir William Striveling, 3rd of Craigbernard, who was granted the Glorat estate in 1508.

The Stirlings sold the site in the 20th century: the castle to woodland developers and the mansion for development as a farm.

Other references: Craigbernard Castle

Craigend Castle (*)

The Lennox & East Dunbartonshire
Ruin or site   OS 64   NS 545778
2.5 miles north of Milngavie, on minor roads between the A81 and A809, 0.25 miles north west of Mugdock Castle, at Craigend.
Craigend Castle is a large mansion of the Buchanans, which was built in 1812. It stands within its own large estate, and replaced or incorporates an earlier castle of the Inglis family.

Craigends Castle (*)

Renfrewshire
Ruin or site   OS 64   NS 417661

Craigend Castle

2.5 miles north east of Kilbarchan, on minor roads south of B790, and east of B789, just south of Gryffe Water at Craigends.
Now gone, the mansion of Craigends may have contained an earlier structure.

Early owners may have included the Knoxes of Ranfurly. They continued to use the title long after the estate came to the Cunninghams in the mid 15th century. The family died out and it came to the Boyles of Kelburn in 1647. The estate passed to other Cunninghams who built the mansion.

Craigievairn Castle *see* Craigievern

Craigievern Castle (*)
The Lennox and East Dunbartonshire
Ruin or site   OS 57   NS 495902
2 miles north east of Drymen, off minor road north of A811, just south of Muirpark reservoir, at Craigievern.
Craigievern was a Buchanan property and consisted of a T-plan 18th century house. A large castle here appears in Bleau's Atlas Novus of the 17th century. Little remains of either structure.

Craiglockhart Castle (*)
South Lanarkshire
Ruin or site   OS 72   NS 875450
0.5 miles north west of Lanark, above the gorge of the Mouse Water, on minor roads and by foot north of the A73, 1 mile east of Cartland.
A fort here is now thought to have had medieval origins, and it is certainly close to the site of Craiglockhart Castle.

It was a property of the Lockharts of The Lee, and in 1900 was described as 'a ruined lofty picturesque tower'.

An early castle here was held by William Wallace prior to an attack on Lanark. He is said to have hidden in a cave within the Mouse Water gorge to the east after killing Hazelrigg, the English Sheriff of Lanark. Wallace's Cave is now inaccessible but lies just to the north of Telford's Cartland Bridge. The nearby village of Cartland is of medieval origin.
Other references: Castle Qua, Qua Castle

Craigmaddie Castle (**)
The Lennox & East Dunbartonshire
Ruin or site   OS 64   NS 575765
2 miles north east of Milngavie, on minor road east of A81, just east of Craigmaddie House.
Only a vaulted basement remains of Craigmaddie Castle, a 16th century tower house. Craigmaddie was a property of the Galbraiths from 1238 or earlier. The estate passed by marriage to a branch of the Hamiltons of Cadzow in the 14th century. They later left for their new castle at Bardowie.

Craigneith Castle – see next page

Craigneith Castle (*)

South Lanarkshire
Ruin or site   OS 64   NS 663553
1.5 miles north east of East Kilbride, by minor roads and foot south of A725, west of Auchentibber, and above the Avon Gorge.
The ruinous stump which remains is a remnant of a small tower, once enclosed by a large mansion, of which nothing remains.

Craignethan Castle (***)

South Lanarkshire
Ruin   OS 72   NS 816464.
4.5 miles north west of Lanark by the A72, 2 miles west of Crossford, and north east from Tillietudlem for 1 mile.
Craignethan consists of a large 16th century tower house within a walled courtyard with supporting towers at strategic points of the perimeter. A second walled courtyard protecting the approach, and a sophisticated arrangement of all-around ditches and gun ports provides further defence. It is sited upon a spur that is protected by a ravine on three sides, the fourth and west side being the heavily defended approach.

The main tower house or keep of the castle is sited as close to the point of the spur as was possible given the nature of the site, and within the inner courtyard. It is thus as far from the awkward approach as possible, and separated from it by several strong lines of defence.

The keep is a parallelogram, about 63 ft by 50 ft, and some 33 ft high. It once had two storeys plus an attic, now lost, above a vaulted basement below ground level. There were four large vaults here, and one smaller, which was possibly a prison. One of the rooms contained the well, and another had a hatch leading

Craignethan Castle (1909) – before clearance and excavation

to the kitchen above for supply purposes. A cramped stairwell also accessing the kitchen supplemented this. The building is divided into two halves by an interior wall stretching the entire length, east to west, of the structure. An unu-

Craignethan Castle – wall of outer courtyard (McGibbon and Ross)

sual feature is that the main rooms are at ground level as opposed to the usual first floor arrangement. The main door is in the west wall at this level, leading to a very large reception area. From this a wide stairway leads to the first floor, with another below to the basement. There is a small guardroom containing a mural stairwell leading to the parapet. The main hall is entered from here, and measures 20 ft by 40.5 ft. It supported a high rounded vaulted ceiling, with two large windows on the south wall for illumination. A fireplace stood supported by a portion of the central wall, now gone. A stair in the south west corner of the building leads to a musicians gallery that is supported by the west wall. A private chamber with fireplace and garderobe is entered from the north east corner, as is a private stair to the first floor. A kitchen with large fireplace and a private suite of rooms for the lord take up the remainder of the floor. Above this section was an additional floor at the level of the vaulting in the hall, and it was supported by wooden flooring. There is an altered serving hatch from the kitchen to the reception area.

The upper floor is ruined, though it appears to have had four rooms with individual garderobes and fireplaces. There remains decorative string coursing and corbelling atop the walls. It is thought that the keep was battlemented, and stone roofed. There are open bartizans at each corner and machiolations over the entrance.

Towers at each corner, and a gate tower strengthen the inner courtyard wall. The western wall reaches 16 ft in thickness, in illustration of the design of the castle as principally for defence against artillery. It once supported artillery batteries, and was battlemented. Much of it is now demolished. The south eastern tower is larger than the others, and is the least ruinous. It is believed that originally this was the chapel, but has acquired the by-name of the 'Kitchen Tower'. This tower has three storeys and is unusually proportioned, 34 ft by 31.75 ft. Its basement is at ground level outwith the perimeter of the castle, while within the ground reaches the first floor. Subterranean vaults support the ground to this level with-

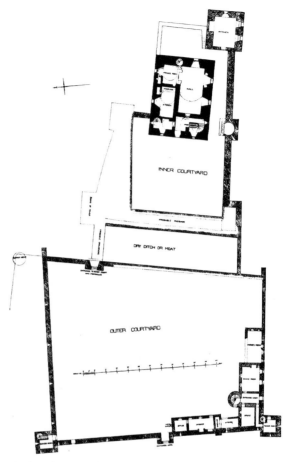

Craignethan Castle – plan before excavation (M&R)

in the yard, these being entered from a door and stair in the south wall. The vaults of the keep may have been entered from these at one time. Each of the towers supported auxiliary accommodation, either for guests or servants. The ground floors would have provided service areas, for bakery, brewhouse and so on.

Access to the inner yard from the outer was via a drawbridge, then a narrow gateway, which led into one of the towers. A ditch supplemented the western defences. At 30 ft wide and 12 ft deep it presented a formidable barrier. In 1962 a unique feature was excavated at the southern end of this ditch. The caponier is a defensive structure which traversed the width of the ditch, and with gun loops allowing fire along the base of the ditch added another obstacle to crossing to the inner courtyard. The caponier was entered via a stair from within the west wall. At the opposite end of the ditch, a wall crossed the ditch, and from this crossfire could be given. It was similarly entered from the west wall.

The outer courtyard was a larger area, and may once have been centred by gardens. It is of later date than the inner courtyard. The walls here were not as strongly built, though could still have prevented smaller assaults. A tower that was named and functioned as the 'Dovecote Tower' strengthens the north east corner. The outer gatehouse is situated midway along the western wall. In the south western corner stands a later house of 1665. It is known as Andrew Hay's house, and has two storeys and an attic. There is a round stair tower off-centre, and it is built against the perimeter wall. Lean-to subsidiary buildings probably surrounded this entire courtyard, and in many places on the interior wall, projecting corbels can be seen which would have supported their roofs.

Formerly known as Draffane, it was a Douglas property until their forfeiture in 1455. It was granted to the Hamiltons, and in about 1530 was given to Sir James Hamilton, 'the Bastard of Finnart'. Sir James was the illegitimate son of the 1st Earl of Arran. As a young man he had toured Europe, and had studied the defensive architecture of several countries. On his return he gained popularity at court, and with his continental experience, became Master of Works to James V. He was an acquisitive character, who frequently appears as a short-term owner of properties in the 16th century. He was willing to trade property with anyone, if the deal suited his personal ambitions at the time.

He began work on Craignethan about 1531, building it as a showcase for his talents and as the most sophisticated ex-

Craignethan Castle – outer courtyard and tower

ample of a castle designed for defence with and against artillery. Some argue that this is the irony, given that the land on the west is high enough to provide an artillery platform from which larger canon could strafe the entire site. Others would argue that the height of the west rampart and the squat nature of the keep prevent this. Either way the castle remains as a unique example of what could be achieved given a talent such as he. In 1540 he was beheaded for treason, obviously his wheeling and dealing had upset the king. The castle was regained by the Hamiltons from the Crown in 1542. The 2nd Earl of Arran added the outer court prior to the coronation of Mary Queen of Scots, when he gained the French title Duke of Chatelherault. He became Regent for Mary during her infancy, but later lost Craignethan and Cadzow to the Crown as he opposed her marriage to Darnley. He returned to regain both and support her after her enforced abdication, helping her escape from Loch Leven in 1568.

Lord Claud Hamilton had her as a guest at the castle, and next day led her forces at Langside. He lost the battle, as well as Cadzow and Craignethan to the Regent Moray. He recaptured the castles in the same year. Hamilton of Bothwellhaugh assassinated the Regent two years later.

The animosity between

Craignethan Castle – tower

those who controlled the young James VI and the Hamiltons continued, and in 1579 they were proclaimed outlaw. They fled to France, and both castles surrendered without a fight. Craignethan's massive west rampart was pulled down along with the north west tower.

The noted Covenanter, Andrew Hay, purchased Craignethan, and built himself a new house in the outer courtyard. The castle was bought by the Duke of Douglas in 1730. Along with Bothwell, it passed through his descendants until in 1949 the Earl of Home gave them into the care of the state.

Sir Walter Scott is said to have used Craignethan as model for 'Tillietudlem' in his novel *Old Mortality*, though he denied this. Of course, the railway companies followed their tradition of naming stations after places invented by Scott, and named the nearby station (now long gone) in honour of this link. The castle has since acquired Scott's invented name as an alias.

A headless spirit is said to haunt the castle, and it is suggested that this represents Queen Mary herself. Andrew Hay's house is also reported to have spectral visitations.

Historic Scotland: open Apr-Sep, daily; Mar & Oct, daily except Thu PM and Fri; closed Nov to Feb.

Tel: 01555 860365 – see page 217.

Other references: Draffane, Tillietudlem

Crawford Castle (**)

South Lanarkshire

Ruin or site   OS 72   NS 954213

0.5 miles north of Crawford, on minor roads east of the A74, just north of the River Clyde, and just south of Castle Crawford Farm.

Crawford Castle is sited upon the large motte of its predecessor, which retains traces of a silted up ditch and large bailey.

The castle consisted of an almost square enclosure within a curtain wall 5 ft thick, and measuring some 80 ft by 70 ft. Plans drawn by McGibbon and Ross show a remnant of a semicircular round tower in the north west corner. Similar towers at the other corners may have existed. The gateway was probably in the south wall, now mostly gone.

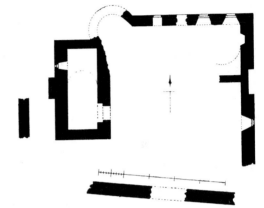

The north east corner of the court was once occupied by a vaulted building of one

Crawford Castle – plan (McGibbon and Ross)

storey. The northern two thirds of the western wall was formed by a large rectangular block of three storeys and a garret, of which only the once vaulted ground floor remains. There may have been a defensive wall to the west of the main block outwith the main enclosure. Much of what remains probably dates

Crawford Castle (McGibbon and Ross)

from the extensive 17th century rebuilding by the Marquis of Douglas.

The castle at Crawford was first recorded as early as 1175, and from an early date the hereditary keepers were the Carmichaels of Meadowflat. They retained the office until at least 1595, despite changes in ownership.

From the 13th century the barony and castle were the property of the Lindsays. Sir William Wallace captured the castle from the English in 1297. In 1488 it was granted to the Douglas Earl of Angus until his forfeiture in 1528. He had changed the name from Crawford Lindsay to Crawford Douglas. It thereafter became a favoured hunting seat of James V, who repaid his keepers hospitality by making his daughter pregnant (see Boghouse). On the king's death in 1542 the forfeiture was revoked, and the estate and castle reclaimed by the Earl of Angus. It was sold to Sir George Colebrooke in the 18th century.

Other References: Castle Crawford, Crawford Lindsay, Crawford Douglas, Tower Lindsay, Lindsay Tower

Crawford Douglas *see* Crawford Castle

Crawfordjohn Castle (*)
South Lanarkshire
Ruin or site   OS 71   NS 879239
3.5 miles west of Abington, in Crawfordjohn, just east of the B740, at its junction with minor roads, on knoll in centre of village.
This is the likely site of Crawfordjohn Castle, of which nothing now remains.

The barony was granted to John of Crawford in 1250. In the 13th century another John of Crawford died, leaving two daughters. One of these married Thomas Randolph, nephew to Robert the Bruce, and the other a Barclay. The castle came into royal possession by 1359, and was granted to the Douglases in 1366. They were forfeited in 1455, and it was given to the Hamiltons. It came to the Crawfords of Kilbirnie, who exchanged it with Sir James Hamilton of Finnart in 1528, and he was granted a licence to build towers within the barony. In 1540 after his forfeiture and execution for treason it was annexed to the Crown (see Boghouse). It returned to the Hamiltons in 1553 and remained with them until 1693.

Crawford Lindsay *see* Crawford Castle

Crookston Castle (***)
City of Glasgow
Ruin   OS 64   NS 524628
3 miles east of Paisley, on minor roads east of the A736, on south bank of Levern Water, just off Tower Avenue.
Sited upon the summit of a hog back ridge, and surrounded by the modern housing estate of Pollok, Crookston was thought to date from the 13th century,

but more modern estimates date it to about 1400. Roughly X-plan, it consists of a massive rectangular central block, once supported at each corner by towers. Only one of these remains intact, and of two there is little evidence.

It stands within a wide and deep ditch, the remnants of the earlier ring work predecessor. This is entered from the south east adjacent to the keepers cottage. The hill on three sides is steep, and on the north is an almost precipitous drop to the Levern Water.

The main block of the castle measures 60 ft by 40 ft, and sections of its walls reach 13 ft in thickness. There is one entrance to the castle, in the main block at the re-entrant with the north eastern tower. A machiolation above provided defence. The door was also defended by two doors and a portcullis, the sockets for drawbars can still be seen. This was cleverly designed, the first door opening outward, and when drawn back and the door opened, the bar would have prevented access to the stair. This straight stairway rises westward within the wall to the first floor. The passage directly facing the door enters a rib vaulted basement. This consists of a large single room, with mural stairs leading to the floor above at various points, and a recess within the wall contains the well. There are several arrow slot windows which provide light and enhance the defensive features of the castle.

Crookston Castle

A recess within the wall at first floor level also allows access to the well. The first floor contained the great hall, also vaulted, which has a large fireplace and windows with stone seats. The intact north eastern tower is entered from here.

The basement of this tower contains a guard room entered from just within the main door, and this room contains the hatch which opens to reveal a pit prison. The upper floors must be entered from the hall. There is a single room to each floor, and you climb by modern wrought iron ladders to the centre of the floor of each. This can be a harrowing experience for sufferers of vertigo, as it is possible to look down to the starting point several floors below! There are four storeys above the basement, each illuminated by long slot windows. The upper story, containing the lord's bedroom, has a larger window to the east. The corbelling which supported a parapet and bartizans at the open sides is continuous, though it is likely that this was added in the renovations which were undertaken to commemorate Queen Victoria's visit to the city in 1847. The view from the roof is well worth the trauma of the climb.

Little remains of the south eastern tower other than a vaulted basement.

The original ring work defences were constructed by Sir Robert de Croc (hence Crookston) of Neilston in the 12th century. The estate was purchased in 1330 by Sir Alan Stewart of the Darnley Stewarts, and his descendants built the castle around 1400. This family gained the Earldom of Lennox in 1425 on the execution for treason of the old Celtic earl and his heirs. In 1489 the family with the Lyles of Duchal went into rebellion against James IV. His reply was severe. Bringing the great bombard Mons Meg from Edinburgh, he destroyed the western end of the castle forcing the submission of the castle. He continued to Duchal, with or without the cannon, repeated his action, and then to Dumbarton, where Lord Darnley, son of the Earl, was in charge.

In 1544 the Regent Arran and Cardinal Beaton laid siege to the castle while the Earl of Lennox was holding Glasgow Castle against would be assailants.

A later Lord Darnley was to become husband of Mary Queen of Scots, and it is beneath an ancient yew tree at the castle that they were allegedly betrothed. This tree was cut down in the 19th century, and its wood used to create a carved model of Crookston, which can now be seen in Pollok House. Darnley was murdered at Kirk O' Field in Edinburgh in 1567.

Crookston passed through various hands, until in 1757 it was sold by the Graham Duke of Montrose to the Maxwells of Pollok.

Sir John Stirling Maxwell was a founder of The National Trust for Scotland, and gifted them Crookston as their first property in 1931. It is still owned by the trust, though administered by Historic Scotland – open to public see page 217.

Crossbasket Castle (**)
South Lanarkshire
Private   OS 64   NS 665599
2 miles south west of Blantyre, and 1 mile north east of East Kilbride, on minor road north of A725 and B7012, above east bank of River Calder Gorge, at Crossbasket.
Crossbasket is a 16th century tower house of three storeys and a garret, within a corbelled out parapet. The superstructure of Crossbasket Castle remains intact, though altered. The interior has been completely rebuilt on the addition of the adjoining 19th century mansion.

The tower remains, albeit with the original doorways blocked and windows enlarged. The continuous corbelling of the parapet may have been renewed at the rebuilding. There are numerous water spouts to drain the wall head. There

Crossbasket Castle

is a square caphouse at the south east corner. The garret storey has large dormer windows. The walls are harled. The hall was originally on the first floor, and the basement vaulted.

Crossbasket was the jointure house of the Lindsays of Mains, though is now operated by the American-based 'Missionaries of the Latter Day Rain' as a warehouse storing charitable donations for Romania. There is a children's day nursery which raises funds to maintain the operation.

Culcreuch Castle (**)
The Lennox & East Dunbartonshire
Private   OS 57   NS 620876
0.5 miles north of Fintry, by minor roads north of B822, 0.25 miles north of Endrick Water, at Culcreuch Castle Hotel.
Culcreuch consists of a 16th century keep, extended to the east and north at the end of the 17th century.

The keep measures 41 ft by 28.75 ft, and is of four storeys including a garret. The walls are about 9 ft thick through which there was a door into the basement at the northern end of the eastern wall. Within the wall on either side of the entrance are small recesses, one of which may have led to an original stair. The basement has two connected vaulted chambers, originally lit by slot windows. There were gunloops.

There was a main entrance on the first floor, entered by removable ladder, above the basement door. The hall had a fireplace in the southern wall which has been replaced by a more modern version. There is an aumbry with moulded ogee arched frame in the west wall. The windows are larger than on the base-

Culcreuch Castle

Culcreuch Castle

ment floor, and in the east wall have been opened up to provide access to the mansion. There remain two windows each in the west and south walls.

The plan of the second and garret floors are similar, having been divided into one small room and one large with access corridor. Each room had its own fireplace, and enlarged windows. The remnants of a garderobe chute have been discovered in the west wall.

The floor of the attic room is 3.5 ft below the level of the wall walk outside. The parapet is supported on chequered corbelling, with a single continuous corbel supporting all. There are many water spouts. The upper part of the parapet wall has been replaced. The stairways between the floors have now gone, access to each being from the mansion. The original stair was probably sited within the wall at the north east corner.

The entrance to the mansion is decorated by worn armorial stones, one dated 1721. The alteration to the windows of the tower and other changes internally, were probably made when the extension was added.

Culcreuch was a major stronghold of the Galbraiths from early times. In 1630 Robert Galbraith sold out to Alexander Seton, who sold it on to Robert Napier in 1632. It was acquired by Alexander Speirs in 1796. He built a large and successful cotton mill on the estate. It passed into other hands in 1896, and is now a hotel – see page 217. It possibly supported a garrison of Cromwell's troops and is allegedly haunted by a harper. The story originates in 1582 when a Buchanan was fatally wounded by Robert Galbraith, son of the then laird. The dying man was accompanied by his mistress and when he died she began to play a clarsach, a wire-strung harp. It is said that sometimes in the dead of night her playing can still be heard. There are also said to be other manifestations.

104

Cumbernauld Castle (**)
The Lennox & East Dunbartonshire
Ruin or Site   OS 64   NS 773759
In Cumbernauld, off minor roads south of A80, east of Cumbernauld Village, at Cumbernauld House.

Cumbernauld House contains much stone from the late 14th century castle of the Flemings. The courtyard now acts as car park for the house. It contains portions of the original wall and subsidiary buildings, including two vaulted chambers. There is a renovated 16th century doocot at the east gate.

Excavations of 1963-4 uncovered the remains of a 15th century rubbish chute, a prison, and a 17th century well house to the north east of the house. The excavation was filled in. A motte of the Comyns sits in the park to the east.

Cumbernauld was originally part of the Comyns great barony of Kirkintilloch. Robert the Bruce granted it to the Flemings of Biggar in 1306. They built the tower towards the end of the 14th century, and extended it later by adding several buildings including a large hallhouse. They replaced the castle by commissioning Cumbernauld House, a mansion by William Adam, in the early 18th century. The house occupies the castle site, stone from the castle being used in the construction. It now provides offices for Cumbernauld Development Corporation.

Robert Fleming was the son of the Lord of Biggar. He was one of the Bruce's strongest friends and allies. He died just prior to Bannockburn, but Bruce had shown his gratitude by knighting his son, Malcolm, and rewarding him with this portion of the Comyn's vast lowland estate. Later Sir Malcolm was given the Sheriffdom of Dunbartonshire, and made keeper of the castle. Finding it simpler to manage his duties as one domain, it was he who arranged that Cumbernauld and the estate become part of the shire of Dumbarton, albeit detached. This curious anomaly persisted in local government organisation until recently, and is honoured in the division of the maps in this book.

About 1371 the family decided to move their main seat from Kirkintilloch to Cumbernauld, this being more central for involvement in national affairs.

In 1440 another Sir Malcolm of Cumbernauld was one of the party of the Earl of Douglas murdered at the 'Black Dinner' at Edinburgh Castle: Douglas and his companions having been accused of treason. Sir John Fleming protested his father's innocence for many years thereafter, and James II may have visited Cumbernauld during his investigations. The outcome did not change recorded history, though at some point Sir John was made a lord of parliament and gained the title Lord Cumbernauld.

In the time of James IV, the second Lord John married Euphemia, a daughter of Lord Drummond. King James had a poorly concealed relationship with this lady's sister Margaret. James made frequent visits to Cumbernauld with the excuse that he was hunting the famous wild white cattle that lived in the woods there at the time. It is supposed that meetings with Margaret Drummond were the real reason for his visits. The relationship led to tragedy as Euphemia, Margaret and their sister Sybilla died after dining at Stobhall or Drummond Castle, each suffering an agonising death with severe abdominal pain. Poison was suspected but never proven – they are buried side by side at Dunblane Cathedral. James subsequently married Margaret Tudor, sister to the English King Henry VIII, for political reasons. She was the choice of James's counsellors, though it is said that James had wanted to make Margaret Drummond his queen. In the end James's marriage to the Tudors led to the Union of the Crowns.

The Flemings importance at court was maintained: Mary Fleming, daughter of Lord Fleming, being one of Queen Mary's four 'Maries' who accompanied her in her flight to France as an infant. James, Lord Fleming, was one of a party of commissioners sent to arrange Mary's marriage to the French Dauphin, though he died with his companions on their return journey. Again poison and English desires for another Anglo-Scottish royal marriage were suspected.

Later Mary visited Cumbernauld, and during the feasting the roof of the great hall collapsed. The next Lord James was Mary's Governor of Dumbarton, who escaped the 'daring raid' of 1571. He had fought at her side at Langside in 1568 and assisted her flight to England.

In 1606 James VI granted the title Earl of Wigtown to John Fleming. The first Earl married Lilias, daughter to the Earl of Montrose. His son, the next Lord Cumbernauld, was therefore friend, ally and cousin to the first Marquis of Montrose. This led to the first Covenant being signed at Cumbernauld, the document becoming known as the Cumbernauld Bond. In due course, Montrose reverted to the side of the monarchy as the aims of the Covenant became more extreme, and war ensued. Following a brilliant campaign, Montrose was finally defeated at Philiphaugh in 1645, his entire bodyguard dying protecting his escape. Among his immediate staff who escaped with him was Lord Cumbernauld, and he subsequently became the Earl of Wigtown.

In 1747 the last male heir died, and the title passed by marriage to the Elphinstones. The house was left for Carberry as the main seat, though a grandson added Fleming to his name in order to gain the title. He was Admiral Charles Elphinstone-Fleming, and a much revered local parliamentarian for Stirling. He died at Cumbernauld House.

In the 19th century the title moved south of the border by inheritance, and eventually the estate was broken up and sold. Cumbernauld was purchased by Lord Inverclyde, but the house burned down before he could move in.

It was later renovated with an altered interior: only the facade remains of Adam's work.

D

Dalzell House (***)

North Lanarkshire
Private   OS 64   NS 765550
1.5 miles south east of Motherwell, on minor roads south of A721, west of Muirhouse, south of Motherwell College, 0.5 miles north of River Clyde, at Dalzell.
Situated on the western edge of a treacherous ravine, Dalzell is a much altered and extended castle. The earliest portion dates from the 15th century, though it was added to at various times until it now encloses a courtyard. There remains a section of moat guarding the western approach to the main entrance.

The oldest section is a three storey keep of the 15th century, with corbelled out parapet and modernised garret. Measuring 39 ft by 32 ft, and 48 ft to the parapet, there is an unusual buttress-like projection in the south west corner. This was 2.75 ft deep and 17 ft wide, and had the original entrance at its centre. There was a portcullis, for which the grooves remain, guarding the door.

Dalzell House (McGibbon and Ross)

The basement was vaulted, as was the hall on the first floor above. The hall has corbels projecting from the wall, suggesting an intermediate wooden floor dividing the room into two storeys. The second floor had mural chambers and galleries.

A straight mural stair from the entrance led up to the first floor, and a turnpike continues from there to the storeys above. The parapet was of chequered corbels supporting open rounds at the corners.

In the 17th century extensions were added to the north and south of the keep, and westward from the southern end of the south extension. This completed two sides of a rectangle, the remainder being made up by a wall, parts of which remain. The extension provided a vaulted kitchen with vaulted cellar space below. There are shot holes throughout.

For three years from 1857 the famed architect R. W. Billings lived in the castle, as he designed and built the northern wing. This was designed to sympathise with the older structures, which he greatly altered in the process, leaving the structure seen today. His

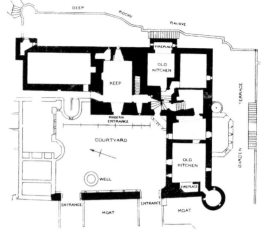

Dalzell House – plan (McGibbon and Ross)

alterations included enlarging the windows of the keep, moving the main entrance to a central position on the west wall, and building a wing out from the south wall to overlook the terraced gardens. He also added a wall along the edge of the ravine and from there along the southern front encasing the gardens until reaching the moat at the western approach. A well was introduced within the courtyard. In recent years the structure has been renovated for use as private flats. Park open to the public – see page 217.

The estate belonged to the Dalziel Earls of Carnwath from the 13th century. In 1649 it was sold to Hamilton of Boggs. This family became Lords Hamilton of Dalzell.

Dalziel House *see* Dalzell House

Dalyell House *see* Dalzell House

Dargavel Castle (**)
Renfrewshire
Private   OS 64   NS 433693
1 mile south of Bishopton, on minor roads south of A8, within the Royal Ordnance Factory, Dargavel.
Dargavel House is a large Z-plan structure of three storeys and an attic, dating in part from 1574, and extended and remodelled in 1670. It was again remodelled by David Bryce in 1849, and subsequently in 1910. It consists of a main block with two round towers projecting from diagonally opposite corners. The entrance was

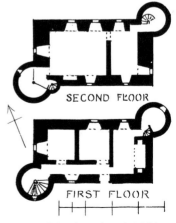

Dargavel Castle – plans (M&R)

in the south wall, from which a corridor led to the south west tower. This contained a turnpike stair to first floor level. From first floor level, a further angle turret was corbelled out of the re-entrant, carrying a turnpike to the floors above. This stair turret has a small window, surmounted by a sundial of 1670. A similar stairway existed within the north east tower.

The ground floor was vaulted and contained a kitchen and two cellars. The first floor had the hall and two private rooms. There was a large fireplace in the east wall of the hall. There were two disproportionate rooms on the second floor. A mansion wing has been added to the south eastern corner, producing an L-plan.

A dated armorial stone of 1584 in the east gable confirms the construction date, and the builders as Maxwells.

Dargavel Castle (McGibbon and Ross)

Darleith House (*)

The Lennox & East Dunbartonshire.
Ruin or site   OS 63   NS 345806.
2 miles north of Cardross, on minor roads north of A814, at Darleith Farm.
This ruinous neoclassical mansion of the 18th century incorporates a much altered 16th century tower house with round bartizans. It was a property of the Darleith family from 1510, until sold in 1670 to the Yuills.

Darngaber Castle (*)

South Lanarkshire
Ruin or site   OS 64   NS 730501
4 miles south of Hamilton, 0.5 miles south east of Quarter, off A723 or B7078, Darngaber.
An 1879 reference stated that only foundations remained of the tower of Thomas, 2nd son of Hamilton of Cadzow. Small cellar vaults were discovered. A motte marks the site.

Darnley Castle (**)
City of Glasgow
Private   OS 64   NS 527586
1.5 miles north east of Barrhead, at Darnley Toll, south of A726, at 'The Mill'.
A round stair tower and adjoining room survived in use as a doocot, then part of a mill, and remain today as part of the renovated mill complex, operating as a restaurant – see page 218.

This was the ancestral home of the Stewarts of Darnley. It was from this property that Queen Mary's second husband, Henry, Lord Darnley, took his title. In 1488 the family became Earls of Lennox, and Darnley's father was Regent for the young James VI until Lennox was murdered.

In 1679 Ludovick Stewart was summonsed for a debt of £11,146, and lost much of the estate. In 1689 the old castle was purchased by the Duke of Montrose, and allowed to fall into ruin. It passed to the Maxwells of Nether Pollok, who demolished most of the structure leaving only the remaining portion, and that roofless. Later it was developed for other uses mentioned.

It has been rebuilt with cleansed original stone, though with some concession to modern requirements. The undressed section of the building represents the castle remains, the other buildings having been whitewashed.

Dennistoun Castle (*)
Renfrewshire
Ruin or site   OS 63   NS 364673
2 miles south of Kilmacolm, south of A721, north of Gryffe Water, at or near Craigends Dennistoun.
Site of an early castle of the Dennistoun family, later of Colgrain.

A motte to the north west may represent the original family seat. The family took their name from the lands, originally Danzieltoun. They still used the property in the 16th century, some 100 years after moving their main residence to Colgrain, the latter being more convenient in their role as hereditary keepers of Dumbarton Castle.

Sir John Dennistoun was uncle to Elizabeth Mure of Rowallan, wife of Robert II, precipitating the proud family boast: 'Kings have come o' us, not we of kings.'

A later member of the family gave their name to an area of Glasgow.

Devon Castle *see* Dowane

Dolphinton Castle (*)
South Lanarkshire
Ruin or site   OS 72   NT 106466?
On A702, 4 miles south west of West Linton, Dolphinton.
Site of a castle, which in the 15th century belonged to the Hepburns.

Dougalston House (*)

The Lennox & East Dunbartonshire
Private   OS 64   NS 565743
East of Milngavie, east of A81, just north of junction with A807, at Dougalston House.
The present house replaced, or may incorporate part of, an older structure, probably fortified.

This was a house of the Grahams from an early date, though there is a suggestion that it once belonged to the Douglases of Mains, which is nearby, and that the name was corrupted. In 1591 Walter Graham of Dougalston became the latest in a long series of local lairds to seriously quarrel with his neighbour Hamilton of Bardowie. On this occasion the outcome does not appear to have been fatal, though several Hamiltons had lost their lives in similar disputes. By 1796 Dougalston belonged to a Crawford.

The present house stands within a golf course, and acts as clubhouse.

Douglas Castle (*)

South Lanarkshire
Ruin or site   OS 72   NS 843318
0.75 miles north of Douglas, on minor roads west of A70, east of the Douglas Water, and 1 mile south of M74.

A round corner tower and vaulted cellars are all that remain of the castle. A later mansion of the Dukes of Douglas, designed by the Adam brothers, is long since gone.

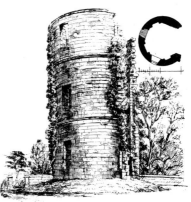

The round tower which remains is thin walled, and of later date, possibly 17th century.

The family took their name from Douglas Water, or 'Black Water' as it translates. This was their original estate before they reaped the rewards of Sir James Douglas's unfailing support for Robert the Bruce.

Douglas Castle (M&R)

First recorded in 1288, the castle was held by the English in 1307, and recaptured by stratagem by Sir James while the garrison were at worship in the chapel. It became known as 'Douglas's Larder' since he had the garrison put to death and the castle burnt and razed.

It had been rebuilt by 1455 when James II had it sacked after the Battle of Arkinholm, at which the Black Douglases were defeated then forfeited.

It was rebuilt allegedly by Clifford, giving it the by-name of 'Harry's Tower'. This tower house was destroyed by fire in 1755 and the round tower is a remnant of this or a surrounding wall. In 1707 the family had been created Dukes of Douglas. Fifty years later they had the Adam brothers build them a grand castellated mansion, on a large scale with various round towers and turrets. The Earls of Home inherited the house and estate. The mansion was demolished between 1937 and 1948 due to subsidence caused by coal mining.

In recent times a historical theme park has been proposed within the parkland around the site, including replicas of a crannog, and a motte and bailey castle. Developments are awaited.

Dowane Castle (*)
South Lanarkshire
Ruin or site   OS 71   NS 857422
1.5 miles south west of Lanark, at Greenrig, 2 miles south west of A72 at Kirkfieldbank.
Between 1180 and 1203 the lands of Dowane were granted by the Abbot of Kelso, Superior of Lesmahagow, to one Constantine, who took the name De Dowane and was son of a priest at Lesmahagow named Gilbert. In 1294 the estate was divided into two, Dowane and Auchtyfardle (at or near Bogside, OS 71 NS 826 409), and each apparently supported its own 'tenement', or tower house. Both properties came to the Weirs, as did much of the area. However, in 1546 Auchtyfardle became a Kennedy holding.
Other references: Devon, Greenrig

Draffane Castle *see* Craignethan Castle

Druid's Temple (*)
Renfrewshire
Ruin or site   OS 64   NS 537574?
2 miles east and south of Barrhead, off B769, in or close to Cathcart Castle Golf Course, Williamwood.
A knoll, once known as Druid's Temple, supported the foundations of a building believed to have been an ancient keep. This structure stood within what remained of a walled circular enclosure.

Drumquassle Castle (*)
The Lennox & East Dunbartonshire
Ruin or site   OS 57   NS 483869.
1.5 miles south east of Drymen, south of A811 or west of A81, on the north bank of the Endrick, at Park of Drumquassle.
Site of a house or castle occupied in the 16th century by the Cunninghams. In 1572 Sir John Cunningham of Drumquassle was keeper of Dumbarton Castle. He had been appointed joint commander of the small force which took it in the 'Daring Raid' of 1571. By 1577 he was Master of the King's Household.

Drumry Peel (*)

City of Glasgow
Ruin or site   OS 64   NS 515711
2 miles east and south of Duntocher, off Drumry Place, Drumchapel, at Drumry Primary School.
Drumry was a three storey tower with a corbelled out turret in the north east corner. It once had an extension to the east, which was removed in 1959. The Peel survived into this century, and is still entered on some Glasgow street atlases, but no trace remains.

It was built in 1530-40 by Lawrence Crawford, and replaced an earlier house. Originally a Wemyss property, it passed to the Livingstones in 1338. Sir Robert Livingstone of Drumry was Lord Treasurer of Scotland until executed in 1447. The last Livingstone laird fell at Flodden in 1513, and Sir James Hamilton, 'the Bastard of Finnart', married his heiress, Margaret. He had no sooner got his hands on the estate than in 1528 he exchanged Drumry with the Crawfords for Crawfordjohn and Kilbirnie. Crawford probably built the Peel, before being accused of treason. It therefore came to Lord Semple in 1545. It was a ruin by 1836, when it was restored, and this may be when the extension was added as farm accommodation. It was demolished in the late 1960s.
Other references: East Kilpatrick

Drumsagard Castle (*)

South Lanarkshire
Ruin or site   OS 64   NS 666597
3.5 miles north west of Hamilton, off A724, 100 yards south west of Hallside village, Cambuslang.
Drumsagard from 'Druim-saigard', hill of the priests.

Nothing remains of Drumsagard Castle, a 14th century stone castle on a rounded, flat topped mound at the end of a ridge. There was an early castle on

Drumsagard Castle – site

this site, John Moray (Murray) of Drumsagard being one of those forfeited by Edward I in 1306 as penalty for supporting Robert the Bruce during the Wars of Independence. This same gentleman had married the heiress of Malise, Earl of Strathearn, in 1299, and their descendants became the Murrays of Tullibardine. They were related to the Morays (Murrays) of Bothwell, descended from Walter de Moravia who had married the Olifard (Oliphant) heiress of the Justiciar of Lothian, owner of the baronies of Drumsagard and Bothwell. The caput of his Drumsagard barony was the impressive motte at Greenlees Hill, just north of the Burnside-East Kilbride road, between Greenlees Road and Turnlaw Road. In common with Bothwell, Drumsagard passed to the Douglases in 1370, though on their forfeiture in 1455, it passed to the Hamiltons. Drumsagard was a ruin by 1796, and the remaining stone used to build the Hallside Farms nearby.

The Hamiltons retained the property until the 1920s, when all the land was sold. Westburn House, built in 1685, had become the main residence of the Drumsagard barony, and was demolished this century. There remains a doocot on Cambuslang Golf Course, and another that is similar on the banks of the Clyde at Daldowie, though this probably belonged to another property.

The Hamiltons also had an 18th century 'lodge' on Dechmonthill, the grounds of which are now used as a firing range by the Territorial Army: something to keep you on your toes when gun fire can be heard from where you write!

The name of the barony was changed to Cambuslang in the 17th century. Other references: Drumsargard, Drumsharg

Drumsargard Castle *see* Drumsagard Castle

Dubs (**)

Renfrewshire
Private   OS 64   NS 516591
Dubs Farm, Dubs Road, off B773, Barrhead.
The defensive potential of this site is obvious. On a knoll, guarded by a burn and only approachable by a narrow looping drive, it was a small two storey fortified house, now with altered facade. Built of roughly hewn sandstone blocks, it retains a well preserved barmkin, albeit with a modern fabricated roof. There is now a conservatory, and enlarged modern windows. Sandblasting of the yellow sandstone walls and extensive modernisation disguise the ancient nature of the house.

Dubs was a Maxwell property for 560 years from 1271. In 1745 Maxwell of Dubs went to fight for the Hanoverians, and trusting neither his family nor bankers hid his fortune high up in Darnley Glen, a rhyme giving a clue to its whereabouts. He never returned to collect it and occasional finds of gold and silver coins in the area give credence to the legend and keep the interest alive:

'Yont Capelrig and Lyoncross, and eke the auld harestane,
There a rowth o' siller lies, who finds a king will sain'.'
Maybe investing in a metal detector would be a good idea ...

Duchal Castle (*)

Renfrewshire
Ruin or site   OS 63   NS 334685
1.5 miles west of Kilmacolm, by minor roads and foot south of B788, on a peninsula created by the confluence of the Burnbank and Blacketty Waters.

Fragments of curtain wall and traces of foundations of a keep are all that remain of a large courtyard castle, probably dating from as early as the 13th century.

The curtain wall set apart all the high ground of the peninsula, giving an internal area of 210 ft by 90 ft. This could only be approached over the narrow neck of land at the western end. Precipitous 20 ft drops guarded the northern edge above the Burnbank Water, while a steep bank protected the east and south.

The remnants of the wall remain on the north. The entrance to the courtyard was assumed to be in the north western angle. A deep ditch was cut across the neck of the peninsula, guarding the approach.

In the south eastern corner of the yard a 20 ft high rocky knoll is surmounted by foundations of a keep measuring 33 ft by 39 ft with walls of 5 ft thickness. This was sur-

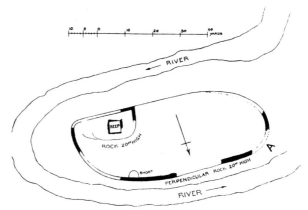

Duchal Castle – plan (M&R)

rounded by its own high curtain wall. The structures are impossible to date due to the poor quality of the remains, which are now overgrown. Although overlooked by higher ground, access to this would have been very difficult and therefore no threat.

Duchal was a property of the Lyle family from the 13th century. Sir Robert was made Lord Lyle in the 1440s. At some point the family were Lords High Justiciar of Scotland. Lord Lyle supported the Lennox rebellion of 1489 against James IV, and James besieged Duchal in the same campaign which saw the fall of Crookston and Dumbarton. Although Mons Meg was used at Crookston, there is no evidence to suggest that it was used at Duchal, and equally scant evidence to show that it was not. Nevertheless the castle fell, and the rebellion was crushed. It is claimed that Duchal may have been ruinous since then. However, James IV returned to stay, and liaise with one of his mistresses, Marion Boyd. They had a son, James Stewart, who became Archbishop of St Andrews and died with his father at Flodden in 1513. When John, 4th Lord Lyle, died in 1544, the estate passed by marriage to Montgomery of Lainshaw, and was then sold to the Porterfield family. Thereafter the castle fell into ruin.

Dumbarton Castle (**)
The Lennox & East Dunbartonshire
Ruin or site   OS 64   NS 400744
On the north shore of the Clyde, south of Dumbarton town centre, off minor roads south of A814 and A82.

Dumbarton from 'Dun Breatan', Fort of the Britons. Built upon a twin peaked volcanic plug which oversees the Firth of Clyde, only a 14th century portcullis arch and some portions of the guard house remain of the medieval royal castle of Dumbarton. The remaining structure is essentially a military fortress of the 18th and 19th centuries.

Dumbarton has been fortified since at least as early as the 5th century, when St Patrick wrote to the subjects of Ceretic, King of Alcluith, castigating them for a piratical raid on his Irish converts and selling Christians into slavery.

It was the capital of the kingdom of Strathclyde, the nation of the Britons, and was besieged on several occasions. In 756 a combined force of Picts and Northumbrians took the castle, only to be annihilated themselves a few days later. The buildings on the rock were burned in 780, though it is not certain whether this was a result of hostile activity.

In 870 a Viking attack led by Olaf the White of Dublin and Ivar the One-Legged led to a four-month siege. They severed the water supply and starved the occupants to submission. The castle was plundered for its wealth and people, 200 longships carrying the booty to Dublin. This marked the demise of the Britons.

They returned to strength in

Dumbarton Castle – 14th century entrance

the 10th century, and extended their territory southwards. In 1018 following the death of Owen the Bald, last king of the Britons, at the Battle of Carham, Malcolm II of Scots was able to set his grandson Duncan upon the British throne. When Duncan succeeded to the Scots throne in 1034, Strathclyde was finally integrated into the Scottish kingdom.

Little is then heard of Dumbarton until 1222 when the burgh charter mentions the new castle. Dumbarton at this time was of significant importance as it guarded the western approaches to the realm from the Viking territories of the Isles and west Highlands. Until their defeat at the Battle of Largs in 1263, the territory of the Norsemen came as close as Kilcreggan on the Rosneath peninsula, where it is likely that a Norse watch tower occupied the site of what is now Craigrownie Castle.

From these early years it is evident that Dumbarton was a royal castle, and as such was a target of Edward I in his invasion of 1296. He subsequently installed sympathetic Governors, such as Sir John Menteith, the captor of William Wallace in 1305. Legend asserts that Wallace was brought here as a prisoner prior to his departure for London, though many think this unlikely.

In 1333, in the aftermath of the Battle of Halidon Hill, the Scots sent their young king David II and his queen Joanna of England to reside here for security. At this point Edward Balliol was attempting to regain his father's former realm for himself with English support. Dumbarton, although on the west coast, was then to become Scottish royalty's accustomed embarkation point for the safety of France, and the young couple departed in early 1334.

As a royal castle under the care of the rebellious Earl of Lennox in 1489, it was again besieged by the young James IV himself, the castle being occupied by Lord Darnley, the Earl's heir. The siege failed as the garrison burnt the burgh, but James returned the same year and was successful. He may have utilised the great bombard Mons Meg in the assault.

The castle remained at the centre of national events, when in 1514, during the minority of James V in the aftermath of Flodden, it was held by the Lord Erskine for the Queen Mother. The Earl of Lennox captured it at this time on behalf of the opposing faction led by the Earl of Arran. The assailants had tunnelled below the north entrance and stormed the garrison.

A year later the Duke of Albany arrived at the castle from France to take up his duties as Governor of Scotland. As the late king's cousin he had been invited to take up the role as a neutral, and immediately arrested Lennox, installing a garrison of Frenchmen. He thereafter used Dumbarton as his regular port of departure to France. In 1523 he arrived with a large French force with the intention of invading England, but the plan was never followed through due to inconsistent support from the Scots. He left the following year with his troops and never returned. The divided Scots nobles squabbled over the castle and control passed among the various parties until James V regained it as a base for several sorties to the west.

In 1548 it again had a royal resident, as the young Queen Mary was brought to the castle to protect her from the effects of the 'Rough Wooing' of Henry VIII. She left for France within five months, where she married the Dauphin, heir apparent to the throne. She returned to visit (didn't she visit everywhere?) in

1563. Her Governor of the castle was Lord Fleming of Cumbernauld, who fled with her to
England after Langside in
1568. He returned in 1570 to be
besieged in the castle by the
Regent Moray. The arrival of a
French fleet and the murder of
Moray relieved him within a
few weeks.

Fleming held the castle for
the queen until 1571, when
Captain Thomas Crawford of
Jordanhill took it for the young
James VI: his assault is re-
corded in detail.

Leaving Glasgow an hour
before sunset on the evening of
31 March, Crawford and about
a hundred men carried ladders
and ropes with iron hooks.
They were armed with mus-
kets. By 1 am they halted a mile
from the castle, and bound
their guns to their backs, and
crossed what was then marsh-

Dumbarton Castle – from Finlaystone

land to the north east curtain wall, at the highest point of the cliff where attack
would be least suspected. Climbing by stages they reached the base of the wall
at dawn, and as the first of the assailants crossed the wall tops, a sentry raised
the alarm. The garrison awoke and were attacked by Crawford's men. Three
died, and the remainder fled. Crawford established his forces on the area known
as the Beak, the summit of the eastern peak, and when no counter attack developed used the castles own artillery against the remaining garrison strong points.
Most of the garrison fled, some were captured, but the Lord Fleming made his
escape by sea. Archbishop Hamilton of St Andrews, one of the exiled queen's
staunchest supporters, was captured, and later tried and executed.

The castle changed hands several times during the Covenanting period, and
the Civil War. It sustained much damage, and required extensive repair by the
time extension and improvement work was begun in 1675.

Thereafter the castle functioned mostly as a state prison, with a few noble
inmates, until it regained some strategic importance as a military installation in
the Jacobite years. From then on military buildings and gun batteries obliter-
ated the medieval castle, as its role continued through the Napoleonic wars

and into the 19th century. It was used as a military prison throughout this period. The constructions of that time represent the bulk of what can be seen today. It remained in use as a military installation until World War II when two bombs were dropped on it during the raids on Clydebank.

Historic Scotland: open all year, daily except closed Thu PM and Fri Oct -Mar Tel: 01389 732167 – see page 218.

Other references: Alcluith, Alt Clut, Clyde Rock

Dundaff Castle *see* Graham's Castle

Dunglass Castle (**)

The Lennox & East Dunbartonshire
Private   OS 64   NS 435735
2 miles east of Dumbarton, south of the A82, on north bank of Firth of Clyde, within Oil Terminal grounds.

Little remains of the 14th century castle with a sea gate, other than a portion of courtyard wall and an incorporated round tower. A turreted house of the late 16th century stands within the north eastern corner of the yard, and this was extended and remodelled in the 19th century.

The house is thought to have been built by Humphrey Colquhoun of Luss toward the end of the 16th century. Although the house is much altered, the

Dunglass Castle (McGibbon and Ross) – since rebuilt

round turret corbelled out from the north west corner is thought to be from this time.

Dunglass was for centuries the main stronghold of the Colquhouns, who took their name from this parish. They later inherited the Luss estates by marrying the heiress. From 1439 to 1478 this was the home of Sir John Colquhoun, Chamberlain of Scotland. In 1592 the builder of the house, Humphrey Colquhoun, was murdered at Bannachra by a MacFarlane archer with the aid of Colquhoun's own manservant.

The Edmonstones gained Dunglass in 1738, but it fell into ruin soon afterwards. In 1783 the castle began to be used as a quarry in the building of a new quay. This process was halted by Buchanan of Auchentorlie who purchased, extended and restored the house.

Due to its location within the oil terminal and the dangerously dilapidated state of the structure, access is denied. Re-roofing is being planned for the near future.

Dunrod Castle (*)

Renfrewshire
Ruin or site   OS 63   NS 224732
3.5 miles south west of Greenock, on minor roads east of A78, west of railway, at Dunrod.
Site of the original stronghold of the Lindsays of Dunrod, who were granted the former Comyn estate of Mains at East Kilbride by Robert the Bruce for their loyalty during the Wars of Independence. John Lindsay was one of those who ensured the death of the 'Red Comyn' when he was stabbed by Bruce in Grey-friars Kirk in Dumfries on 10 February 1306.

Dunrod was sold by his descendant, Alexander Lindsay of Dunrod, to Archibald Stewart of Blackhall. Lindsay died in poverty, and an old rhyme describes the attitude towards one member of his family:

'In Innerkip the witches ride thick,
And in Dunrod they dwell,
But the greatest loon among them a',
Was auld Dunrod himsel'.'

Dunsyre Castle (*)

South Lanarkshire
Ruin or site   OS 72   NT 073482?
At or near Dunsyre, 6 miles east of Carnwath, on minor roads north of A721 at Newbigging, east of A702 north of Dolphinton.
Near the parish church stood a three-storey tower with vaulted basement and mural turnpike stair.

William de Newbygging held the lands until granted to the Douglases in 1368. In 1444 they gave a half portion of the property to Hepburn of Hailes, later Earl of Bothwell, who exchanged the remainder for Hermitage Castle in Liddesdale in 1492. This, among many other properties, changed hands in a deal which saw the Douglases regain Bothwell, and increase the Hepburns landholding in an area where he already held Elsrickle, Dolphinton and Walston. Dunsyre later passed to the Lockharts of The Lee. It was the seat of the barony, and courts were still held there until 1740 despite its ruinous state: at which time it retained its 'instruments of torture'. Of eight other towers in the parish mentioned in *Castles of Scotland*, one reference states that four were sited at Hills, Torbrex, Westhall, and Todholes, while elsewhere stating that one stood at Todholes, two at Westhall, and five at Easter Saxon. Entries within this book which are within the parish are at Weston, Walston, Westhall, Torbrex, Elsrickle, Dolphinton, Dunsyre, Hills, Ogs Castle, Todholes and Edmonston.

Duntarvet Castle *see* Duntervy Castle

Duntervy Castle (*)
South Lanarkshire.
Ruin or site   OS 72   NS 828401
4.5 miles south west of Lanark, 1 mile east of M74 and Lesmahagow, off minor roads south of B7018, just north of Brocketsbrae, at Dumbraxhill.
Site of a 15th century castle, occupied in the 16th century by the Durham family. The head of this family built part of Lesmahagow's first post-Reformation church, which section was known as the Durham Aisle.
Other references: Duntarvet Castle

Duntreath Castle (***)
The Lennox & East Dunbartonshire
Private   OS 64   NS 536811
4 miles north of Milngavie, and 1 mile north of Blanefield, just west of the A81, and east of Blane Water, at Duntreath.
Duntreath, pronounced Duntreth, lies in the Blane Valley close to the lofty conical mound of 'Dungoiach', guarding the southern approaches to the heartland of the great Earldom of Lennox. This was therefore a position of strategic importance in early centuries, forming a gateway to and from the Highlands. It consists of a large keep of the 15th century, once with extensive additions of the late 16th and early 17th centuries which created a large quadrangular courtyard castle and external measurements of 120 ft by 100 ft. Much of the 17th century

Duntreath Castle (McGibbon and Ross)

structure has gone, replaced in part by extensions of the 19th century.
    The western wall of the courtyard was broken centrally by an arched gatehouse of three storeys with turnpike stair and round corner towers defending

the outward approaches. This was adorned by a heraldic panel bearing the arms of Edmonstone.

The keep stands in the north western corner of the former courtyard, and is of three main storeys and a garret. Measuring 48 ft by 26.5 ft, it is an excellent example of a 'double tower', each floor being divided by a thick central wall providing two rooms to each. There is a further stair in the north western corner which entered each floor. There are machiolated projections in the southern and northern fronts which may have served as garderobe chutes.

The parapet is crenellated, and is supported by a single course of corbelling 39 ft above ground level. The entrance at the eastern edge of the south front has an unusual projecting porch. This is on a small scale, allowing space above for a turnpike stair. This projection of the wall recedes to merge with the wall as it rises and the width of the stair narrows. Rather than creating a stair tower, the impression is given of a buttress. There is a round caphouse above this dating from the Victorian renovations. The garret and roof were rebuilt around the same time. The keep represents all that remain of the older buildings.

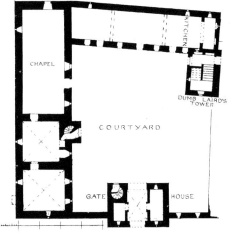

To the east of the keep the northern perimeter was continued by a large ruinous chapel of the 17th century, which may have been built out of an earlier hall block, perhaps of the 14th century.

Going south from this at the north eastern corner was a long, two storey utility range containing three rooms per floor. The ground floor contained the kitchen, the block culminating in the 'Dumb Laird's

Duntreath Castle – plan (M&R)

Tower' of the early 17th century. This tower had two floors above the basement, and contained a scale and platt stairway to first floor level, with access to the upper floor via a stair turret corbelled out from the re-entrant with the kitchen block. The entrance to this tower was on the north front within the courtyard, and was surmounted by a heraldic panel.

The south side of the courtyard may never have been completed, and the remnants of whatever structure lay there were replaced by a mansion dating from the 19th century.

Duntreath was part of the early estates of the Earls of Lennox. In 1360 Earl Donald granted the estate to his brother Murdoch. When in 1425 Earl Duncan was executed for treason, James I granted the estate to his sister Princess Mary Stewart, and her husband William Edmonstone of Culloden. The castle was gradually enlarged by this family until creating the large courtyard described. In 1578 the Earl of Argyll, acting as Justice General of Scotland, granted Sir James Edmonstone, 6th Laird, the power to hold justice courts at Duntreath. Sir James died in 1618, by which time he had added the later restored gatehouse as the final addition to the house before the restoration of the 19th century. William, 9th of Duntreath, was titled 'the Dumb Laird', being both deaf and dumb from birth. It was in his honour that the tower was named. This was his residence, although his handicap meant that he could not take up his full title. He was, however, reported to have exceptional intelligence and overcame his handicap, communicating his will to others and administering the estate with some skill. He died toward the end of the 17th century.

Thereafter the family removed to their Irish estates at Redhall, and Duntreath fell into ruin. Possibly during their absence, the chapel suffered 'a crash' during a church service. The family sold Redhall returning to live at Colzium House, which they had built for themselves in 1783. About 1863 Sir Archibald Edmonstone, the 13th of Duntreath and 3rd Baronet, had the castle renovated and extended, reoccupying it soon afterward. In 1958 all of the older work, excepting the original keep, was demolished. The keep and mansion are what remain today. The family remain in occupancy, and are believed to have been descended from a branch of the Seton family, who were granted the estate of Edmonstone in Midlothian around 1248.

E

Eaglesham Castle (*)

Renfrewshire
Ruin or site   OS 64   NS 574520?
North west of Eaglesham, 4 miles south west of East Kilbride by the B764, and by minor roads through village.
Site of an early castle of the Montgomerys. Sir John, 9th of Eaglesham, captured Henry 'Hotspur' Percy at the Battle of Otterburn in 1388. He held him for ransom, using the money to build himself a new castle at Polnoon. The two had become firm friends, and Hotspur helped in the design of Polnoon. The family became Earls of Eglinton in 1508.

The clues as to the original site lie to the north west of the present village. It is likely that the castle stood near Castlehill Farm, with the farm of Boreland (another term indicating the mains or home farm of the castle) nearby. There is also a man-made mound of ancient origin a little to the north, which may have been the moot (or court) hill, or even the gallows hill.

The present village was laid out in 1796 by the 12th Earl of Eglinton to provide accommodation for the work force of his new cotton mill. This lies some way south east of the original village, of which no trace now remains. The Eaglesham Castle or House to the north of the village is a grand sprawling mansion, with no fortified core. In 1960 the village was the first in Scotland to be designated a place of special historic interest.

East Arthurlie Castle *see* Arthurlie

Eastend Castle (**)

South Lanarkshire
Private   OS 72   NS 949374
7 miles south east of Lanark, and 1.5 miles west of Thankerton, on minor road south of A73, just south of Glade Burn, at Eastend.
Eastend incorporates a 16th century tower house, to which tall corbiestepped gabled wings of 1673 have been added. There is also an 18th century bow-fronted range encasing one side of the tower, and a late 19th century castellated extension.

The tower is of three storeys and a garret. There is a corbelled out, crenellated parapet with open corner rounds. It once had a vaulted basement, removed on complete reconstruction of the interior.

This was a Carmichael property from early times. The house is occupied.

Easter Cochrane Castle *see* Johnstone Castle

Easter Greenock Castle (*)

Renfrewshire
Ruin or site   OS 63   NS 300755
1.5 miles east of Greenock, 0.25 miles south of Firth of Clyde, south of A8, close to railway line, east of Bank Street, Wellpark.

Only a well of 1629, and some gate piers of 1635 remain of this much extended L-plan tower of the late 15th or early 16th century. The original entrance is believed to have been in the re-entrant as was usual, this giving access to a stair tower and vaulted basement.

Numerous extensions were added, including an 18th century mansion block designed by James Watt. Some of the extensions and door lintels were dated 1635, 1637, and 1674. The mansion block was of the 1730s.

Easter Greenock Castle (McGibbon and Ross) – demolished

McGibbon and Ross, looking retrospectively at plans and drawings supplied by Lord Cathcart, described the older part of the building as 'a picturesque assemblage of corbiestepped gables and chimneys'.

In 1540 Sir Alexander Schaw of Sauchie was given a grant of the lands of Wester Greenock Schaw by James V. These were part of the estates of the forfeited and executed 'Bastard of Finnart', Sir James Hamilton. The lands of Finnart, from which he acquired his title, lay a little to the west, and had once belonged to the Stewarts of Castlemilk. The grant included the 'auld castellsteid, castell, tour and fortalice and manor place new buildit'. Indication here that the oldest structure on site was already of some antiquity and had recently been extended. It passed through the family to a descendant, Lady Cathcart, who commissioned Watt to add the mansion. The family moved to Ardgowan in 1745 and let the property to various tenants. In 1886 it was demolished on the building of the Caledonian Railway.

Other references: Wellpark, Greenock Mansion House, Wester Greenock Schaw

The top floor contained a single room. There is a large cupboard within the south western wall, and windows above those in the hall. There are remains of a fireplace in the south western wall. No detail remains of the parapet.

A second house was built within the courtyard, and it was the demolition of this in 1815 which destroyed any evidence of the courtyard detail. A new mansion was built at this time, a little further down the hill.

The estate of Edmonston and Candy were resigned

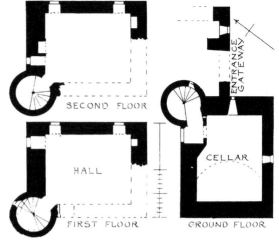

Edmonston Castle – plans (M&R)

by William of Edmonstone, with the consent of his superior Gilbert Fleming of Biggar, in favour of Sir James Douglas in 1322. The Douglases retained the property until selling to Baillie of Walston in 1650. By the start of the 18th century it had passed to one Lawrence Brown, whose descendants retained it until 1867, when it was purchased by the Wodropps of Elsrickle and Dalmarnock.

Eilean Mhore *see* Eilean Vhow

Eilean Vhow Castle (**)

The Lennox & East Dunbartonshire
Ruin or site   OS 56   NN 332128
About 5 miles north of Tarbet, and 2 miles south of Ardlui, just east of A82, on Island I Vhow, Loch Lomond.
Eilean Vhow means the 'island of the cows', and located here is a ruined 16th century tower on a Z-plan. It was a house of the MacFarlanes, and little survives above the basement. Of what remains there are two vaulted chambers. A stairway from the north east corner led to the first floor.

A ruin by the 19th century, it apparently provided a roof for a recluse, giving it a by-name of the 'Hermit's Cave'.
Other references: Eilean Mhore

Elderslie *see* Wallace's Buildings

Elliston Castle (*)
Renfrewshire
Ruin or site   OS 63   NS 392598.
3 miles south west of Johnstone, on a minor road north between the A737 and B776,
0.5 miles south of Howwood, in a private garden.
Only a section of one wall remains of Elliston, a large 15th century tower within
a small courtyard. Formerly measuring about 35 ft by 30 ft, there was a vaulted
basement, which is now filled with debris of the ruin. There may have been
mural chambers and a stair within the thickened south eastern wall.
   It was a property of the Semple family, who abandoned it to move to Castle
Semple in 1550. It was demolished to its present state about 1735.

Eliotstoun *see* Castle Semple

Elsrickle Castle (*)
South Lanarkshire
Ruin or site   OS 72   NT 062435?
5 miles east of Carnwath, on A721, 2 miles west of junction with A702, at Elsrickle.
Site of a castle or fortified house, which in the 15th century belonged to the
Hepburns, but by the 18th century had passed to the Wodropps of Dalmar-
nock.

Elphinston Tower *see* Baronial Hall

Erskine Castle (*)
Renfrewshire
Ruin or site   OS 64   NS 462720
0.5 miles north of Erskine, on minor roads north of A726, and south east of Erskine
Bridge, on south shore of River Clyde.
Site of a castle. Erskine gave its name to the family who owned the estate from
1266 or earlier. It was sold to Sir John Hamilton of Orbistan in 1638, and then to
the Stewart Lords Blantyre in 1703. It was this family who commissioned the
great mansion of 1828, which since 1916 has served as 'the Princess Louise Scottish Hospital for Limbless Sailors and Soldiers'.

F

Farme Castle (*)

South Lanarkshire
Ruin or site   OS 64
NS 624624
In Rutherglen, off
minor roads north of
A724, 0.5 miles east of
Farme Cross, the
junction of A724 and
A730.

Farme Castle was a
simple keep of the
15th century, possibly

Farme Castle (McGibbon and Ross) – demolished

with an older core. Later the keep acted as one corner of a courtyard formed by
an extension in the form of a castellated mansion. High walls and subsidiary
buildings completed the courtyard. There was an ornate arched gateway to the
courtyard adjacent to the keep. The old keep was of three storeys and a garret
above a corbelled out parapet with machiolations and water spouts. An old
ceiling was removed in 1917 to reveal an ancient wooden ceiling, which carried
writing alluding to the Stewarts, and the date 1325.

Robert the Bruce granted the Farme estate, which extended from Dalmarnock to Cambuslang, to Walter the Steward. It later passed to the Douglases.
From 1482 to 1599 it belonged to the Crawfords, and became known as Crawford's Farme. By 1645 it belonged to Sir Walter Stewart of Minto, then in turn to
the Flemings, and Dukes of Hamilton. It finally passed to local industrialist
James Farie and his descendants. It remained their property into the 20th century. It was one of their colliery managers who discovered the ancient ceiling
while resident in the house. It was finally demolished in the 1960s, by which
time it was being used as a repository for redundant mining equipment.

Faslane Castle (*)

The Lennox & East Dunbartonshire
Ruin or site   OS 56   NS 249903

0.5 miles north east of Faslane Port, adjacent to railway line, just south east of
Greenfield by minor road and foot east of A814 and Gareloch.
Only a motte remains of this 12th century castle of the Earls of Lennox. They
had another stronghold at Shandon ('old fort') three miles to the south. There
remains a medieval chapel of more ancient origin a little to the south, where it

is alleged Henry, Lord Darnley, 2nd husband to Mary Queen of Scots, was christened. The Earls moved their main seat to Balloch in the 13th century, and the Faslane and Ardincaple estates granted to Auley, progenitor of the MacAuleys of Ardincaple.
Other references: Shandon

Fatlips Tower (*)
South Lanarkshire
Ruin or Site   OS 72   NS 969340
5 miles south west of Biggar, by minor roads and foot west of A73, just north west of Tintoside, high on side of Scaut Hill, north of Lanimer Burn.
This curiously named tower house of the 16th century survives only at basement level, and is as curiously sited as it is named. Little is known of its history, and its site is secretive and remote. It would nevertheless have provided an excellent vantage point from which to observe any movement along this strategically important stretch of the Clyde Valley, where the Rivers Clyde and Tweed almost meet. This provided a main invasion route from England to both west and east coasts. All that can be said is that the basement appears to have had two chambers, one with a fireplace and probably the kitchen. It had walls 6 ft thick and measured 37 ft by 26 ft. No other detail is discernible.

Ferme Castle *see* Ardardan

Findlaystone *see* Finlaystone House

Fingalton Castle (*)
Renfrewshire
Ruin or site   OS 64   NS 499550?
3 miles west of A77, and 1.5 west of B769, by minor roads south west of Newton Mearns, and south east of Neilston, at or near Craigton.
This once large estate was held by a family of Hamiltons from the 14th to 16th centuries. The superiority of the estate was held by the Maxwells of Nether Pollok, and his Hamilton vassal had to seek the agreement of his chief before taking up feudal agreements and submitting himself to Maxwell. A castle here is very probable, and Craigton an obvious site, though nothing remains to prove the assumption.

Finlaystone House (*)
Renfrewshire
Private   OS 63   NS 365738
3 miles east of Port Glasgow, and 2 miles west of Langbank off minor roads just south of the A8, at Finlaystone.
Finlaystone House is an 18th century mansion by John Douglas, extended and

remodelled between 1898 and 1903 by J. J. Burnet. It stands on the site or incorporates a castle of the 15th century.

This was the main seat of the Cunningham Earls of Glencairn. In 1556 the 5th Earl had John Knox as a guest, and Knox 'ministrat the Lordis Table'.

The Earl sided against Mary Queen of Scots at the Battle of Carberry Hill in 1567. The 9th Earl led a rising for Charles II in 1654, but the rebellion failed. After the Restoration Charles made him Chancellor of Scotland. Robert Burns was a great friend of the then Earl, and scratched his initials on a window pane in the library. On the Earl's death in 1791 Burns wrote a lament, and in his own words,

'In loud lament bewailed his lord,
Whom death had all untimely ta'en
But I'll remember thee Glencairn,
And a' that thou hast done for me'

The estate and house passed to the MacMillans, and General Sir George MacMillan had the grounds opened to the public. There is a visitor centre with Clan MacMillan exhibits, a doll museum, and a Celtic Art display.

Gardens and grounds open all year; house open Apr-Aug, Sun.

Tel: 01475 540285 – see page 218.

Fintry Castle (*)

The Lennox & East Dunbartonshire
Ruin or site   OS 57   NS 642864
1.5 miles east of Fintry, by foot 0.5 miles north of the B818 at Camalt, north of Endrick Water, in Fintry Hills.
Little remains of Fintry Castle, other than some rubble sitting astride a high knoll. The walls appear to have been about 4 ft thick, and the tower measured roughly 26 ft by 45 ft. It probably dates from around 1460 when Sir Robert Graham was granted this portion of the Graham estate by Patrick, Lord Graham, his nephew. The castle was ruined by 1724.

Folkerton Castle (*)

South Lanarkshire
Ruin or site   OS 71   NS 866364
4.5 miles south of Lanark, off minor roads off A70 or B7078, 0.5 miles west of Douglas Water, at or near Tower Farm.
Site of a 'tenement', or tower house. In 1147 the lands of Poneil and Folkart were granted to Theobold the Fleming. In 1270 the Abbot of Kelso granted them to William de Douglas. They were won back by litigation by Alexander de Folkart in 1311. The family disappeared from the site in about 1495. A further house at Poneil (NS 840343) is very probable.

G

Gallowhill House (*)

Renfrewshire
Ruin or site   OS 64   NS 499650
About 1 mile south of Renfrew, on minor roads east of A741, off Gallowhill Road, near Arkleston Road, north of Paisley.
The last Abbot of Paisley granted most of the lands of the abbey to his 15 year old nephew in anticipation of the Reformation. Lord Claud Hamilton built one of his houses at Gallowhill. It was replaced by a mansion in 1867. In the mid 17th century it was owned by the Cochrane Earls of Dundonald. The estate was divided in 1866, and nothing remains of the house.

Garrion Tower (**)

North Lanarkshire
Private   OS 64   NS 797512
2.5 miles south of Wishaw, on minor roads south of A71, on north bank of River Clyde, at Garrion.
Garrion Tower is a small 16th or 17th century tower which had become a ruin until restored and extended by the addition of a large mansion of the 19th century. There was probably an earlier house here, used as a summer residence by the bishops of Glasgow in the 15th and early 16th centuries.

The tower is an L-plan structure measuring 25 ft by 19.5 ft, excluding the stair tower. It is of three storeys plus an attic, access to all floors being by a turnpike stair within the wing at the north east corner.

The entrance was originally into the base of the stair tower in the re-entrant. However, with the extension closing in this

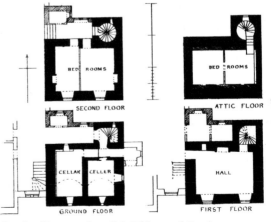

Garrion Tower – plans (McGibbon and Ross)

angle, a new entrance has been opened to the stair base from the east wall, where a porch was added. The stair to the first floor rises within a square cavity to first floor level, and above this within a rounded cavity. There are shot holes below the sills of the stair tower windows.

The ground floor contained two rooms, entered from a link corridor, both were vaulted, and illuminated by slot windows.

The hall, as usual, occupied the entire first floor, and was illuminated by two windows in the south wall, opposite which were a fireplace and an aumbry.

The second floor has been subdivided to provide two bedrooms, which are now entered from the extension and have no access to the stair tower. Each has a window in the south wall above those of the hall, and there is an aumbry in the west wall of the western room, with the other room mirroring this arrangement.

The attic has also been divided into two rooms, one entering from the other. The eastern room is entered from the stair tower.

The church owned the estate as part of its diocese of Glasgow. It may have been let to the Forrest family, but by 1530 'Garyn' was occupied by Sir James Hamilton of Finnart (yes Hamilton again: he's been to more castles than Queen Mary herself!). It is likely that he built the tower. In 1605 a grant was issued under the Great Seal to another 'James Hamilton of Garrion and Elizabeth Haye, his spouse, and the longest liver of them, and to their heirs, of the lands of Garrien, held of the Archbishop of Glasgow'.

The later Episcopalian bishops may have repossessed the house for a time.

Garscadden Castle (*)
City of Glasgow
Ruin or site   OS 64   NS 522710
1.5 miles south west of Bearsden, on minor roads north of the A82, in Drumchapel, 0.5 miles north of Garscadden Road.
Garscadden was a 15th century tower incorporated into a mansion of the early 18th century. Until 1369 this was a property of Patrick, second son of Malcolm Fleming of Biggar. He exchanged it with Sir Robert Erskine for the lands of Board, near Croy. In 1444 it was acquired by the Galbraiths of Gartconnel. Thereafter it passed in succession to each of the captains of Dumbarton castle. In the 17th century it was held by Archibald, 2nd son of Colquhoun of Camstradden.

In the 18th century it was given to the artist Henry Colquhoun of Kilermont. He extended it into the mansion later known as Garscadden House. It was demolished in the 1970s.

Toward the end of the 18th century, at the end of a drinking session in Law, the laird of Kilmardinny remarked on the pale appearance of the laird of Garscadden. To this their host replied that Garscadden had been dead for over two hours, but he had not mentioned it for fear of disrupting such good company. This event is reputedly responsible for the Glaswegian phrase 'as gash as Garscadden', meaning deathly pale.

Gartconnel Castle (*)
The Lennox & East Dunbartonshire
Ruin or site   OS 64   NS 537732
In Bearsden, close to the junction of the A810 and A809, south of Gartconnel Avenue, in the grounds of Bearsden Academy.
Site of a 14th century keep of the Galbraiths of Culcreuch. Traces of a ditch survive.

Gartlea Castle (*)
North Lanarkshire
Ruin or site   OS 64   NS 765648?
In Gartlea, Airdrie, 3 miles north of A80, and 1 mile west of A73, exact site not known.
Probable site of a 16th century castle or tower of Crawford of Rochsolloch.

Gartness Castle (*)
The Lennox & East Dunbartonshire
Ruin or Site   OS 57   NS 502868?
2 miles north east of Drymen, on minor road west of A81, south of Endrick Water, at or near Gartness.
Nothing remains of this 15th century castle of the Napiers. They gained the estate in 1495, and a stone reportedly taken from the castle bears a date of 1574. Nearby is the 'Pots of Gartness', a waterfall on the Endrick Water, famed for leaping salmon toward the end of the season.

Gartsherrie House (*)
North Lanarkshire
Ruin or site   OS 64   NS 726659
In Coatbridge, 2.5 miles east of A752, just north of Gartsherrie Road, at the Container Base.
The estate of Gartsherrie was granted by David II to Ranulphus de Colt in the 14th century. It is very likely that the house here was fortified. It remained the main residence of the Colts, although they later gained estates in Lothian. The early house was replaced by Gartsherrie House, which probably occupied the same site.

The family built a bridge over a local burn, and inadvertently gave the town of later years its name, or so the story goes. The lands and mansion were purchased and developed by the Baird family, industrialists at the forefront of the iron and steel industry of the Monklands. Their foundries stood close to the house. The vast sea of tarmac which constitutes the container base now covers the site.

Gartshore House (*)

The Lennox & East Dunbartonshire
Private   OS 64   NS 692737
1.5 miles south east of Kirkintilloch, off minor road south of B8048, 1.5 miles west of Drumgrew Bridge.
Gartshore was a mansion house of the 17th century, and represented an example of the transitional phase when the need for defensive features diminished, and comfort became more of a priority. It probably had replaced an earlier fortified house.

Gartshore House (McGibbon and Ross)

Consisting of a double tenement block, each has its own corbiestepped gables, sitting side by side, creating a V shape. The blocks were joined on their longest sides, and internally were separated by a thick central wall, effectively creating two houses in one. The entrance was centrally placed below the V of the roof. There was a large heraldic panel above the door. Each block was of two storeys and an attic with dormer windows. Each floor had a series of large windows. A smaller two storey T-plan structure adjoined one of the blocks centrally on one side of the structure. This met the main building at one end of the head of the T. The other end and the base of the T were also corbiestepped. The house was demolished in the mid 20th century.

A life rent of the estate of Gartshore was sold by charter of the Duke of Chatelherault to his eldest daughter Barbary Hamilton in 1553. By 1579 John Gartshore, alias Golfurd, was in possession, and was cautioned by the Privy Council. By 1594 the family are referred to as Gartshore of that Ilk, and John Gartshore acted as surety for 'certain burgesses of Kirkintilloch'. The laird held various important positions in the mid 17th century, including Commissioner of Supply, Commissioner of Loans and Taxes, as an MP for Dunbartonshire, and on the Committee of War from 1647-8.

By the 18th century the estate had passed to the Starks of Auchenvole.

Geilston House (**)

The Lennox & East Dunbartonshire
Private   OS 64   NS 340780
3.5 miles north west of Dumbarton, by A814, just east of Cardross, at Geilston.
Geilston House is a two storey, L-plan house of the 18th century and later. It may incorporate work from as early as the 16th century. The walls are harled and it has corbiestepped gables. There is a beautiful walled garden. In the 16th

Geilston House

century this was a property of the Woods family, who held a tower here. By the 19th century it had passed through various owners until coming to the Henrys. In 1983 the gardens were granted to The National Trust for Scotland by a Miss Henry – see page 218. The house remains a private residence.

Gilbertfield Castle (**)

South Lanarkshire
Ruin or site   OS 64   NS 653558
2.5 miles north west of East Kilbride, off minor roads south east of Cambuslang and south of A724, on north side of Dechmont Hill at Gilbertfield Farm.
Gilbertfield is a ruined 17th century L-plan house of three storeys and an attic. All chambers on the ground floor were vaulted. The gable and northern wall of the south eastern wing collapsed in the 1950s.

The house consists of two blocks, the larger running east to west, joined at the western half of the north side by the other, which has the entrance in the re-entrant. The door leads to a small lobby, which provides access to a turnpike stair within a square well. To the left a door leads into a larder with service stair in the south western corner leading to the dining room or hall on the floor

Gilbertfield Castle

above. A door in the east wall accesses the kitchen within the south wing. This has a gunloop and window which.guard the main door, a large fireplace with oven and seat, and a stone sink with conduit drain. To the right of the lobby another door leads to a chamber, possibly used as a wine cellar, which has two small slot windows in the north and east walls.

The first floor of the southern wing is entirely composed of the dining room or hall, which measures 27 ft by 17 ft and 14.25 ft to the ceiling. There was a fireplace in the north wall which at some point had been reduced in size. A corridor leads past the stair well to a parlour in the north wing. The entire floor is illuminated by a series of large windows on all sides, many with gunloops. Access to the stair is from the north western corner of the hall. The plan on the floors above was similar, with three bedrooms to each.

Externally there is a heraldic panel above the door, and originally two round corner turrets at the south eastern and north western corners. Of these only the supportive corbelling of the latter survives. The roof and corbiestepped sections of the gables have now gone, though the stepping itself was adapted to accommodate the corner turrets. There was no parapet, access to

Gilbertfield Castle (McGibbon and Ross)

the turrets being from the rooms of the attic storey.

The house stands within the ancient barony of Drumsagard, and is dated 1607. It was presumably constructed by the Hamiltons. By the turn of the 18th century it was occupied by the retired soldier turned poet, William Hamilton of Gilbertfield. He was responsible for the translation of Blind Harry's epic poem *Sir William Wallace* from the old Scots. This work of 1477 provides a biography of Scotland's national hero, in somewhat exaggerated terms, and its translation by Hamilton brought it to national attention. The screenplay of 'Braveheart' is based directly upon it. As a poet Hamilton was admired by Burns.

'And wouldst thou have me dissipate my grief;
While Scotland weeps, weeps out her dearest blood,
And floats to ruin down the crimson flood.'

Gilkersceugh House (*)

South Lanarkshire
Ruin or site   OS 72   NS 900236?
2 miles south of Abington, on minor road south of M74, at Duneaton Bridge to B740, 2 miles east of Crawfordjohn, at or near Gilkerscleugh Mains.
Site of a 17th century L-plan tower of three storeys. It was altered and modernised, though then demolished in 1958 after a fire. There was a round stair tower projecting from one corner, and round corner turrets and corbiestepped gables. The estate belonged to the Hamiltons from 1598 until the 19th century.

Gillbank House (*)

South Lanarkshire.
Ruin or site   OS 71   NS 706426
Above the south bank of the Avon Water, 2 miles south of Strathaven, off minor roads west of A726 or west of A723.
In 1852 the last vestiges of the old tower were removed due to their 'dilapidated condition'. For centuries it was the property of the Auchinleck family, one of whom was a friend of William Wallace, and they reputedly raided Lanark from here. Legend asserts that because of his friendly welcomes here, Wallace frequented the area when fugitive, often hiding out in this part of Lesmahagow parish. A cave in the hills to the north of Douglas Water bears his name. Another property of the same name exists on the east bank of the Clyde at Rosebank, but is less likely to be the site referred to in references.

Glanderston Castle (*)

Renfrewshire
Ruin or site   OS 64   NS 501560
2 miles south of Barrhead, on minor roads south of A736, on west side of Duncarnock Hill, south east of Glanderston Mains.
Glanderston Castle was demolished in 1697, and replaced by a tall, castellated

mansion, now also demolished.

It was a property of the Mures of Caldwell, and resulted in a 50 year feud with the Maxwells of Nether Pollok who disputed ownership. Over the period there were many skirmishes, law suits, and even a riot in Paisley in 1490. It was a property of the Stewart Earls of Lennox by 1507.

Glasgow Castle (*)
City of Glasgow
Ruin or site   OS 64 NS 603655
In Cathedral Square, just south of Glasgow Royal Infirmary, north of St Mungo's Museum and west of Glasgow Cathedral.
A stone bearing a brass engraving illustrating the castle stands at the centre of the square formed by the cathedral, hospital and museum. This marks the position of the great keep, though the site was much more extensive. The stone was taken from the castle itself, and other decorative stones from the castle are on display within the crypt of the cathedral.

This was a royal castle in 1258, but was the seat of the Bishops of Glasgow by the Wars of Independence. It was recaptured from the English by William Wallace in 1296, but garrisoned by Edward I in 1301. The great keep was built by Bishop Cameron in the 15th century and was five storeys high. The castle was extended by the addition of a courtyard and a gatehouse with round towers. It changed hands six times during the various conflicts between 1513 and 1568 with the final defeat of the Hamiltons and other supporters of Queen Mary at Langside. It was abandoned and used as a prison in the 17th century, though was demolished to clear the site for the Royal Infirmary in 1792.

The nearby cathedral is the only Scottish medieval cathedral to survive the Reformation, St Magnus in Kirkwall on Orkney having been built when the islands were not yet part of Scotland.
Other references: Bishop's Castle, Glasgow, Castle of Glasgow

Glassford Castle (*)
South Lanarkshire
Ruin or site   OS 64   NS 728473?
2 miles west of Stonehouse, on minor roads north of A71, just north of Glassford.
Site of a castle, which is now occupied by housing.

Glenane Castle (*)
South Lanarkshire
Private   OS 71   NS 812421
At Kerse, 1 mile north of Lesmahagow, off B7078, west of River Nethan.
The mansion of Kerse replaced a tower house known as Glenane. There was a disposition by Thomas of Thomastoun granting this property to Ralph Weir, 'portioner of Auchtygemmil' in 1612. He later became superior of Poneil

(Saddlerhead), Daldaholm and Clannachyett, other local properties.

Glendorch Castle (**)
South Lanarkshire
Ruin or site   OS 71   NS 871189
3.5 miles south of Crawfordjohn, by minor road and track south of B740, west of
Glendorch burn, at Glendorch.
Enough remains of this 16th century bastle house of the Foulis family to show
that it was occupied by a family of at least moderate means. The laird at
Glendorch was known to have been involved in the mining of gold and lead in
the region.

Glengonnar Castle (*)
South Lanarkshire
Ruin or site   OS 71   NS 899201
In Glengonnar, just east of B797, 4 miles north of Leadhills, 0.5 miles south of
Lettershaws.
Site of a 16th century bastle house of the Bulmer family, who were known to
have made their wealth from mining gold and lead.

Glenochar Castle (**)
South Lanarkshire
Ruin or site   OS 78   NS 951139
2 miles south of Elvanfoot, by foot west of A702, west of Daer Water, near Glenochar
Farm.
Glenochar was a bastle house, and enough remains to show a vaulted ground
floor and internal stair to the floor above. The site has been excavated. A hoard
of coins was uncovered close to the house, including a few Elizabethan six-
pences.

Glenrae Castle (*)
South Lanarkshire
Ruin or site   OS 71   NS 833185
5 miles north east of Sanquhar, off B740, and 0.5 miles by foot east of burn, 0.5 miles
south west of Nether Whitecleugh.
Site of a castle, of which a remnant remained until the 19th century.

Glorat House (*)
The Lennox & East Dunbartonshire
Private   OS 64   NS 642778
1 mile north west of Milton of Campsie, and 1 mile east of Lennoxtown, about 0.75
miles north of A891 by minor roads, at Glorat.
Glorat House is a late 19th century mansion, which may incorporate parts of

the 16th century tower house of the Stirlings.

The Stirlings of Glorat are descended from a second son of Sir William Stirling, 3rd of Craigbarnet, who was granted the estate in 1508. Another branch of the same family held the estate from 1430, and one of these was armour bearer to James I. In 1547 George Stirling of Glorat died of wounds received at the Battle of Pinkie. Stirling of Glorat killed Malcolm Kincaid in 1581. At some point the Glorat branch became chiefs of their name, inheriting the title from the Craigbarnet line. The house remains occupied by the family.

Gourock Castle (*)

Renfrewshire
Ruin or site   OS 63   NS 239773?
East of Gourock, off minor roads south of A770, about 0.5 miles south of Kempock Point on south shore of Firth of Clyde.
Site of a small and unimportant castle, of which some remnants survived until 1875. It was a Douglas property until their forfeiture in 1455, and passed to the Stewarts of Castlemilk. They sold it to a family named Darroch. Gourock Mansion, a plain house of 1747, was built nearby.

Graham's Castle (**)

The Lennox & East Dunbartonshire
Ruin or site   OS 57   NS 682859
6 miles east of Fintry, Just north of B818, by forestry track at western end of Carron Valley Reservoir, Carron Valley.
Atop a steep sided spur of the hillside is an unusual, almost square motte with sides 77 ft by 75 ft, within a similarly shaped dry moat 10 ft deep and 30 ft wide.

Sir David de Graham was in possession of the barony of Dundaff in 1237. This site is regarded as that of the peel of Sir John de Graham, who fought alongside Wallace at Stirling Bridge in 1297 and died at the Battle of Falkirk the following year. His tomb lies in Falkirk Kirkyard close to the grave of another fallen hero of Falkirk, Sir John Stewart of Bonkyl.

The Graham's epitaph reads:
'Here lyse Sir John the Graham, baith wight and wise,
Ane of the chiefs who saved Scotland thrise,
Ane better knight not to the world was lent,
Nor was gude Graeme of truth and hardiment.'
A second inscription translated from the Latin reads:
'Of mind and courage stout,
Wallace's true Achates,
Here lies Sir John de Graham,
Felled by the English baties (dogs).'
The summit was reached from the hillside to the north, and there is slight

Graham's Castle

evidence of a ditch across the approach. A drawbridge would have controlled access to the castle from this side. There are fragmentary remains of a later house above the motte, which may represent the remains of the Grahams' later castle of Dundaff. This appears to have had walls of up to 2 ft thick, and sat on one side of a rectangular court, which in places can just be traced below the grass. There may have been corner towers on the perimeter wall.

Sir John's descendants became Viscounts Dundaff and eventually Marquises of Montrose, and frequently crop up in Scottish history.

The valley itself was once a very fertile and productive place, now bleak since the reservoir dam was built and the water drowned much of it. It nevertheless retains a rugged and remote beauty, which seems strange given its proximity to the industrial heart of Scotland.

The site itself had strategic importance lying west of the meeting place of the few roads that allowed a crossing of the hilly barrier of the Campsie, Touch and Kilsyth Hills. Before the flooding of the reservoir, the courses of the Carron and Endrick rivers passed within a few yards of one another just below the motte. Again emphasising the strange atmosphere of the place as one emptied via Lomond into the Clyde on the west coast, and the other into the Firth of Forth on the eastern seaboard. This is well worth a visit if only to absorb the view and atmosphere.

Other references: Dundaff, Sir John de Graham's Castle

Greenock Castle (*)

Renfrewshire
Ruin or site   OS 63   NS 280765.
In Greenock, near present course of A8, on south shore of Firth of Clyde.
Site of a castle which seems to have been held in common ownership with
Easter Greenock.
Other references: Wester Greenock

Greenock Mansion House *see* Easter Greenock

Greenrig Castle *see* Dowane

Gryffe Castle (*)

Renfrewshire
Private   OS 63   NS 385663
0.5 miles north of Bridge of Weir, on minor road north of A761, just west of junction with B790, at Gryffe.
Gryffe Castle is a small asymmetrical mansion of 1841, which may incorporate
part of an earlier castle. In the 19th century it was a property of the Barbours.

Grymm's Castle (*)

Renfrewshire
Ruin or site   OS 63   NS 377676?
2 miles south east of Kilmacolm by the A761, and north 1 mile by minor roads, at or near Barlogan Farm.
Site of a castle which appears as a ruin on Bleau's Atlas Novus of the 17th
century.

H

Haggs Castle (***)

City of Glasgow
Private   OS 64   NS 560626
*In Pollokshaws, just north east of junction of B768 and B769 with St Andrews
Drive, and east of south eastern entrance to Pollok Country Park.*
Haggs is a much altered 16th century L-plan house of three storeys and an attic.
There are a plethora of both square and round gunloops. There is much decorative moulding, particularly around the door and windows. It has corbiestepped
gables and corbelled out stair turrets above first floor level.

The small wing contains a turnpike stair, reached from an entrance in the east
wall, in the re-entrant. A
door in the connecting
wall leads to the vaulted
basement of the main
block. A passage runs
west to east, two thirds
of the length, terminating at a door which
opens into the kitchen.
This had a centrally
placed fireplace in the
east wall, which measured 19 ft by 5 ft. Above
this a large chimney
stack rises within the
walls. To the north of the
passage are two doors,
which access separate
chambers. There are a
few small recesses
within the walls in each
of these rooms. Orig-

Haggs Castle (McGibbon and Ross) – then ruinous

inally this floor was illuminated by slot windows, of which a few remain, the
others having been enlarged.

The main stair terminates at first floor level, where access is gained to the
former hall. This had three windows and a large fireplace in the south wall.
From the recess of the large west window, access is gained to a mural chamber
measuring 10 ft by 4 ft, from which a private stair led to the cellar below. At the

eastern end of this floor, a dividing wall created a private room. This was reached via a porch-like structure which was formed by a corbelled out staircase turret at the south western corner of the hall. Within the private room was a garderobe within the north wall, the chute for which serviced similar closets on the floors above. A further round stair turret was corbelled out in the western wall at the junction of the two wings, at the south western corner of the hall. The dormer windows of the attic appear to have been enlarged, and retain some of the original elaborate decorative moulding. Similarly the cornicing at the eaves is highly detailed.

Until restoration in the 19th century, the floors above were comp-

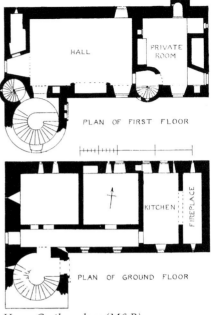

PLAN OF FIRST FLOOR

PLAN OF GROUND FLOOR

Haggs Castle – plans (M&R)

letely ruined, and so a fair assessment of the internal plan cannot be given. The exterior walls above have been much altered at this restoration, with the addition of more modern windows. A small half octagon extension was added out of the south wall just east of the stair turret. This provides another door at ground level and a new main stair to all floors. Above the original main door a highly decorative heraldic panel declares 'Sr. John Maxwell of Pollok Bart. and Dame Margaret Cunninghame his wife bigget this hous 1585'.

The house was built by Sir John Maxwell to replace the Laigh Castle to the west. Haggs was abandoned on the completion of Pollok House around 1753, and fell into ruin until restored in the late 19th century. For a while it served as a private residence, then was acquired by the city. It was used in the 20th century as a Museum of Childhood. It was sold to a private developer in the late 1990s, and has now been converted into private flats, a process which again has meant much internal remodelling.

The Maxwells were powerful locally and for many years they were involved in a feud with the Johnstones of Annandale. The house was used by Covenanters in the 17th century for which the family only escaped paying a hefty fine because of the Revolution of 1689.

Hallbar Tower (***)

South Lanarkshire
Private OS 72   NS 839471
2 miles south west of Carluke and 0.5 miles south west of Braidwood, on minor road just east of B7056.
Commanding a hilltop site above the Fiddler's Burn, Hallbar is a semi-ruinous tower of the 16th century which is often attributed origins as ancient as the 11th century. A courtyard once measured 93 ft by 40 ft, with walls 4 ft thick. The tower has four storeys and a garret over walls 5 ft thick. Each floor consists of a single room. The garret is gable ended and is flanked on the east and west sides by crenellated parapets with walks supported on

Hallbar Tower (McGibbon and Ross)

corbels. There is square caphouse in the south eastern corner. Although it has lost its courtyard it does retain a few unusual features.

Square in plan, each side measuring 24.75 ft, the entrance is centrally placed on the southern wall, unusually at ground floor level. This door gives entry to a vaulted chamber. Light is provided by an arrow slot in the north wall.

From the door a steep straight stair rises eastward within the wall to reach first floor level at the south eastern corner of the building. From here a mural corridor leads northward in the eastern wall to its midpoint. Doors open to the hall on the left, and right to the exterior once accessing a wall walk around the perimeter wall.

The hall measures 14 ft square, and has the only fireplace in the house. This sits on the northern wall in the north east corner. Light is provided by a single window in the south wall, which enhances the defence of the main door below. A mural chamber was reached by a short stair in the south west.

A similar straight mural stair rises from the doors in the eastern wall to enter the second floor room from the north east corner. This floor had a second hall, with garderobe in the south western corner. This projected on the exterior on corbels, and may have doubled as a machiolation.

From the north west corner another straight stair rose southwards in the western wall to the third

Hallbar Tower – restoration

147

floor bedroom. The door was set along the south wall, a mural corridor having wound around the south west corner. The stair continued to the garret room from this door.

At the stair head was a slot window. Within the bedroom a deep window recess provided further space. This floor was vaulted to support the weight of the stone flagged garret and roof.

At roof level the stair terminates in the caphouse, which once had a pyramid-shaped roof. A door gives access to the eastern battlement, and midway along this a door opens into the garret room. The western battlement is entered by a door midway down that side of the room. Central in the south wall, a small oriel window projects to the exterior and was supported on machiolated corbels. On the exterior north gable nesting boxes for a doocot are built into the wall itself. The walls of the doocot and a service walkway were supported on projecting timbers. Access to the walkway was via a door from the north east corner of the garret. This walkway may also have had a defensive function.

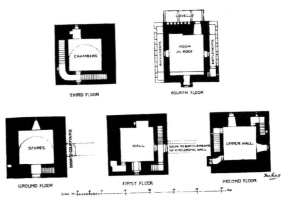

Hallbar Tower – plans (M&R)

Hallbar was the stronghold of the important barony of Braidwood. This was a property of the Earls of Douglas, which was acquired in 1581 by the Stewarts of Gogar. Harie Stewart was the brother of the infamous Earl of Arran, James Stewart, who was Chancellor to James VI. It passed to his main rival, Maitland of Thirlestane, who developed his own notoriety. The Douglases briefly regained the property before selling to the Lockharts of The Lee, on whose property it remains. The tower fell into ruin following the building of Braidwood House, a more modern mansion, nearby. It is presently being restored with the aid of a National Lottery Grant. Holiday accommodation is available and the tower can be visited – see page 218.

Hallcraig House (*)

South Lanarkshire
Ruin or site   OS 72   NS 829500?
1.5 miles west of Carluke, on minor road west of A73, on north bank of Jock's Burn, at or near Hallcraig.
Hallcraig House was a mansion which possibly incorporated part of a castle. It was demolished in the 20th century.

Hamilton Palace (*)

South Lanarkshire

Ruin or site   OS 64   NS 726557

In Hamilton Low Parks, on minor roads off B7071, 200 yards south of Mausoleum, north of Hamilton.

This luxurious mansion of the Hamiltons was demolished earlier this century. There are references to earlier buildings on this site dating back to at least the 15th century. From about 1590 it is almost consistently referred to as 'The Orchard', and later as 'The Palice'. The building of this time is often described as being fortified, and on demolition, to allow mining, the foundations of an 18th century wing were found to have been supported by much older work with walls up to 10 ft thick. It is possible that this was the castle at Hamilton dismantled by the Regent Morton's forces in 1579, though Cadzow is also a candidate.

Hamilton Palace – demolished

Hawkhead Castle (*)

Renfrewshire

Private   OS 64   NS 501626

1 mile east of Paisley, on minor roads north of the A726 and south of the A737, just east of Hawkhead Road, at Ross House within the grounds of Hawkhead Hospital.

Site of a large keep, which in 1634 was extended by ranges to form a quadrangle and remodelled in 1782.

Originally part of the Steward's great estates of Renfrewshire, Robert II continued to divide these and granted this portion to the Ross family. They built the great keep, and retained possession until 1866 when the lands were divided. What was then known as Hawkhead Asylum was built on this part of the site, now more modernly known as Hawkhead Hospital.

Hazelside Castle (*)

South Lanarkshire.

Ruin or site   OS 72   NS 815289

Off minor road, just north of A70, 0.5 miles east of Glespin, and 1.5 miles south west of Douglas, at or near Hazelside.

Site of a large castle which appears on Bleau's Atlas Novus of the 17th century.

High House of Edmonston *see* Edmonston Castle

Hill of Ardmore *see* Ardmore

Hills Castle (*)
South Lanarkshire
Ruin or site   OS 72   NT 049481?
5 miles east of Carnwath, at or near East Hills, 4 miles north east of A721 at Newbigging, off minor roads.
Site of a tower house. In 1299 the lands were granted to Allan de Denume, before passing to Baillie of Lamington, then the Hamiltons, and finally the Lockharts.

Holm Castle (*)
South Lanarkshire
Ruin or site   OS 64   NS 746474
At Holm, 0.5 miles east of Stonehouse, off A71, north of Avon Water.
Site of a castle, ruined by the early 19th century, which appears on Bleau's Atlas as Holmhead.
Other references: Holmhead

Holmhead Castle *see* Holm Castle

Houston Castle (**)
Renfrewshire
Private   OS 64   NS 412672
1 mile north east of Bridge of Weir, just north of Houston, on minor roads west of B790, and east of B789.
Houston was a 16th century courtyard castle of the Earls of Lennox. Of this there remains only a 17th century block which once formed the east side of the yard. There was originally a high arched gateway in the south front of the courtyard. A tall tower stood at the north west corner of the 'Palace', as the house became known. The remain-

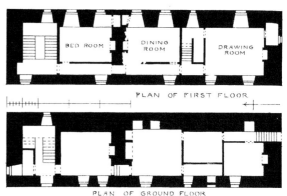

Houston Castle – plans (M&R)

ing range is of two storeys and an attic.

The block has its entrance in the northern end of the west front, giving access to a wide stair within a square well. To the south of this a door opens into the smaller of two large rooms, the second of which is subdivided into several smaller rooms. There is a secondary entrance in the south gable, with service stair to the first floor. The floor above is similarly divided, the smaller of the rooms acting as a bedroom, and the divided room providing dining room and drawing room. The exterior walls are about 5 ft thick where they formed the outside of the former courtyard, and 3 ft on the west within the yard. The 5 ft thickness continues on the main interior dividing wall. Drawings of the mid 18th century show the remains of massive corbelling along the top of the eastern wall. The building has corbiestepped gables at the north and south ends. The house is dated 1625.

In the 18th century one Captain Macrae purchased the estate, and removed three sides of the courtyard when modernising the house. He also funded the reconstruction of the village further from the house than its original site.

From 1782 it belonged to the Spiers of Elderslie, who used it as a shooting lodge, until in 1872 a new mansion was built to the south. At this time many original outbuildings were removed, and the house substantially altered both inside and out. Further changes were made in 1893-5.

Houston Palace *see* Houston Castle

$$I$$

Inch Castle (*)
Renfrewshire
Ruin or site   OS 64   NS 515675
0.5 miles east of Renfrew, north of A877.
Elderslie House, a long vanished 18th century mansion was built about 40 yards from the ruin of this entry on Bleau's Atlas.

The lands originally belonged to David I who had a castle here, hence King's Inch (island), then he granted them to the Stewarts. They built Inch Castle in the 15th century: a four storey keep with corbiestepped gables and a centrally placed round stair tower supported by corbels at first floor level. It was ruined by 1770 when Elderslie House was built. This was named after the place of that name near Paisley. The house later came to the Spiers family who remodelled and enlarged it, though it was later demolished and nothing remains.

The site is no longer an island, and is occupied by Braehead Power Station.

Inchgalbraith Castle (**)
The Lennox & East Dunbartonshire
Ruin or site   OS 57   NS 369904
On the island Inchgalbraith, Loch Lomond, 1.5 miles south east of Luss, and 0.5 miles east of A82 at Bandry.
Only fragments of the northern block or a turret remain to second storey level of a 15th century courtyard castle of the Galbraiths. It seems to have been built within a courtyard measuring some 49 ft by 39 ft with walls 4.5 ft thick. There may have been as many as three blocks, and traces remain of a building to the south. There is evidence of a portcullis groove.

The Galbraiths anciently owned the Bannachra Estate, Inchgalbraith being their stronghold. In the 16th century the estate passed to the Colquhouns of Luss who built Bannachra Castle, leaving the island stronghold to fall into ruin.

Inchinnan Castle (*)
Renfrewshire
Ruin or site   OS 64   NS 480698?
1 mile south east of Erskine, and 0.5 miles north of Inchinnan, on Newshot Island on south shore of Clyde, at or near Garnieland.
Site of a castle of which there were considerable remains in 1710, though no evidence now remains.

It was held by the High Steward in 1151, but passed to the Stewart Earls of

Lennox. It was rebuilt or enlarged by Matthew, 2nd Earl, in 1506, and passed to the Crown in 1571. It returned via several members of the Stewart family to the Earls of Lennox and Richmond. They sold out to the Campbells of Blythswood. Inchinnan, with nearby Govan, were early Christian sites, both producing a variety of burial sites and ancient coffins from archaeological digs.

Inchmurrin Castle (*)

The Lennox & East Dunbartonshire
Ruin or site   OS 57   NS 373863
3 miles north of Balloch, at the western edge of Inchmurrin Island, Loch Lomond.
Inchmurrin was a late 14th century keep or hallhouse of the Earls of Lennox. One estimate puts the dimensions of the main building at 34 ft by 53 ft. The first document confirming its existence is dated 1400. It sits on a high knoll at the western end of Inchmurrin, allowing effective control of traffic on Loch Lomond. There remains a small portion of wall, including a window, which may have been reconstructed from the rubble.

In 1425 James I executed the Earl of Lennox and his male heirs for their part in the corrupt regency of the Duke of Albany, Murdoch Stewart. His widow, became dowager Duchess of Lennox, being the daughter of the executed earl. She was imprisoned in Tantallon for two years before being released to live out her retirement on Inchmurrin until her death in 1460. The executions of 1425 brought about a division of the Lennox estate, a portion going to the Napiers of Merchiston and another to the Haldanes of Gleneagles. The remaining estate and title went to the Stewarts of Darnley: they gained the castle on the death of the Duchess.

In 1439 Sir John Colquhoun and his retinue were murdered by Highlanders in the castle.

James IV visited in 1506, and in 1585 James VI stayed. James was related to

Inchmurrin, Loch Lomond

153

the Earls of Lennox as his father was Lord Darnley. James's grandfather had been the Regent Lennox until he was killed in 1571. Following the Union of the Crowns, James stayed at the castle in 1617 during his only return visit to Scotland as a guest of his cousin Ludovick Stewart, to whom he had granted the Earldom.

This part of the Lennox later passed to the acquisitive Dukes of Montrose in the early 18th century. The Earldom is now one of the titles held by the Duke of Richmond and Gordon.

Inchneuk Castle *see* Inchnock Castle

Inchnock Castle (*)
North Lanarkshire.
Ruin or site   OS 64   NS 718694
2.5 miles north of Coatbridge, off minor roads, 2.5 miles east of A752, east of Marnock, north of Glenboig near Inchneuk Farm.
Some rubble remaining at a spot known locally as 'the rocks' is all that is left of Inchnock Tower.

Inchnock was built in the late 16th century by the Forsyths of Dykes. At the Reformation the Lords Boyd gained this parish of Medrox and divided it into four portions. The best at Bedlay they kept for themselves, another may have led to the building of a castle at Old Yetts to the south, and this third was feud to the Forsyths. No information is available on the fourth portion.

Inchnock later passed to Hamilton of Dalyell, then to John Hay.
Other references: Inchneuk

Inverkip Castle (***)
Renfrewshire
Ruin or site   OS 63   NS 205728
5 miles south west of Greenock, and 0.5 miles north of Inverkip, on minor roads west of A78, near Ardgowan House.
Standing on a cliff overseeing the Firth of Clyde, Inverkip is a ruined 15th century square keep of three storeys and formerly a garret.

The square tower has a double course of chequered corbelling supporting a crenellated parapet with open rounds at three corners. The basement

Inverkip Castle (McGibbon and Ross)

154

was vaulted, and entered by a door below the original main entrance at first floor level. This is reached by a stone stair of later date. There are various key-hole-style arrow slots, particularly guarding the doors.

A 13th century castle here was held by the English during the Wars of Independence, and it was to here that Sir Philip Mowbray fled after being routed by the Black Douglas. Robert III granted the estate to his natural son Sir John Stewart in 1390, and his family built the present castle. The estate was created a baronetcy in 1667, and the lands remain with Sir John's descendants, the Schaw Stewarts. The castle was superseded by nearby Ardgowan House in the 19th century, and fell into ruin thereafter.

Inveruglas Castle (*)

The Lennox & East Dunbartonshire
Ruin or site   OS 56   NN 323096
3.5 miles north of Tarbet, east of A82 at Inveruglas, on Inveruglas Isle, Loch Lomond.
Site of a castle of the chief of the MacFarlanes, which was burnt to the ground by Cromwell in the 1650s.

The 11th chief died at Flodden in 1513, and the 13th, Duncan, was slain at the Battle of Pinkie in 1547. The clan were in the Regent Moray's army at Langside in 1568 when Queen Mary was defeated and fled to England. They fought with Montrose at Inverlochy in 1645, when he defeated the Marquis of Argyll, chief of the Campbells.

J

Jerviston House (***)

North Lanarkshire
Private OS 64 NS 757583
1 mile north east of Mother-
well, by minor roads north of
A723, on north bank of
Calder Water, at Colville
Park.
Jerviston is an L-plan
house of the 16th century
with a corbelled out stair
turret above first floor level
within the re-entrant. It has
corbiestepped gables, and
formerly had bartizans in
the north west and south
east angles, of which only
the corbels remain.

The entrance is in the
north face of the wing at

Jerviston House (McGibbon and Ross)

the re-entrant. A wide turnpike stair leads from here to the first floor. Above the
door was a heraldic panel, which once held the initials R. B. and E. H.

Above the stair on each floor of the wing were bedrooms. These were entered
from the stair turret. The turret originally had a conical roof, as had the bartizans.

The basement of the main block is vaulted, and contained the kitchen and a
cellar. Above this on the first floor was the hall. The top floor provided further
private apartments or bedrooms.

The property belonged to the Baillies, the initials representing Robert Baillie
and his wife Elizabeth Hamilton. The house was abandoned in favour of a later
mansion nearby, and fell into partial ruin.

Jerviswood House (***)

South Lanarkshire
Private OS 72 NS 884455
1 mile north of Lanark, on minor road north of A706, on south bank of Mouse Water.
Defensively sited high above the Mouse Water on Cartland Crags, Jerviswood
consists of a late 16th, early 17th century L-plan house of three storeys and a

garret, below a steeply pitched roof. McGibbon and Ross drew the ruins of a much more ancient castle adjacent to the house 100 or so years ago.

The lower sections of the walls of Jerviswood show signs of having originated in a much earlier period than the remainder of the house.

The basement was not vaulted, and contains the kitchen fireplace and oven within a 12 ft arch. A *Jerviswood Castle (McGibbon and Ross)*
square stair rises to the floor above. Much of the original interior was destroyed as the house was converted to house farm labourers. Of the remaining external features, an arrow slot in the north wall, heraldic panel of the door, and the generally fine workmanship of the building are notable.

The older castle would have been constructed by the original Livingstone owners. It was purchased in 1636 by a branch of the Baillies of Lamington. George Baillie rebuilt the house in the early 17th century, and a later extension was added to the east.

He was succeeded by the Covenanter Robert Baillie who hid in a recess within the walls before being captured, then hanged, drawn and quartered for high treason in 1684. The parts of his body were displayed in Edinburgh, Lanark, Ayr and Glasgow. The Lanark folk rescued their part of his body and gave it a decent burial. Before his death he wrote to his son George, and stated 'if ye have a strong heart ye may go and see me nagled; but if ye have not the heart for it, ye may stay away'.

George married the daughter of the Earl of Marchmont, and so the family eventually inherited Mellerstain, and later still became Earls of Haddington.

A heraldic panel bearing the arms of George Baillie is built into the wall of the Mains Farm. The house has been restored and reoccupied as a private home. It received a Civic Trust Commendation in 1984.

Johnstone Castle (***)

Renfrewshire
Private   OS 64   NS 425623
In Johnstone, on minor roads south of A737, just south of Quarrelton, in Tower Place.
Johnstone is an altered L-plan tower house of the 16th century. It consists of a main block of three storeys and a garret, and an altered wing, which now rises

a further storey. This wing has been Gothicised. A two storey bartizan crowns the gable of the main block, and a massive chimney stack dominates the east gable. There is a watch house in the re-entrant. There are corbiestepped gables and many arrow slits.

The entrance in the re-entrant has a porter's lodge. This was guarded by a machiolated projection from the floor above. The door leads to a vaulted passage from which the two basement rooms are reached. A bricked-up portion of this passage probably led to the stair. The eastern most of these rooms is the kitchen, with a wide arched fireplace. The room to the west was a wine cellar, and had a service stair which rose within the wall to the hall on the floor above. Although much altered, the hall retains a garderobe and a deep window recess. There is a decorated heraldic panel high on the wall below the watch house.

Originally named Easter Cochrane, Johnstone was a property of the Cochranes who in 1669 became Earls of Dundonald. The Houstons of Milliken Park bought it in 1733, and changed the name to Johnstone. They extended the castle in 1771 and in 1812 had it remodelled, possibly by James Gillespie Graham. Frederick Chopin apparently visited in 1848. The estate and mansion were taken over by the local council in the 20th century, and in 1950 they ordered the demolition of the mansion. This left only the old core, with some modifications to the wing. It now stands within a housing estate, and was used as a store by the council.

Jordanhill Castle (*)
City of Glasgow
Ruin or site   OS 64   NS 538683
In the grounds of Jordanhill College, on minor roads south of A82, to the west and north of Glasgow.
Site of a tower house of the 16th century of the Crawfords, which they retained until the 19th century.

In 1571 Lord Fleming held Dumbarton Castle against the Regent's forces for Queen Mary. Captain Thomas Crawford of Jordanhill led a small force against the castle on the 31 March. Approaching before sunrise, his men fixed their muskets across their backs. Choosing the north east section of the wall, since the garrison 'suspected nocht the heighest part of the crag', he and his men scaled the walls with iron hooks, ropes and ladders. A few, once over the walls, disposed of the sentries and allowed the others up. Crawford and his force then took the part of the castle known as the Beak. By this time the garrison was alert to the attack, but failed to counter attack. Crawford then used their own artillery against the remaining parts of the castle, and won it. Lord Fleming escaped to sea, but Archbishop Hamilton of St Andrews was captured and later executed.

In 1577 Crawford became Provost of Glasgow, and was responsible for the building of the bridge to Partick over the Kelvin. He died in 1603. By the late 18th century the property belonged to the Houstons.

K

Kat Castle *see* Cot Castle

Kelly House (*)
Renfrewshire
Ruin or site   OS 63   NS 198690?
2 miles south of Inverkip, on minor road east of A78, north of Kelly Burn, at or near Kelly Mains.
Site of a mansion which stands on the site of an earlier house or castle. Kelly was held by the Bannatynes from the 15th century until 1792 when it was purchased by John Wallace. A new house was built in 1793 and later occupied by Sir James 'Paraffin' Young, pioneer of oil technology. Another new house by William Leiper was built in 1890, but was burned down in 1913, probably by suffragettes.

Kemp Castle *see* Cot Castle

Kenmuir (*)
City of Glasgow
Ruin or site   OS 64   NS 660622
On south side of M74, 1 mile east of Carmyle, 0.25 miles north of River Clyde, off minor roads east of A763, south of Glasgow.
Site of a castle which appears in Bleau's Atlas Novus of the 17th century. The site is now occupied by what were formerly farm buildings, though is now surrounded by a land fill site, sewerage works and the M74. The occupier has a display of building facades built from restored sandstone dumped in the land fill, and originating from the now demolished tenements of Glasgow. They provide a conspicuous and attractive landmark adjacent to a very unsightly and malodorous stretch of the motorway.

Killallan House (**)
Renfrewshire
Private   OS 63   NS 383689
1 mile east of Kilmacolm, on minor roads east of A761, 0.5 miles south east of Lawfield Dam, at Killallan.
Killallan House is a stout 17th century two storey house with attic and corbiestepped gables. There is a projecting round tower with turnpike stair. The roof

is steeply pitched, and there are later single storey extensions to both east and west gables.

The main block runs east west and is a rectangular structure. At its east end the stair tower projects to the north. To the rear of this in the south wall is the entrance, an unusual feature. Some of the windows have been enlarged, though a few retain their original moulded recesses. The door is similarly set within mouldings, and gives entry to the foot of the stair.

The basement was not vaulted, and opens from a door to the left. The kitchen has been converted into a public room, with a smaller moulded fireplace than the original. This has been reset from a room on the floor above. There is an aumbry in the northern wall. Beyond the kitchen is a private room.

The plan on the first floor is the same. Above the kitchen was the hall, with a bedroom beyond. In the garret are two rooms, one with a large dormer window built into the roof.

The house was renovated and extended in 1783, 1921, and again in 1963.

Adjoining the house is the ruined church of St Fillan, established in the 8th century. A hollowed stone and well nearby are named St Fillan's seat and well in his honour. The house was originally the manse of the parish, and is now used as a farmhouse. In 1659 the Reverend Alexander Jamieson was ordered to remain in the house by the Privy Council. He was later alleged to have suffered at the will of the 'Witches of Pollok'.

Killallan Manse *see* Killallan House

Kilmacolm Castle (*)
Renfrewshire
Ruin or site   OS 63   NS 361693?
South of old part of Kilmacolm, near A761, east of River Gryffe.
Site of an old castle which may have been held by the Porterfields.

The family tomb dated 1560 was repositioned within the graveyard on the rebuilding of the Old Kirk in 1831.

Kilmahew Castle (**)
The Lennox & East Dunbartonshire
Private   OS 63   NS 352787
1 mile north of Cardross by minor roads north from A814, 0.5 miles east of Kirkton, just north west of Kilmahew House.
Kilmahew consists of a ruined 15th century keep of five storeys and a garret. The south and west walls were rebuilt in the 19th century with a view to incorporating the keep in a Gothic mansion, which was never completed. Only the north and east walls to the wall head, with the northern most portion of the west wall including the door, remain of the 15th century work. Some of the internal features of the original remains were also altered, including a fireplace

in the west wall and a variety of recesses.

The keep measured 46 ft by 25 ft, the main door on the ground floor being guarded from above by a machiolated projection at parapet level. The lintel above the door once carried the inscription, 'The peace of God be herein'. The staircase originally rose from just within the doorway, and the basement rooms do not appear to have been vaulted. The kitchen may have been in the north wall, the fireplace recess remains. The hall as usual was on the first floor. Some of the parapet corbelling survives.

The estate was held by the Napiers from the 13th to 19th

Kilmahew Castle (M&R)

centuries. In 1820 they sold the estate in portions, which were repurchased by John Burns to form a single estate by 1859. While in other hands, plans were drawn up to have the castle included in the unbuilt mansion. However, on purchasing the site, Burns built the present Kilmahew House instead.

Kilmaronock Castle (**)

The Lennox & East Dunbartonshire
Ruin or site   OS 57   NS 456877
1 mile west of Drymen, north of A811, on south bank of Endrick, at Kilmaronock.
This ruin stands to the level of the second floor. Vaulting remains in the basement and partially, as well as at second floor level. Its walls vary in thickness from 7 to 8 ft.

Formerly of four storeys, this large keep had its entrance by removable ladder on the east side of the second floor. This led directly into a vaulted hall of 27 ft by 19 ft. A stair in the south eastern corner led to the floors below. Another in the north eastern corner led to the floors above.

In the hall over the main entrance and entered from the rising stairway was a musicians gallery. There was a large fireplace in the western wall. Either side of this in the north and south walls were two large windows with stone transom and mullion, unusual in a secular building of this date. Both windows boast stone seating within their recesses.

The basement was vaulted and consisted of two chambers of unequal size. The smaller narrow chamber was reached only by a small stairway from the kitchen above, and may have been the prison. The larger was probably a wine cellar and was illuminated by three small slit windows.

The first floor again had two disproportionately sized chambers. The smaller had its own vaulting, and fireplace. Very narrow, this appears to have been the kitchen, and had no windows. At one of its narrow ends was the base of the staircase from above, which at its head had a passage to the prison. A doorway from the kitchen led to a larger vaulted chamber with three small windows and the stairway to the wine cellar.

The third floor also had transom and mullion windows, this time with arched heads. The single large room of this floor had many mural chambers and recesses. On the southern exterior wall is a projection, which provided further space on the first and upper floors, and may have been used for garderobes.

The base of the keep was wider than that of the structure above. This sloping outward on all sides was known as a talus, and provided extra stability on soft ground. There may originally have been a moat supplied with water from the Endrick a few yards away.

The lands were anciently part of the Earldom of Lennox, but were granted to Sir Malcolm Fleming in 1329. Sir John de Danyelston, or Dennistoun, gained them by marrying Malcolm's daughter, with the lands as dowry. His son, Sir Robert, was one of the hostages held by the English as ransom for David II in 1357. As reward the family were granted the hereditary keepership of Dumbarton Castle, large grants of land, and the

Kilmaronock Castle (McGibbon and Ross)

Sheriffdom of Lennox. The Dennistouns probably built the keep. Sir Robert died toward the end of the 14th century, and the estates were divided between his two daughters. The male line continued through the Dennistouns of Colgrain. Kilmaronock passed to Margaret, wife to Sir William Cunningham of Kilmaurs.

This family became Earls of Glencairn, but passed the barony of Kilmaronock to the Cochrane Earls of Dundonald. The 1st Earl granted the property to his second son, William. The estate was broken up to various smaller tenants, the keep passing to one John M'Goune in the 18th century. From then the castle deteriorated and was ruinous by the mid 19th century.

The remains of the castle stand within the grounds of Kilmaronock House, a mansion of 1901.

Other references: Mains of Kilmaronock

Kilsyth Castle (*)

The Lennox & East Dunbartonshire
Ruin or site   OS 64   NS 717776
Just south of Allanfauld Farm, west of Allanfauld Road, on the banks of the Garrel Burn, Kilsyth.

The castle was garrisoned and strengthened against Cromwell, who stayed the night here after its capture in 1650. He then blew up the main tower, and burnt the rest. It was subsequently used as a quarry, providing stone for most of the dykes in the area. Some of the more interesting blocks have made their way to the Colzium House Museum.

The site was excavated in 1976, and has revealed details of the development of the castle. William Livingstone, 1st of Kilsyth, built a substantial tower house here in the 15th century, and he died in 1459. In 1500 his successors built a court with kitchens and an L-plan corner tower. In 1600 a three storey domestic range was added.

The excavations also surrendered a coin of Charles I, a green glazed pot, a bronze spoon, and a basket hilt from a broadsword, among other things. These have gone to various museums, including Colzium, the Hunterian, Kelvingrove, and to Castle Cary.

The Livingstones were created Viscounts Kilsyth in 1661, but were forfeited for backing the Jacobites in the rising of 1715.

Kincaid Castle (*)

The Lennox & East Dunbartonshire
Private   OS 64   NS 650760
Just south of Milton of Campsie, and just west of B757, and south of Glazert Water, at Kincaid House Hotel.

Site of a castle which lay some way west, probably at Castlehill (NS 632753), which was replaced by Kincaid House.

The lands known as Kincaid lay between the Glazert Water and the River Kelvin. They were Galbraith property, but in 1290 were sold to a local family who adopted the name as their own. In 1690 they abandoned their original castle and built Kincaid House. One of the family married the heiress of Woodhead, and adopted the joint surname of Kincaid Lennox. Their son built the grandiose mansion of Lennox Castle to impress his remote claim to the ancient Earldom of Lennox, a claim which failed. The family mausoleum is one of several ancient graves in the church yard at Clachan of Campsie.

The house was extended in 1712 and 1812, and is now the Kincaid House Hotel – see page 219.

Kirkintilloch Peel (*)
The Lennox & East Dunbartonshire
Ruin or site   OS 64   NS 655740?
In Kirkintilloch, south of A803, at confluence of Luggie Water and River Kelvin.
Nothing remains of a 13th century castle or peel of the Comyns. The barony of Kirkintilloch was granted to the Comyns in 1211, though then to the Flemings after the Wars of Independence. They preferred the Cumbernauld site at the other end of the estate, where the Comyns had a motte. They subsequently built their castle there, though by 1747 had sold the Kirkintilloch portion to the Kennedys. A further early castle of the Comyns is thought to have stood on the hill where Lenzie Railway Station now stands, though there are no remains.
Other references: Lenzie Castle

Kirkton Hall *see* Ballanreoch

Kirkton of Carluke (*)
South Lanarkshire
Ruin or site   OS 72   NS 844502
0.25 miles west of Carluke, close to railway station, on minor roads west of A73.
This mansion was demolished in the mid 20th century. It had as its core an altered three storey tower house. The older section had a projecting tower with narrow turnpike stair. It had replacement windows and a new roof. There was a vaulted basement and the hall was, as usual, on the first floor.

It was a property of Weir of Stonebyres, but passed in 1662 to the Lockharts of The Lee.
Other references: Carluke

Knightswood Castle (*)
City of Glasgow
Ruin or site   OS 64   NS 530695
2 miles east of Clydebank, off A82, at or near Knightswood Cross, Glasgow.
Site of a 15th century tower house. The 'Knights' were the Knights Templars, who in early days kept this ground as their hunting forest. They had their Temple at what is now Anniesland, and part of that area retains the name Temple.

Knockderry Castle (*)
The Lennox & East Dunbartonshire
Private   OS 56   NS 218836
1 mile north of Cove, on minor road just off B833, on east shore of Loch Long, at Knockderry Castle.
Perched on a rocky outcrop, Knockderry Castle is a mansion of 1855 which was enlarged in 1886. It is said to be built upon the foundation of a Norse watch-tower of the 13th century, and alleged to be haunted by ghosts associated with its dungeons.

Knownoblehill Castle (*)
North Lanarkshire
Ruin or site   OS 64   NS 794589
1 mile south east of Newarthill, off minor roads south of A723, 0.5 miles west of Knownoble, at Knownoblehill.
Site of a tower house of the Cleland family, of which the vaulted basement was still visible just prior to 1880.

Kot Castle *see* Cot Castle

L

Laigh Castle *see* **Pollok House**

Lamington Tower (**)

South Lanarkshire
Ruin or site   OS 72   NS 980230
5 miles south west of Biggar, on minor roads north of A72 at Lamington, just east of River Clyde.
Portions of the south and west walls remain of Lamington Tower, a 15th century house of the Baillies. The remains indicate a rectangular keep of 38.75 ft by 31.75 ft, which had bartizans on at least two corners. One remains, though it has been replaced on the south east corner, and was not present in the days of McGibbon and Ross. This has been put on top of an already ruinous wall, and so at a lower level than originally set. The north west bartizan, which was recorded as being in situ by the intrepid architects, now lies broken within a field

Lamington Tower (McGibbon and Ross)

close to the site. The walls that have gone must have contained the entrance, stair and hall fireplace, since no trace of these remain. The basement was vaulted, though this was demolished. The hall was as usual on the first floor, and had a window with arched recess in carefully dressed stone. There was also a window in the south wall. There are remnants of a garderobe, and a mural chamber was partly built up to strengthen the ruin. A heraldic stone bearing the arms of the Baillies was removed to the Episcopal chapel at Lamington. An engraving there states it was removed from Wallace's Tower at Lamington.

This serves to remind of the connection of the estate with Marion Braidfute, heiress of Lamington, and from whom the Baillies claim descent. She was the wife of William Wallace, who after receiving her aid by escaping the English through her house in Lanark, avenged her execution by the English Sheriff Hazelrigg, by killing him, and then torching his stronghold in the town.

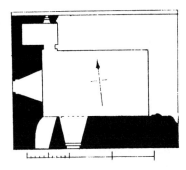

It was this event which allegedly sparked his campaign to release the nation from English occupation.

Lamington Tower – plan (M&R)

Lamington takes its name from Lambin Asa, the original Flemish settler granted the barony by Malcolm IV. William Baillie acquired the estate in 1368. Another William Baillie was Master of the Queen's Wardrobe to Mary Queen of Scots, who visited in 1565, and he was forfeited after taking her side at the Battle of Langside in 1568.

The tower was occupied in 1750, but in 1780 was blown up so that the stone could be used for dyke building. The Baillies became Lords Lamington in 1880, and built a small mansion, Lamington House.

Lanark Castle (*)

South Lanarkshire
Ruin or site   OS 72   NS 876435
In Lanark, 0.75 miles south of A73, off minor roads, at Castlebank, at Lanark Thistle Bowling Club.
A huge motte remains of this 12th and 13th century castle. It is now topped by the greens of a bowling club.

The 12th century kings of Scots visited the castle, but it was occupied by the English during the Wars of Independence. Wallace torched the castle after taking revenge on Hazelrigg, the English Sheriff for the death of his wife, Marion Braidfute. It was presumably rebuilt, since it was recaptured from the English by Robert the Bruce in 1310, and pulled down as part of his policy of rendering major strongholds indefensible. The summit was excavated and levelled in the 18th century to create the greens, and a formidable ditch to the north filled in.

Lanrig Castle (*)

Renfrewshire
Ruin or site   OS 64   NS 536550
3 miles south east of Barrhead, off minor roads east of A77, and south of Newton Mearns, in woodland behind the former site of Mearnskirk Hospital.
Site of an early castle which is likely to have been the Maxwells' original site at Mearns. They built their new castle and vacated the old site in 1449. This site

has been excavated on two occasions, and was described as a rectangular enclosure defended by crags and steep slopes augmented by ditches. The abutment for a wooden bridge was still visible over the southern ditch in 1982. An alternative site for the original Mearns castle is on the hill now occupied by Paidmire Gardens, which is recorded in 1791 as being known as Castlehill. This link may be a little tenuous.

The Maxwell family of Caerlaverock gained the estate of Mearns by marriage to the Pollok heiress around 1300. James II granted a licence to build the new castle in 1449. One of the family died at Flodden in 1513, and another was imprisoned in the Tower of London while Ambassador to France in 1542. He was ransomed. The Maxwells of Nether Pollok inherited in 1648, and it later came to the Schaw-Stewarts of Ardgowan and Inverkip.

Lauchope House (*)
North Lanarkshire
Ruin or site   OS 64   NS 782619?
3.5 miles north east of Motherwell, off minor roads, north of A8 and south of B799, south of Chapelhall, at or near Lauchope Mains.
Site of a strong tower house of the Muirheads, which was later incorporated into a mansion, now demolished.

The tower gave refuge to Hamilton of Bothwellhaugh in 1570 after his assassination of the Regent Moray in Linlithgow. Muirhead was his brother-in-law. The house was burned as a result.

The first Muirhead of Lauchope was renowned as a hero nationwide, if the legend of the notorious robber baron Bertram of Shotts is to be believed. Bertram was a giant among men, deemed capable of fighting a dozen men at once, and winning!

The Crown was so concerned by his piratical antics that they offered a substantial reward for his removal. Muirhead was their man. Dumping a cart load of heather close by a well that the giant was known to use, Muirhead lay in wait for his victim. Sure enough Bertram came to drink, and after examining the curious pile, he bent over to sup from the well. Muirhead emerged from below the heather and struck the giant a fatal blow to the head with his sword. The story continues that Robert II was so grateful that Muirhead was granted the Lauchope lands as a result.

This same hero supposedly died at Flodden some 140 years later. Obviously the tale has gone astray, and for the sake of a good story say that it might have been Homildon Hill, and that a descendant died at Flodden. The existence of a Bertram of Shotts has never been shown in fact, though the legend warranted a mention in Sir Walter Scott's epic *The Ballad of the Battle of Flodden Field*.

Law Castle (*)

The Lennox & East Dunbartonshire
Ruin or site   OS 64   NS 515738
1 mile west of Bearsden, off minor roads north of the A810, east of Duntocher.
Site of a 16th century tower. Law was a property of the Livingstones, passing by marriage to Sir James Hamilton of Finnart after 1513. He sold it to the Stirlings of Glorat about the time that he exchanged his other local property of Drumry with the Crawfords for Kilbirnie.

Law's Castle (*)

North Lanarkshire
Ruin or site   OS 65   NS 826612
4 miles north east of Wishaw, 1 mile south of B7066 at Salsburgh, by foot, or 0.5 miles by foot east of minor road at Jersay, on eastern slope of the hill 'Law's Castle'.
Site of a large castle which appears on Bleau's Atlas Novus of the 17th century.

Lee Castle (*)

Renfrewshire
Ruin or site   OS 64   NS 579591
4 miles north west of East Kilbride, on the east side of the B767 (Clarkston Road), in Beechgrove Park, Netherlee.
This is the most likely site of the 14th century castle of Lee. It was a property of the Cochranes of Lee in the 15th century, but had passed to Pollok of Balgray by the 16th.

This site has been excavated, and produced pottery of the 14th and 15th centuries. In 1840 the foundations were removed and revealed a number of human bones which the *New Statistical Account* described as being of 'superhuman magnitude'.
Other references: Overlee.

Lee Castle – site

Lee Castle *see* The Lee

Lenzie Castle *see* Kirkintilloch Peel

Leven Castle *see* Castle Levan

Lickprivick Castle (*)
South Lanarkshire
Ruin or site   OS 64   NS 616525
In East Kilbride, 2 miles south of A726, and 1.75 miles east of B764, west of Greenhills, and east of Newlandsmuir, off minor roads, near triangulation point.
A mound remains which is associated with the 14th century castle of the Lickprivicks of that Ilk. They were granted the estate by Robert I, though the estate passed to another family, probably the Maxwells of Calderwood. There was a later castle here, mostly dating from the 17th century, though incorporating an earlier keep.

Lindsay Tower *see* Crawford Castle

M

Maiden Castle (*)
The Lennox & East Dunbartonshire
Ruin or site   OS 64   NS 643785
3.5 miles north west of Kirkintilloch, and 1 mile north east of Lennoxtown, on lower sloes of Campsie Fells, just north of Glorat House.
A small traditionally pudding bowl shaped motte remains of a 12th century castle. It was probably one of a series commissioned by the Earls of Lennox guarding traffic ways from north to south, and guarded the southern end of the Campsie Glen pass.

Mains Castle (*)
The Lennox & East Dunbartonshire
Ruin or site   OS 64   NS 535752
1 mile north west of Milngavie, on minor rod east of A809, just north of Mains housing estate, at or near Douglas Academy.
Site of a castle, replaced by a mansion, itself pulled down to clear the site for the present school. It was a property of the Galbraiths of Culcreuch, and passed by marriage to the Douglasses of Dalkeith in 1373. They retained the property until the 20th century.

Mains Castle (***)
South Lanarkshire
Private   OS 64   NS 627560
1 mile north west of East Kilbride, and just west of Stewartfield, off minor roads north of A726, and south of A749, just south of Comyn's Castle.
Mains is a plain rectangular keep of the 15th century. It once had a courtyard and substantial outbuildings. It has three storeys and a garret, with a square cap house above a corbelled out parapet.

The structure measures 37.5 ft by 26.8 ft, and reaches a height to the parapet of 41.25 ft, the garret adding a further 12 ft to this height. The entrance is at

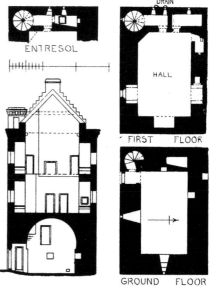

Mains Castle – plans and elevation (M&R)

the western end of the south wall, and is through a round arched doorway. This gives access to a turnpike stair within the walls which leads to all floors. At the head of the stair, the square caphouse with corbelled supports for the roof, opens out onto a parapet walk flanked by a corbelled out parapet which once supported a crenellated wall. The roof is stone flagged, and the garret had corbiestepped gables which supported chimney stacks at each end.

Mains Castle (1910?)

The basement is vaulted, consisting of a single chamber with an entresol. The lower section was illuminated by two arrow slits, and the entresol reached from a passage from the stair. From this passage, an opening led to a dungeon within the walls, which had a small opening of about 1 ft square to the ground floor. This has been sealed for many years.

The hall on the first floor has a garderobe in the north wall, and a plain fireplace in the east. There are two windows with stone seats. The hall may also have served as the kitchen, since in the access passage from the stair there is a stone sink with conduit drain. There is a mural chamber in the west wall. The floor above has been subdivided into two rooms, each with fireplace and there is a garderobe and mural chamber above those in the hall.

The entire site was surrounded by a deep ditch which remained visible 200 years ago, and was crossed by a drawbridge to the east. This was guarded by an arched gateway bearing a stone with the

Mains Castle

Royal Arms. This stone was taken to Torrance House.

The estate originally belonged to the Comyns, but was granted to the Lindsays of Dunrod in 1382. One of the family was present at the death of the Red Comyn in Dumfries Kirk, after his famous altercation with Robert the Bruce.

A later Lindsay of Mains was angered by one of his servants while curling on the nearby pond, ordered a hole to be cut in the ice, and the man held under until drowned. They sold the property in 1695 to pay off debts. It was unroofed in 1723 and fell into ruin. Some repairs were carried out in the 19th century, and in the 20th century it was restored and remains occupied as a private house.

The castle is reputedly haunted by a variety of ghosts, one of which is said to represent a woman strangled by her jealous husband.

Mains of Kilmaronock *see* Kilmaronock

Mearns Castle (***)

Renfrewshire
Private   OS 64   NS 553553
3 miles south west of Barrhead,
just east of Newton Mearns,
and 0.25 miles north of Earn
Water, off minor roads south of
A77, at Mearns Parish Church,
immediately west of Mearns
High School.

Sited on the edge of a precipitous drop, Mearns is a 15th century rectangular keep of three storeys, which is now connected to a modern church building and serves as the church hall. Lord Maxwell already had a castle on this estate but on the building of his new house, moved both kirk

Mearns Castle – illustration and plans (M&R)

and village. It may be that this site was occupied by a previous structure, since the wall to the head of the basement door is of rough rubble, while the structure above is of dressed ashlar block (compare Lanrig).

Situated on a level platform, the site is defended on the west and north sides by a severe drop, and once had a wall and ditch on the remaining sides. The site was reached by a drawbridge.

The tower measures 44 ft by 29.5 ft, and reaches 45 ft in height to the corbels of the parapet. At the ground floor the east wall reached 10 ft in thickness and the others to 8 ft They thin to 6.5 ft at the top storey. An entrance at ground floor level in the east wall is now closed, and the main arched entrance immediately above to the hall on the first floor has been adapted to create a window. A connecting corridor has been built from the church, and enters the castle in the west wall.

From the passage into the basement at the ground floor entrance, a straight stair rises northward within the wall, turning at first floor level to create a turnpike to the floor above within the north east corner.

The vaulted basement room was illuminated by splayed arrow slots in west and south walls. The hall occupied the whole of the floor above, and internally measured 27.75 ft by 16.5 ft. It reached 21 ft to the vault, allowing the introduction of a musicians gallery or entresol high on the east wall. This was entered from the turnpike stair by a passage, and illuminated by its own window above the door. The hall had a closet in the east wall adjacent to the main door, and the fireplace was centrally sited on the west wall. Two arrow slots in the closet and on the north wall, plus larger windows with stone seats in the north and south walls, provided illumination.

The top storey was similar in plan to the hall, though from the closet a machiolated projection through the south wall allowed drainage and use as a garderobe.

Mearns Castle

The supporting corbels remain.

The stair to the parapet and caphouse have now gone, though there remain impressive machiolated corbels at the wall head around the entire structure. Internally there are sockets for support of massive roof beams, though it is not now possible to say exactly what form the roof took. The licence to build Mearns implies that it was flat.

This document was granted by James II to Herbert, Lord Maxwell, on the 15 March 1449. The document permits Lord Maxwell 'to build a castle or fortalice on the Barony of Mearns in Renfrewshire, to surround and fortify it with walls and ditches, to strengthen it by iron gates, and to erect on top of it all the warlike apparatus necessary for its defence'. This may have meant that the castle was supplied with mangonels or similar weapons, indicating the flat roof from which they would operate.

The estate belonged initially to the local Celtic lords, widely assumed to be the Polloks. It passed by marriage to the Maxwells of Caerlaverock in 1300. Lord John Maxwell died at Flodden in 1513. His son Robert was imprisoned until ransomed in the Tower of London after capture at Solway Moss. This while acting as Ambassador to France in 1542.

In 1589 James VI wrote from Craigmillar to the catholic William, 5th Lord Herries, demanding the surrender of his castles at Caerlaverock, Threave, Morton and 'the place and fortalice of Mearns'.

The estate was sold by the then Earl of Nithsdale to the lesser house of Sir George Maxwell of Pollok in 1648, and then to the Stewarts of Blackhall, later Schaw Stewarts of Ardgowan and Inverkip. It was abandoned and fell into ruin until renovated and incorporated into the present Church of Scotland building in 1971.

Middleton Castle (*)
Renfrewshire
Ruin or site   OS 64   NS 452652
2.5 miles north east of Johnstone, 1 mile west of Linwood, off minor roads north of A740, at or near Middleton.
Site of a tower house which appears on Bleau's Atlas Novus of the 17th century.

Middleton of Colquhoun *see* Tressmass

Milton of Colquhoun *see* Tressmass

Moat (*)
South Lanarkshire.
Ruin or site   OS 71   NS 846396
At Moat, off minor roads 3 miles east of M74, 2 miles east of Lesmahagow.
The Old Statistical Account of 1794 describes a building 30 ft by 15 ft, which could be surrounded by water, to resist Annandale thieves. It was vaulted, and 'loopholed in the lower part'.

Moat (*)
South Lanarkshire
Ruin or site   OS 72   NS 941272
2.5 miles north of Abington, at Moat, 1 mile south of Roberton, on A73.
The motte here has been excavated and shown to have been constructed during the 14th century. The ground below surrendered pottery of this date, negat-

ing the theory that this had been the caput of Robert the Fleming in the 12th century. It is believed that his site lies just north of the parish church in the village, and its remains are represented by faint earthworks.

Moat is now thought to have been constructed by Mary of Stirling, who supported the Balliol faction during the reigns of Robert I and David II. She had been compelled to provide herself and her followers with a fortified base in this area. She resigned her lands at Roberton in 1346 in the hope of a pardon from David II.

Monkland House (*)
North Lanarkshire
Ruin or site   OS 64   NS 730633
1 mile south of Coatbridge, on minor roads west of A725, at Shawhead.
Monkland House has been demolished, though it had been an impressive L-plan house of the late 16th or early 17th century. The house was built against a slope, so that the main entrance at ground level on the north, actually entered at the first floor proper. A later porch had been added at the entrance. There was no entrance at ground floor level.

The building consisted of a long main block, running east to west, with round towers at both of its southern corners. On the north side against the slope, a square wing was joined by half its length at the western corner. In the re-entrant, a round stair tower reached a turnpike stair from the door. This led downwards to the basement of the main block, and upwards to third floor level. The main block rose to three storeys and an attic for two thirds of its eastern end. However,

Monkland House (McGibbon and Ross) – demolished

an additional storey rose at the western third. The wing had three storeys, and supported a wide chimney flue on its northern wall. All of the gables were corbiestepped and topped by chimney stacks. The windows on each floor had been enlarged in the 18th and 19th centuries, and dormers provided for the attic rooms of the lower section of the main block. There were many gun loops around the building.

All of the ground floor rooms were vaulted and protected by external walls

reaching 5 ft thick. The kitchen occupied the basement of the wing,
and through the stair tower a door
led to the three chambers of the main
block.

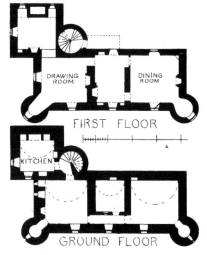

Each floor of the wing appears to
have had a single room. On the first
floor of the main block was a drawing room, a dining room, and a
smaller connecting room between
the two. The rooms of the round towers were continuous with those to
which they were connected. Access
to the room in the wing was via a
door in the northern connecting wall,
behind the stair tower. The private
chambers would have occupied the
floors above.

Monkland House – plans (M&R)

Originally part of the extensive Monklands Church property, under the superiority of Newbattle Abbey, the estate passed to the Kerrs of Ferniehirst at
the Reformation. The Hamiltons then obtained them before being acquired by
Sir James Cleland of Monkland, who built the house.

Several fires in the 20th century caused the building to be demolished. A
housing development now occupies the site.

Moss Castle (*)
South Lanarkshire
Ruin or site   OS 71   NS 845227
*2.5 miles west and south of Crawfordjohn, on minor roads north of B740, 1 mile west
and north of Eastertown Farm, at Mosscastle.*
Site of a castle which appears on Bleau's Atlas Novus of the 17th century as
'The Tour of Mausonly'. A vestige of the castle remained in the 19th century but
has now gone.

Mugdock Castle (***)
The Lennox & East Dunbartonshire
Ruin or site   OS 64   NS 549772
*1.5 miles north of Milngavie, on minor roads west of A81, 0.5 miles west of Mugdock
village, in Mugdock country park, on west side of Mugdock Loch.*
Mugdock Castle is sited upon a narrow level ridge some 320 ft long, which
once formed a steeply banked peninsula into the now partly drained loch.

There remains a fairly intact slim tower adjacent to the section of wall containing the gateway, and nearby to the north the vaulted basement of a second

tower. A small portion of the gatehouse survives. Parts of the original wall mark out the site, which at the opposite and northern end of the ridge has the remains of the chapel and latrine tower. There was probably a wide ditch with a drawbridge guarding the entrance. The castle dates from the 14th century with several later additions. Other ruins adjacent to the tower represent the remnants of the mansion house of J. Guthrie Smith, an eminent local historian of the Victorian era. A stone arched bridge over the gateway joins the first floor of the tower to the mansion into which it had been incorporated.

The tower is an irregularly shaped structure of four storeys and 24 ft in diameter. It reaches a height of 59 ft to the parapet and probably represents one of several lesser towers of a very ruined large courtyard castle.

The ground floor room contains a mural garderobe which probably drained via a conduit to the ditch. It had no internal access to the floor above. The first floor is rib vaulted and supports the main entrance, formerly entered by way of a removable ladder and now by external stone stair. From here a turnpike stair within the east wall at the south east corner leads to the second floor. The second floor stands at the same height as the top of the courtyard wall. From here a straight stair within the east wall leads the floor above and then to the battlements. The parapet wall

Mugdock Castle

is straight and not crenellated. The roof within is a replacement in similar form to the original. To the east of the tower is a more modern gateway to the mansion.

From the tower to the west runs a substantial portion of the enceinte, including the arched gateway with portcullis grooves. This is 8.3 ft wide, and retains the marks of a pair of folding doors, one outside the portcullis , and one inside.

From the north side of the tower, a portion of lofty wall flanks the entrance route, terminating with the vaulted basement of a second tower. At the northern end of the ridge and at the crest of a steep drop, lies a remnant of a latrine tower and the wall. Seemingly outwith this are the remains of a thin walled chapel which measured 40 ft by 17.25 ft. The castle was extended in the 15th century with a high curtain wall enclosing an outer courtyard. In 1655 further extensions were added, which were replaced by the mansion.

Mugdock was a Graham property from the early 13th century. It may have been the birthplace of James Graham, 5th Earl and 1st Marquis of Montrose. He succeeded his father in 1626, and joined the Covenanters in 1638. As they became more extreme he opposed Scottish intervention in the English Civil War. Lord Sinclair sacked Mugdock during Montrose's imprisonment in 1641. Montrose went on to conduct a remarkable campaign against the Covenanters in 1644-5. He won the battles of Tippermuir, Aberdeen, Inverlochy, Auldearn, Alford and Kilsyth. He was finally defeated at Philiphaugh by David Leslie, and escaped to the continent. During his campaign, the Buchanans 'harried' the castle, and after this the northern portion and that facing the loch were allowed to become ruinous. Montrose returned in 1650 and was defeated at Carbisdale, being captured and then hanged at Edinburgh. The family was forfeited, and Mugdock gained by Montrose's greatest enemy, the Campbell Marquis of Argyll. The Grahams retrieved the castle when in 1661 Argyll was himself executed. The family then moved to Buchanan Castle in the 18th century. The castle remained occupied until J. Guthrie Smith built his castellated mansion in 1875, and damaged or destroyed much of the old castle in the process. The mansion became derelict after being used by the government in World War II and passed to the local council who turned the estate into a country park – see page 219.

Murdostoun Castle (***)

North Lanarkshire
Private OS 65 NS 825573
1 mile north of Newmains, off minor roads north of A71, 1 mile north west of Bonkyl.
A 15th century keep forms the rear half of the south east wing of a large mansion which is now a hospital.

Alexander III granted the barony of Shotts to the Scotts. The Inglis family gained it in 1446 and built the keep. The keep is rectangular of sandstone rubble, and has a parapet and simple cornice. It was originally built around a central court, which was enclosed by later extensions of the 1860s and 1900s.

In 1719 it passed to a nephew, Inglis Hamilton, and was purchased in 1856 by former Glasgow Provost, Robert Stewart, who was responsible for Glasgow's Loch Katrine water supply.

N

Nemphlar (**)
South Lanarkshire
Ruin or site   OS 72   NS 854447
2 miles north west of Lanark, on minor roads south of A73, north of River Clyde, at Nemphlar.
This 17th-century bastle house has a vaulted basement with a blocked-up stair, while the upper floor has been modernised and is still occupied.
Other references: Halltown of Nemphlar

Nether Arthurlie *see* Arthurlie

Nether Pollok *see* Pollok House

Newark Castle (****)
Renfrewshire
His Scot   OS 63   NS 331745
In Port Glasgow, on north side of A8, on south shore of Firth of Clyde, at Newark.
Newark consists of a collection of buildings of the 15th, early 16th and late 16th centuries, forming three sides of a courtyard, the enclosing wall of the remainder has now gone. It is a remarkably well preserved structure, and well worth the care of Historic Scotland.

   The oldest section of the structure stands at the south east corner of the building and is a four storey keep, dated about 1484. It measures 29 ft by 23 ft and reaches a height of 48 ft to the present parapet, though this is now a storey

Newark Castle

higher, an extension having been built up from the original single corbels of the parapet. The entrance to the keep was at its north west corner. This original doorway remains and is reached from a lobby within the 17th century range. The ground floor is vaulted and had two entresol floors built high within the vault, each illuminated by widely splayed arrow slot windows, though this feature may be a later adaptation. A turnpike stair within the wall of the north east corner leads to all of the floors above. Renaissance windows have replaced the originals in order that it reflected the style of the later extension. Each of the upper floors was a single room, sharing a collection of garderobes, mural chambers and fireplaces.

Midway down the west side of the square courtyard is a gatehouse of the early 16th century measuring 23.5 ft by 20 ft. This features an arched vaulted entrance tunnel at its southern end, within which is a stone seat and a door leading to a vaulted chamber which functioned as guard room. From this a pair of arrow slots provided defence of the approach on the west, and that from the north. A turnpike in the north eastern corner led to the two floors above. These have a single room to each, with stone seats within the window recesses. These rooms display similar features to those of the keep. Adjacent to the garderobe on the first floor is an ogee-arched aumbry. The garret is framed by corbiestepped gables topped by chimneys, and a dormer window has been added at a later date in this room. The

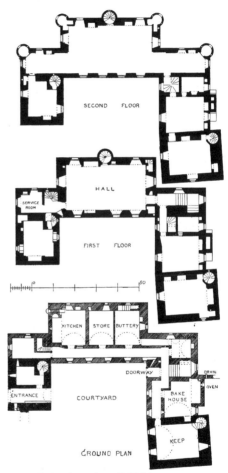

Newark Castle – plans (M&R)

entire south face of this structure adjoins the western end of the late 16th century block. The courtyard wall continued south from this structure, before turning to complete the square by meeting the keep on its west side. There remains a round doocot tower and fragments of the old barmkin wall at the north eastern corner of the site. The north and east sides of the yard were enclosed by a long L-plan block of three storeys with an outward projecting central section. Each of the four northward facing corners has a round turret corbelled out from

181

first floor level, and centrally placed in the projecting wing is a matching stair turret. All of the chambers of the ground floor are vaulted, a door from the courtyard in the east side of the re-entrant giving the only access. Above this an engraved stone gives the date 1597, and the hopeful inscription, 'The blissings of God be herein'. A dormer of the garret carries a date of two years later.

A long corridor ran around the courtyard side of this block. Directly opposite the door, a wide scale and platt stair ascends to the first floor. Southward the corridor led to a vaulted bakehouse, whose oven stood outwith the exterior wall and is now ruined. Above this rises a tall chimney stack built against the gable. At this end of the corridor is the door to the old keep. Within the northern and longest side of this range, the corridor terminates at each end with small vaulted chambers. The western of these was adjacent to a small stair leading to a service room on the floor above. On the northern side of the corridor doors open to the kitchen, a store, and a buttery or wine cellar. The kitchen has a wide fireplace with recess in the northern end, and the wine cellar has a small service stair to the hall above.

Newark Castle (1905?)

On the first floor the central projecting wing is completely occupied by the hall. The room measures 37.25 ft by 20.75 ft. There are a number of Renaissance style windows on all sides, and a wide decorated fireplace in the north wall. This measures 8.6 ft wide by 7.5 ft high. Adjacent on the east of this is a door to the round stair turret. There is a small closet of about 2 ft by 3 in the south east corner, from which a spy hole or gunloop guards the entrance to the block from the yard. The wing to the west of the hall contains the service room mentioned, and that to the east contains the stair from the ground floor and a pair of small rooms. Next to the smaller of these a turnpike rose to the floor above. The larger of these sat above the bakehouse, and has its own garderobe and fireplace. The storey above had the same floor plan at this section of the building.

The long northern section of the second floor contained a single massive room, possibly used as a function suite on grand occasions. The area could be divided by use of removable screens or doors, which separated the wings from the area above the hall. A further possibility is that screens were used to subdivide this area into bedrooms, since a fireplace is available for each. All of the walls of this block support a number of gunloops.

The estate was a property of the Danzielstouns, or Dennistouns. It passed to the Maxwells of Calderwood in 1402 at the same time as Kilmaronock passed to the Cunninghams. When the Dennistoun laird died, his estate was shared between his two daughters who took them to their new families. The entire structure can be attributed to the Maxwells. They were distantly related to royalty through the Dennistouns, and so James IV visited on several occasions. In 1495 he lodged here on his way to quell disturbances in the Western Isles. In 1497 he paid four shillings and eight pence for 'ane bote fetch wine fra the schip twys, quhen she lay at New Werk'. A year later he paid another boatman 6 shillings to take his gear to Newark from the royal castle at Dumbarton, across the river.

Patrick Maxwell was involved in feuds leading to the murders of Patrick Maxwell of Stanely in 1584, and the Montgomery Earl of Eglinton in 1596. In 1668 another Patrick Maxwell sold the surrounding land to the magistrates of Glasgow, allowing the building of a new port for the city. At this point the name of the hamlet changed from Newark to Port Glasgow. The castle itself passed to the Schaw Stewarts, and in the 18th century fell into partial ruin. Part of the castle remained habitable and in the 19th century was the residence of several poorer families while the roofless portions were used as a midden. It came into State care in 1909, and has been restored, although the floors of the garret rooms have never been replaced.

Historic Scotland: open Apr-Sep. Tel: 01745 741858 – see page 219.

Newton House (*)

South Lanarkshire
Ruin or site   OS 64   NS 663613
1.5 miles north east of Cambuslang, off minor roads 1 mile north of A724, and 1 mile east of A763, north of Westburn Road, at Westburn.
Newton House was probably fortified. It was a house of the Hamiltons of Silvertonhill. Built in 1602, the house burned down in 1684. It was replaced by a mansion which appears on maps of the 20th century compiled as recently as the 1970s. Only the gate posts remain.

Northbar (*)

Renfrewshire
Private   OS 64   NS 481693
2 miles north west of Renfrew, on minor roads north of A8, south of River Clyde, north of Inchinnan, at Northbar.
Northbar is a three storey, corbiestepped mansion of about 1742. It stands on the site of a castle of which nothing remains.

The lands were sold to the MacGilchrists in 1672, and were acquired by the Semples in 1741. They sold on to the Buchanans in 1798, and they were bought by the Stewart Lords Blantyre in 1812.

O

Ogs Castle (*)
South Lanarkshire
Ruin or site   OS 72   NT 032447
4 miles east and south of Carnwath, and 2.5 miles west of Elsrickle, off minor roads
north of A721, just east of South Medwin Water, at Ogs Castle.
Site of a castle, remnants of which survived in the 19th century, though nothing
now remains.

Old Ballikinrain (**)
The Lennox & East Dunbartonshire
Private   OS 64   NS 561880
1 mile south east of Balfron, on minor roads north of B818, south of Endrick Water,
at Old Ballikinrain.
Now much altered and having an 18th century facade, Old Ballikinrain incor-
porates a 17th century fortified house, and retains a drawbar to defend the
entrance.
   This was a Napier property from the 17th century until 1862. Ballikinrain
Castle, which stands nearby, is a 19th century Scots baronial castellated man-
sion, designed by David Bryce. It was built around a steel frame, and was burnt
out in 1913.
   It has been restored, and now operates as a Church of Scotland Residential
School.
Other references: Ballikinrain

Old Bishopton *see* Bishopton House

Old Place (*)
The Lennox & East Dunbartonshire
Ruin or site   OS 64   NS 690780
1.5 miles west of Kilsyth, off minor roads north of A803, just north of Queenzieburn
at Old Place Farm.
Site of a hallhouse of the Livingstones.

Old Place of Balgair *see* Balgair

Orbistan House
North Lanarkshire
Ruin or site   OS 64   NS 732580
At the northern edge of Strathclyde Park, minor roads west of A71, Motherwell.
The lands were originally owned by the Olifards (Oliphants) in the 12th century, but like so much of Lanarkshire passed to a branch of the Hamiltons. They sold out in 1827 due to insurmountable debts. There was a 19th century mansion here, but of the earlier tower only a portion of the north east wall survives, with a stone sink and conduit drain to the outside. Opinions vary as to the date of the tower, and it can only be surmised with an certainty that it was built between the 12th and 17th centuries, though the site was certainly occupied throughout. There were vaulted chambers on the lower and second storeys. In the days of the Regional Council restoration was planned, but it is not clear if this is still intended. The ruin is a category C listed building.
Other reference: Orbiston House

Orbiston House *see* **Orbistan House**

Overglinns Castle *see* **Balgair Castle**

Overlee Castle *see* **Lee Castle**

Over Pollok *see* **Pollok Castle**

P

Palacerigg (*)
The Lennox & East Dunbartonshire
Ruin or site   OS 64   NS 783733?
1 mile south east of Cumbernauld, Palacerigg Country Park, Cumbernauld.
The exact site of the house of a cadet branch of the Flemings of Cumbernauld has not been located. As the name implies, it is believed to have been a hall house. It is recorded in the early 17th century, though may have been older.

Parkhall (*)
South Lanarkshire
Private   OS 72   NS 863330
2.5 miles north east of Douglas, on minor roads south of A70, 0.75 miles east of junction with M74, south of Douglas Water at Parkhall.
Parkhall, a modern mansion, stands on the site of a castle.

Partick Castle (*)
City of Glasgow
Ruin or site   OS 64   NS 557664?
In Partick, on west bank of River Kelvin, and north of River Clyde, off minor roads south of A814, at east end of Castlebank Street.
Partick Castle has long gone though it stood on the site of an ancient manor of the Bishops of Glasgow. Despite earning the name of 'Bishop's Castle' once ruined, the castle was of the early 17th century. The contract for its construction survives, and describes the structure in detail. It was commissioned by George

Partick Castle (McGibbon and Ross) – demolished

Hutcheson, the well known city benefactor, and he employed William Millar 'the masoun in Kylwynning' as builder. The contract dates the castle firmly at 1611. It was an L-plan building, some 33 ft high. It had two storeys plus a garret and a vaulted basement.

The contract states that some of the foundations and walls were previously built, and that these were to be removed, new walls to be erected of sufficient thickness as to serve a vaulted house.

The work requested was as follows:

'a mayne hous and ane jamb, turnpykis, and all other easiments, the walls of the mayne hous being maid thrie futtis and ane half of the said George's awin fute' longer than the gables already laid. The jamb or wing was to be 16 ft between walls, and to contain an arched fireplace. The turnpike was to be at the north east re-entrant. The doors were to be arched and the passageways of the basement vaulted. There were to be cellars and a kitchen in the basement, and a pantry on the first floor with service stair to the east cellar. A variety of small windows were to be inserted providing plenty of light. The room in the wing off the hall on the first floor was to be called the 'chalmer of daiss', and a variety of gargoyles and water spouts were to adorn the corner angles of the building. The mason had either to provide a high arch built in the north wall so that a gallery could be formed above the hall, serviced from the room over the 'chalmer of daiss', or turn this into an independent room for a wardrobe room for Mrs Hutcheson in the garret of the wing. Dormer windows were to provide light for the top floor bedrooms.

The house survived as a ruin until the early 19th century.

Patrickholm (**)
South Lanarkshire
Ruin or site   OS 64   NS 756500
0.5 miles south west of Larkhall, off minor roads and track west of B7078, above west bank of Avon Water.
A ruinous 19th century house contains vaulted cellars from a previous building on site. A property known as Patrickholm appears in Bleau's Atlas.

Plotcock Castle (*)
South Lanarkshire
Ruin or site   OS 64   NS 741502
2 miles west of Larkhall, and 0.25 miles east of Plotcock Bridge, by minor roads and foot, 3 miles west of A723 and 0.5 miles west of Thinacres, above east side Powforth Burn gorge.
Scant ruins survive of a 16th century tower house. This may be the same site as Thinacres, though separate sites are very possible.

Pollok Castle (*)

Renfrewshire
Private   OS 64   NS 522570
1 mile west of Newton Mearns, and 2 miles south east of Barrhead, east of Balgray reservoir, by minor roads west of B769, on Pollok Castle Estate.
Pollok Castle was a mansion dated 1686 and 1687 which incorporated a keep of the 15th century. It burned to a shell in 1882, and was restored.

Sited on the edge of a crag high above the valleys of Clyde and Cart, the house provided extensive views reaching as far as distant Ben Lomond. The castle was described in 1710 as having been 'a handsome old tower, according to the ordinary model, with a large battlement'. When Sir Robert Pollok decided to build himself a large new house in the 17th century, he demolished the east and south walls, using the remainder to form part of the south west corner of his stately C-plan mansion. These walls were incorporated into the new house. There were a few original features, such as a straight mural stair in the north wall from ground floor to first, then

Pollok Castle (McGibbon and Ross)

a turnpike within the north west corner wall to the floors above. A few small windows survived, adding to the illumination of the new hall, as well as a mural chamber.

The mansion was a large four storey house, much decorated with fancy stonework, and with numerous stone garden features such as sundials, pavilions, and ornate gateways. It was notable because of the careful dating engraved on successive additions and alterations, of which Sir Robert made many. The building was demolished in 1947.

Within the bounds of the garden is a motte, probably the original 12th century residence of Fulbert de Pollok, progenitor of the line. The estate remained with the family, and in 1568 Sir John Pollok fought for Queen Mary at Langside. His son, another John, was killed at Lockerbie while supporting the Maxwells in a feud with the Johnstones. The Polloks were a turbulent lot, and crop up in reports of feuding throughout this area with numerous other local families.

Pollok House (*)

City of Glasgow
Ruin or site   OS 64   NS 549619
Off minor roads in Pollok Country Park, north of Haggs Road and west of Dumbreck Road, 0.75 miles south of M77 at Dumbreck Interchange.

The remains of the Laigh Castle of the Maxwells constitute part of the garden wall near the stable block. The Maxwells had an earlier castle somewhere nearby, possibly just south of the White Cart, on what is now a golf course. The site was destroyed when the gardens were laid out.

In its original state there was a ditch with drawbridge, the river supplementing the defences to the south. The Maxwells abandoned the site in favour of their new castle at Haggs in 1585, but returned in 1750 when Pollok House was built. It was extended in 1890.

The Maxwells of Pollok were the branch of the family which gained Mearns by marrying a Pollok heiress in the 13th century, Pollok being a division of the original estate. The family became the main branch of the local Maxwells, and became very influential in local affairs.

In 1966 after many years of selling portions of the estate off for development, Sir John Stirling Maxwell gifted the house and park to the city.

The house is used as a museum, and exhibition centre for local events. There is a hand carved model of Crookston Castle, fashioned from a branch of 'The Crookston Yew' under which Queen Mary is alleged to have pledged her troth to Henry Stewart, Lord Darnley.

The famous Burrell Collection is situated within the park and displays a fraction of Sir William Burrell's collection of artwork, armour, weaponry and other antiquities. The collection is so large that it could not conceivably be displayed at one time, and so is changed frequently. Even after numerous visits there will always be something new to see.

The park also contains a highland cattle enclosure, the Strathclyde Police Dog Handling School, Mounted Division, and other areas of interest.

In 1676 Sir George Maxwell took part in a witch trial at Gourock. Shortly afterwards he believed himself bewitched, suffering a 'hot and fiery distemper'. A local dumb girl disclosed that his effigies were to be found stuck with pins at the house of Janet Mathie, widow to the miller of Shaw Mill. Janet, her son John Stewart (a warlock), her daughter Annabel and another three women were tried in Paisley in 1677. Annabel was only 14 years old, and was released, the others burned at the stake. Sir George recovered but lived for only a few short months. Janet Douglas, the dumb informant, recovered her speech. The story has been dramatised for the stage.

Open Easter-end Sep.
Tel: 0141 632 0274 – see page 219.
Other references: Laigh Castle, Nether Pollok

Polnoon Castle (*)

Renfrewshire
Ruin or site   OS 64   NS 586513
3 miles south west of East Kilbride, 1 mile south east of Eaglesham, off minor roads south of the B764, on the west bank of the White Cart, at Polnoon.
A little rubble and a motte are all that remain of this 14th century castle of the Montgomerys.

The castle consisted of a large keep built upon a small motte, which had to be reinforced with walling to take the weight. This was surrounded by a large courtyard supporting the numerous subsidiary buildings. It all stood above a ravine of the Polnoon Burn which wound its way around three sides of the site. Originally a ditch protected the other side, separating the main castle from a second outer court which stood between the ruin and later farmhouse. From burn to battlement the keep is thought to have reached a full height of about 100 ft, an impressive stronghold.

Sir Henry 'Hotspur' Percy was captured by Sir John Montgomery of Eaglesham at the Battle of Otterburn in 1388. Held for ransom by his captor, Hotspur befriended him and helped design his new castle, and paid for it from his own ransom. Polnoon became the chief residence of the Montgomerys until they removed to Eglinton Castle at the beginning of the 16th century.

Sir John had married the Eglinton heiress and gained that family's large Ayrshire estate. The Montgomerys became Earls of Eglinton in 1508.

Poneil Castle (*)

South Lanarkshire
Ruin or site   OS 72   NS 840343
Off minor roads, 0.75 miles west of M73, 2.5 miles north of Douglas, at Poneil.
Site of a 'tenement', or tower house. In 1147 the lands of Poneil and Folkart were granted to Theobold the Fleming. In 1270 the Abbot of Kelso granted them to William de Douglas. They were won back by litigation by Alexander de Folkart in 1311. The family disappeared from the area in about 1495. A further house at Folkerton is very probable.

Possil (*)

City of Glasgow
Ruin or site   OS 64   NS 584703?
3 miles north of Glasgow, west of Bishopbriggs, by foot west of A879, at north end of Possil Loch.
Site of a castle or fortified house of the Crawfords. In 1612 Crawford of Possil was imprisoned in Edinburgh Castle for taking the law into his own hands. He tried to recover a debt owed to him by the late Earl of Eglinton by attacking his castle at Corslie. Possil was later divided into Easter and Wester Possil.

Provanhall (***)

City of Glasgow
Private   OS 64   NS 667663
3.5 miles west and north of Coatbridge, off B806, 60 yards west of Auchinlea Road,
Easterhouse, in Auchinlea Park.

Described by The National Trust as 'Probably the most perfect pre-Reformation mansion house in Scotland', they claim a 15th century origin for this house, while other sources suppose it originates from the 16th century.

The house and its later successor form the north and south perimeters of a square courtyard, which originally stretched to the shore of Provan Loch, long since drained and now represented by a duck pond to the south. The more modern house is probably late 17th century, and was renovated by Dr John Buchanan in the form of a plantation house, reflecting the source of his wealth in the tobacco trade. This part of the property is properly known as Blochairn House, though picked up a by-name of Coach Mailing, as it was a rest stop for the Glasgow-Stirling mail coach.

The older house contains a huge fireplace in the kitchen, very similar to that in Provand's Lordship, the oldest house in Glasgow, which fireplace is dated firmly at 1460.

The house is of two storeys, and a garret, the ground floor having three vaulted rooms, the vaulting in the kitchen running north to south, and that in the dairy and hallway east-west. This unusual feature gave added strength to the floor above, and the vaulting in the kitchen is reckoned as one of the finest surviving examples in the country. The hallway provided access to the round 'stair tower' in the north east corner of the building, though no evidence shows that a stair

Provanhall

existed, and it is supposed that access to the floor above was by removable ladder. In the base of the round tower are an arrow slot and a gunloop that afforded protection against attack from the blind side of the house. A further gunloop and arrow slot are at first floor level.

The first floor contains two rooms, each with a fireplace. The room to the east was the main living room, and was supplied from the dairy below by a primitive form of dumb waiter. This room was at the exit from the stair tower, though a later external stair and door provides access direct from the courtyard. A curious hollow in the floor, just off centre, puzzled the historians for many years, until it was realised that this was the resting-place of the ladder that originally led to the garret space. The room to the west provided sleeping quarters, and contained a later stair to the attic, with its servants quarters.

The small courtyard, itself, has an unusual feature in that the gateway is protected by a lookout window above the gate in the eastern wall, this being reached by a flight of stairs which is flush to the wall. The stair also provides access to a gunloop, which could provide covering fire across the approaches. A later gate in the western wall

Provanhall – courtyard

leads to a walled garden. There are faint traces of what may have been a ditch surrounding the whole.

The lands of Provan were originally part of the prebendary of Barlanark, a division of the Bishopric of Glasgow. One of the canons of Barlanark was James IV, who wisely chose church duties as penance for his part in the Battle of Sauchieburn in 1448, providing himself with some of the best wild-fowling grounds in the west of the country. In this battle James took the side of the rebellious nobles who defeated James III, his father, who subsequently died in suspicious circumstances in the aftermath of the battle.

It is claimed that his granddaughter, Mary Queen of Scots, also stayed here, and either planted or sat under an old yew tree which stood just a little way from the stair tower.

At the Reformation the lands passed to the Baillies, and Sir William Baillie is widely credited with the building of the house, though rebuilding is more likely. His daughter married a Hamilton, Sir Robert, and his initials appear with the date 1647 above the gate. Sir Robert was a Royalist in the Civil War, and the house was attacked as a result. It then passed through various owners, the last resident owner being Reston Mathers who is reported to haunt Blochairn House, having been seen and heard on various occasions.

It is also said that one of the lairds murdered his wife and son in the first floor bedroom, and her image as the 'White Lady' has allegedly been seen and heard at the garden gate, calling for her son.

The property passed to the city in 1667, and in 1937 was privately restored and given to The National Trust for Scotland, though still cared for by the city. It provides local community facilities, and is impressively decorated annually for Halloween in the fashion of a chamber or horrors, when the local children visit in appropriate costume.

The property had a small secondary house at Ruchazie (Rough Hazy) though it is less likely that this was fortified.

Open all year, except closed 25-26 Dec, and 1-2 Jan, and when special events in progress.

Tel: 0141 771 4399 – see page 219.

Other references: Blochairn House, Coach-Mailing.

Q

Qua *see* **Craiglockhart**

Queen Mary's Castle *see* **Tower Rais**

R

Rais Tower *see* Tower Rais

Ralston House (*)
Renfrewshire
Private   OS 64   NS 507642
2 miles east of Paisley centre, off minor roads south of Paisley Road and A737.
The mansion was built in 1797 and extended in 1864, replacing earlier structures, probably fortified. Hew de Ralston (or Ralph's town) subscribed to the Ragman Roll in 1296. The Ralstons of that Ilk remained on site until 1704, when it passed to the Cochrane Earls of Dundonald, then Hamiltons, and finally the Orrs, who built the mansion – which itself was demolished in 1934.

Ranfurly Castle (*)
Renfrewshire
Ruin or site   OS 63   NS 384652
0.5 miles west of Bridge of Weir, on minor roads south of A761, on Ranfurly Golf Course.
Ranfurly consists of a ruined 15th century keep, once extended to the east by a long block with centrally projecting semi circular tower, and a further block to the south, forming a courtyard.

The original keep survives only to the second storey, though without the west wall. It measured 22 ft square, and had walls 5 ft thick. Extending from the south east corner are the overgrown foundations of a later extension about 43 ft long, which had two rooms in the basement. Protruding centrally from the south wall of this was a semi circular stair tower. Facing the

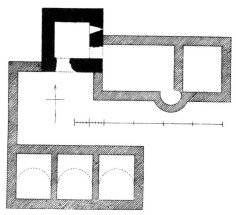

Ranfurly Castle – plan (McGibbon and Ross)

south side of the keep and enclosing a courtyard about 15 ft wide, are the remains of another block whose basement once had three vaulted chambers. The enclosing wall between this and the keep is traceable.

The estate belonged to the Knox family from the 15th century or earlier. The reformer John Knox was a relative or descendant. In 1665 the barony was alienated to the 1st Earl of Dundonald, William Cochrane. It was later sold to the Aitkenhead family.

Raploch Castle (*)
South Lanarkshire
Ruin or site   OS 64   NS 763515
North of Larkhall, near B7078, east of Avon Water, at Raploch.
Site of a castle. This was Comyn property until they were purged by Robert the Bruce. In 1312 he gave the lands to the Hamiltons who built the castle. It was destroyed after the Battle of Langside in 1568 because of the family's support for Mary Queen of Scots.
Other references: Roplock Castle

Renfrew Castle (*)
Renfrewshire
Ruin or site   OS 64   NS 510684
In Renfrew, just west of A741 (Ferry Road), just south of River Clyde.
Site of the 12th century castle of Walter Fitzallan, progenitor of the Stewart dynasty, and High Steward of Scotland. It was attacked by Somerled, King of the Isles, in 1164, but he was assassinated nearby before the castle was taken. It remained in use in the 15th century, and the ditch was visible in 1775. Nothing now remains.

Ridford Castle (*)
Renfrewshire
Ruin or site   OS 64   NS 455635?
Off minor roads north of A761, south of A737, 2.5 miles north west of Paisley, 0.75 miles west of Ferguslie Park, near Barskiven Hill.
Site of a tower house which appears on Bleau's Atlas Novus of the 17th century. It may have been a Hamilton property.

Ringsdale Castle (*)
South Lanarkshire
Ruin or site   OS 64   NS 750485
2 miles south of Larkhall, on minor roads north of A71, on west bank of Avon Gorge.
Site of a castle, of which only a few fallen stones remain.

Rochsoles House (*)
North Lanarkshire
Private   OS 64   NS 756678
Off minor roads 0.5 miles east of Glenmavis, 1 mile west of A73, 1 mile north of Airdrie.
A 19th century stable complex was formerly attached to Rochsoles House, home of the Gerard family. It probably replaced an earlier fortified structure of the Crawfords.

Rochsolloch Castle (*)
North Lanarkshire
Private   OS 64   NS 754649
1 mile south west of Airdrie town centre, south of A89, near Rochsolloch Road, at Rochsolloch Farmhouse, Victoria Place.
The renovated 19th century Rochsolloch farmhouse stands on the site of earlier structures. It is very likely that one or more of these were fortified.

The church owned the lands as part of its Monkland property. Rochsolloch was leased to a Crawford, who from 1547 was granted the powers of Baron Baillie in this parish. His seat was at Rochsolloch, using his own dungeon as gaol and holding courts in the house. The family retained these powers post-Reformation. In 1647 the estates and baronial authority passed to James Hamilton of Dalyell. The estate changed hands in 1685, going to John and Walter Aitchieson, and then by marriage to Mr Alexander of Kentucky.

Roplock Castle *see* Raploch Castle

Rosneath Castle (*)
The Lennox & East Dunbartonshire
Ruin or site   OS 63   NS 272823
1 mile south east of Rosneath, on minor roads east of B822, at south end of bay at Castle Point.
Site of a 15th century castle of the Campbells of Argyll. They owned the property from 1489. In 1633 it was remodelled as a more comfortable house, but burned down in 1802. A large elegant mansion of 1806 replaced it, and this was sold on the death of Princess Louise, dowager Duchess of Argyll, in 1939. It came into use as an administrative centre for the American Navy, who were based here during World War II, but was abandoned before being blown up in 1961. The site is now a caravan park.

Rossavon Castle *see* Ross House

Rossdhu Castle (*)

The Lennox & East Dunbartonshire
Private   OS 56   NS 361896
2 miles south of Luss, on west bank of Loch Lomond, on peninsula to east side of Rossdhu Bay, west of A82 at Rossdhu House, on Loch Lomond Golf Course.
A single high section of wall remains of a plain 16th century tower of the Colquhouns. It was visited by Mary Queen of Scots, and in 1602 James Colquhoun led his men to defeat against the MacGregors in the Battle of Glen Fruin. It was inhabited until 1770 and was used as a source of stone when Rossdhu House was built in 1774. Samuel Johnson and James Boswell visited during their *Tour of the Hebrides* though Lady Helen Colquhoun found the Doctor boorish and his manner insufferable.

Ross House

South Lanarkshire.
Private   OS 64   NS 739558
Just south east of confluence of Clyde and Avon rivers, 1.5 miles east of Hamilton.
A large tower here appears on Bleau's Atlas. It was part of the royal hunting forest of Cadzow in the reign of David I, but was granted to the monks of Kelso in 1222. It was given to a branch of the Hamiltons in 1339. These Hamiltons gained the parish of Carmunnock on the forfeiture of the Douglases in 1455.

Ross House

Hamilton of Rossavon had an important role in the passing of the Act of Reformation at the Scottish parliament, his chief the Earl of Arran being at the forefront of the Lords of the Congregation, who voted the 1560 Reformation through parliament. Another Hamilton of Rossavon had a role at the Battle of Drumclog. The family died out in 1856, and it came to the Aikman or Aitken family.

A Georgian mansion was built on the site in 1788, and a Scots baronial mansion replaced it in 1830. This remains occupied as a private residence.
Other references: Rossavon

Rossland Castle (*)
Renfrewshire
Ruin or site   OS 64   NS 442707?
1 mile north west of Erskine, off minor roads south of M8, 1 mile east of Bishopton, on north bank of Craigton Burn, at or near Rossland.
Site of a tower house which appears on Bleau's Atlas Novus of the 17th century.
Other references: Rostad

Ross Priory (*)
The Lennox & East Dunbartonshire
Private   OS 56   NS 415877
3.5 miles north east of Balloch, on southern shore of Loch Lomond, 1 mile north of Gartocharn, by minor roads north of A811, at Ross Priory.
Ross was a 14th century castle of the Buchanans, rebuilt as a mansion in 1693, and remodelled in 1810-16 by Gillespie Graham. Sir Walter Scott was a frequent visitor when writing *Rob Roy*. It is now owned by the University of Strathclyde.

Rostad Castle *see* Rossland

Ruglen Castle *see* Rutherglen

Rutherglen Castle (*)
South Lanarkshire.
Ruin or site   OS 64   NS 616618
In Rutherglen, 0.25 miles west of A749, and 0.25 miles east of A730, north of Main Street, just north west of junction of Castle Street and King Street.
Once a large and important royal fortress the last remnants of the foundations of Rutherglen Castle were removed in 1759 for the creation of a vegetable plot. It was a 13th century castle of enceinte with several towers, the walls being 5 ft thick.

The English held the castle during the Wars of Independence, and it was at the Old Kirk of St Mary nearby that Sir John Menteith was informed of William Wallace's hiding place at Robroyston and set off to make his infamous capture.

The castle was recaptured by the Scots for a while in 1309, and hosted a sitting of parliament, before recapture by the English. It was retaken by Edward Bruce, the king's brother and future King of Ireland, in 1313. Only the great tower survived when it passed to the Hamiltons of Elliston, lairds of Shawfield. They supported Mary Queen of Scots and as a result it was burned in

1569 by the Regent Moray in the aftermath of Langside.

A recent excavation prior to new housing development on part of the site, produced only a few shards of pottery.

Other references: Ruglen, Castle Ru

Rutherglen Castle – site

S

Semple Castle *see* **Castle Semple**

Shandon *see* **Faslane Castle**

Shieldhill (**)
South Lanarkshire
Private OS 72 NT 008407
About 3 miles north west of Biggar, on minor roads west of B7016, at Shieldhill.
A massive square keep, allegedly dating from as early as 1199, has been incorporated into a sprawling building dating mostly from the 16th century, but of various styles. It was extended in the 17th century and in 1820, and is now a hotel – see page 220.
   It was a property of the Chancellor family. It was at a fort nearby that William Wallace addressed his men before the Battle of Biggar.
   It is said to be haunted by the ghost of a daughter of one of the Chancellor Lords. She fell pregnant by a gamekeeper's son, and it is said that the child was born dead and taken from her, and in a cruel act was buried without her permission. She wept herself to death, and her ghost has been seen in recent years.

Snar Castle (*)
South Lanarkshire
Ruin or site OS 71 NS 863200
3 miles south west of Crawfordjohn, on minor roads and track south of B740, on east bank of Snar Water, at or near Snar Farm.
Site of a 16th century bastle house of the Douglases. The property appears on Bleau's Atlas Novus of the 17th century, and remnants remained in the 19th century.
   Douglas of Snar made his money from mining gold and lead.

Sir John de Graham's Castle *see* Graham's Castle

Stanely Castle (***)
Renfrewshire
Ruin or site OS 64 NS 464616
1 mile south west of Paisley, on minor roads west of B775, in Stanely Reservoir.
Originally surrounded by marsh, and now standing in water which floods its basement, Stanely is a ruined L-plan keep of the 15th century.

Internally the building is completely gutted. It was formerly of four storeys and a garret. The entrance is in the re-entrant, and the ground floor has several gunloops with circular eyelets at the base. There is a continuous corbel around the wall top which

Stanely Castle (McGibbon and Ross)

once supported the parapet, and rounded bartizans at each corner. At parapet level above the door the corbelling is machiolated. There are a variety of small windows on each floor.

Stanely was a property of the powerful Danzieltoun or Dennistoun family, and passed through one of the two heiresses to Maxwell of Calderwood, along with Newark, in 1402. The Maxwells built the castle, but sold it to Lady Ross of Hawkhead in 1629. It passed by marriage to the Boyle Earls of Glasgow in about 1750. In the early 19th century it was abandoned, and in 1837 the surrounding marsh was flooded to create the reservoir. It can be assumed that since McGibbon and Ross's time the water level has risen, since they described the site as being an island, whereas now the lower level of the building is completely flooded.

Stewart's Rais *see* Tower Rais

Stonebyres House (*)
South Lanarkshire
Ruin or site   OS 72   NS 838433?
2.5 miles west of Lanark, on minor roads west of B7018, and south of A744, just south of Stonebyres holdings.

Stonebyres House was a large castellated mansion of 1850, which encased a 15th century five storey tower. It was demolished in the mid 20th century.

The old keep occupied one end of the rectangular structure, and had been considerably modified to match its extension, sharing a

Stonebyres House (M&R) – demolished

201

new roof, and receiving corbelled out corner turrets and a centrally placed round stair turret in the gable from the second floor upward.

The walls of the keep were 8-9 ft thick, and it measured 34 ft by 29 ft, compared to the 34 ft by 70 ft of the completed mansion. The entrance was at ground level with an adjacent turnpike, within the wall, leading to the second floor. Across a landing another turnpike led to the floors above. Each floor had a single room, except the third, which was irregularly divided into two. The ground and second floors had small fireplaces, while the first, presumably the hall, had a larger example. The basement walls were pierced by gunloops, and the hall was famed as one of the finest in the country.

The De Veres or Weirs of Stonebyres held the property from the 15th century until 1845. It was sold to the Monteiths. It was remodelled and extended in 1840 and 1906-14, but pulled down in 1934.

Stonelaw Tower (*)

South Lanarkshire
Ruin or site   OS 64   NS 619609
Off Stonelaw Road, south of Greystone Avenue, off A749 or A730, Rutherglen.
An L-plan tower of four storeys, which is thought to have originated in the 15th century, was later extended by a T shaped single storey mansion, the supporting leg of the T extending out from the re-entrant, the remainder at right angles on either side of the main block. Photographic records show arrow slits on the open sides of the main block at fourth floor level, above which a corbelled out battlement with machiolations is evident around both wings.

Stonelaw Tower – remains

The tower was built by the Spens family, one of whom, General John Spens planted the surrounding woodland. Several members of the family became provosts of Rutherglen, and remained in possession for centuries. The last resident was a local Nationalist councillor, Alan Titson, who had it from the 1930s until 1963, when it was taken over by the Power Petroleum Company. It was then badly vandalised, and the company had it demolished in 1965. The postern gate with gunloops and a large part of the enclosing wall, and arrow slots, are all that remain. A filling station and a block of flats now occupy much of the site.

Strathaven Castle (**)

South Lanarkshire
Ruin or site OS 71 NS 703445
*Just south of the A71, east of
junction with A726, in
Strathaven.*

Standing upon a largely artificial mound above the village, Strathaven Castle consists of the remains of a large rectangular block with a round tower at one corner. Much of the north wall remains, and fragments of the others.

The building itself was rubble built and measured 70 ft by 38 ft running east to west. It was three storeys high and retains few original features. A fragment of corbelling remains, in a style dated to the fifteenth century. The four storey round tower sits at the north west corner, and there was a projecting wing at the south east corner. The round

Strathaven Castle

tower retains a selection of gunloops which are widely splayed externally, allowing a wider angle of fire. The basement was vaulted.

Excavations at the site uncovered part of the foundations of a surrounding wall and portions of the rest of the structure.

Strathaven, or Avondale, was a property of the Bairds, then the Sinclairs and Douglasses. At their forfeiture in 1455, the previous castle was sacked and surrendered to James II. It was granted to Andrew Stewart in 1457, an illegitimate grandson of the Duke of Albany. Stewart later became Lord Avondale and built or remodelled the present castle. In the 16th century the estate passed to Sir James Hamilton, 'the Bastard of Finnart'. It remained with the Hamiltons until 1717, when it was abandoned and fell into ruin. Accessible at all times – see page 220.
Other references: Avondale Castle

Strathblane Castle *see* Ballagan Castle

T

Tarbet Castle (*)
The Lennox & East Dunbartonshire
Ruin or site   OS 56   NS 209483?
At north end of Loch Lomond, east of A82, probably on Tarbet Island, 0.75 miles east of Tarbet.
Site of a 14th century castle of the MacFarlanes, also known as Claddach.
Other references: Claddach Castle

Tarbrax Castle *see* Torbrex Castle

The Lee (*)
South Lanarkshire
Private   OS 72   NS 854465
2.5 miles north west of Lanark, on minor roads south of A73, north of the Auchenglen Burn, at Lee Castle.
The Lee is a 19th century mansion, and possibly includes parts of an earlier castle of the Lockharts.

The family held the lands from as early as the 12th century, and legend asserts that they gained their name because Sir Simon Lockhart carried the key to the casket containing Bruce's heart when Sir James Douglas carried it on crusade. However, the family were already known as Loccard in the 12th century when another Simon and his brother Tancard, gave their name to the villages of Symington and Thankerton.

'The Lee Penny' is a healing amulet, consisting of a dark red gemstone set within a shilling. It was acquired by a member of the family while on crusade. It is said to heal bleeding, fever, animal ailments, and the bites of mad dogs (and, presumably, Englishmen!)

Alan Lockhart of The Lee was killed at the Battle of Pinkie in 1547, and George Lockhart of The Lee was an ardent Jacobite. The property passed from the family in the 20th century.
Other references: Lee Castle

The Orchard *see* Hamilton Palace

The Peel *see* Belltrees Peel

The Peel *see* Busby Peel

The Peill *see* Busby Peel

Thinacres (*)
South Lanarkshire
Ruin or site   OS 64   NS 737503?
1.5 miles west of Larkhall, on minor roads 3 miles south east of A723 and Meikle Earnock.
Probable site of a tower house of the 16th century, though references may have misled and mean the confirmed site at Plotcock, 0.25 miles south east.

Thorril Castle (*)
South Lanarkshire
Ruin or site   OS 72   NS 864309
2 miles east of Douglas on the east side of the A74, near Parkhall Burn, east of Parkhead at Thorril.
Foundations of a two storey 16th century bastle house were discovered during the 1990 M74 Fieldwork Project. A rectangular block stood within a courtyard.

Tighvechtichan Tower (*)
The Lennox & East Dunbartonshire
Ruin or site   OS 56   NN 312045
At or near Tarbet and Arrochar railway station, on minor road north of A83 at Tighvechtichan.
Site of a tower of the MacFarlanes manned to exact 'mail' from traffic on the drove road that traversed the glen.

Tillietudlem Castle *see* Craignethan

Todholes Castle (*)
South Lanarkshire
Ruin or site   OS 72   NT 038461
4 miles east of Carnwath, on minor roads north of A721, south of Weston, at or near Todholes.
Site of a castle, measuring 20 ft by 15 ft, within a ditch, which was demolished in the 19th century. Occupied by a family of Douglases in 1572, Todholes had passed to the Baillies by 1649.

Tollcross House (*)
City of Glasgow
Ruin or site   OS 64   NT 637637
Tollcross Park, Tollcross, off A89, to east and south Glasgow.
David Bryce built the present mansion for James Dunlop in 1848. It replaced a

Tollcross House

series of earlier houses, at least one of which may have been fortified.

The estate was granted to the family of Bishop William Corbett about 1242 by Alexander II, and remained with the family until sold to Dunlop in 1810. It passed to the city in 1897, being used as the centrepiece of the park (see page 220) until converted for use as special needs housing in recent years.

Torbrex Castle (*)
South Lanarkshire
Ruin or site   OS 72   NT 027552
Off minor roads west of A70, 7 miles north of Carnwath, at or near Tarbrax.
Site of a castle of the Somervilles, which had passed to Lockhart of Cleghorn by 1649.
Other reference: Tarbrax Castle

Torrance Castle (***)
South Lanarkshire
Private   OS 64   NS 654526
1.5 miles south east of East Kilbride, off A726 in Calderglen Country Park.
Torrance Castle is a sprawling mansion which preserves an altered keep, possibly of 14th century origins, at its eastern end.

The old castle is essentially a 16th century L-plan tower house of four storeys and a

Torrance Castle

garret with a tall square stair tower within the re-entrant. This contains a turnpike stair to all floors and a small room on each floor at the east side of the tower. Many alterations have taken place, includ-ing enlargement of the windows. This on the southern face gives the building a Georgian feel and appears similar to Auldhouse, although on a larger scale.

A porch has also been added at the main door, and an arched gateway. The new main door has the armorial stone re-moved from Mains Cas-

Torrance Castle

tle, which still supports the Royal Arms of Scotland.

This was a Hamilton property, but passed to the Stewarts of Castlemilk in the 18th century.

Once used to house the offices of the Development Agency of the new town, the mansion is now in private ownership and has been refurbished. The out-buildings house a visitor centre for the park – see page 220.

Tower Lindsay *see* Crawford Castle

Tower of Caldwell *see* Caldwell Tower

Tower of Hallbar *see* Hallbar Tower

Tower Rais
Renfrewshire
Ruin or site   OS 64   NS 511594
0.5 miles north of Barrhead, just west of Darnley Road (B773), 0.25 miles east of A736 junction, off lane.
Rais is an old Scots word for rise. This small square tower with vaulted base-ment was built prior to 1449 by the Darnley Stewarts to guard the important Levern ford. They later used it as a hunting lodge. Local romanticists associate it with Queen Mary, and name it unjustifiably Queen Mary's Castle. A ruin by

the time Richardson's map of Glasgow was published in 1796, it remained a familiar local landmark until a reluctant Burgh Council demolished it in 1932 to preserve the safety of the local children for whom it represented a romantic play area. At the time regret was expressed that the funds could not be raised to preserve the building.

Other references: Queen Mary's Castle, Stewarts Rais, Rais Tower

Tressmass (*)

The Lennox & East Dunbartonshire
Ruin or site   OS 64   NS 428753?
2 miles east of Dumbarton, on minor roads north of A82 and Milton, north of Loch Bowie, at Middleton.

This was the site of the original castle of the Colquhouns before they moved to Barnhill House in 1543. The parish was known as Colquhoun long before the family adopted the name as their own. They gained the Luss estates when one of their number married the heiress of Luss. The Lorane family became tenants for several centuries.

The castle was a ruin by 1810, when a wall 3ft thick and 7 to 8 ft high still survived to the north east of the farmhouse. By 1868 only foundations remained, and excavation revealed a 10 foot long length of wall which was 3 to 4 ft thick. Nothing now survives.

Milton village, as its name suggests, was the Mill Town of Colquhoun parish, and the remains of a large 18th century mill complex sit high above the village as a picturesque Gothic style ruin. Middleton was the Middle Town of the parish, and nearby are the remains of the 14th century chapel.

Other references: Middleton of Colquhoun, Milton of Colquhoun

V

Valence Tower *see* Bothwell Castle

Valence Tower, Bothwell Castle

W

Walkinshaw House (*)
Renfrewshire
Ruin or site   OS 64   NS 464666
2 miles east of Renfrew, at Glasgow Airport, off A726, near the meetings of Black Cart and Gryffe Waters, north of West Walkinshaw Farm.
Dungallus was granted the lands by Paisley Abbey in 1235. His descendants became the Walkinshaws of that Ilk. There was an early 16th century tower here, which was extended about 50 years later. In 1791 a mansion by Robert Adam replaced it, which was extended and renovated in 1825. It was demolished in 1927.

Wallace's Buildings (*)
Renfrewshire
Ruin or site   OS 63   NS 444632
In Elderslie, north of Johnstone, near A727, on south side of Main Street, 1 mile east of Black Cart.
A few foundations and a monument to Sir William Wallace are all that remain on the site of a 17th century building with vaulted basement and associated farm buildings. The house was demolished in the 1970s.

Ellerslie, later Elderslie, was a property of the Wallace family from the 13th century until 1850. This is alleged to be the birthplace of Scotland's national hero. Sir William's father was properly styled 'of Auchenbathie and Ellerslie', and a 17th century society claimed the site to be Ellerslie in Ayrshire, now long gone and over run by Kilmarnock. The Ayrshire claim is maintained to this day.

Sir William was the instigator and leader of the resistance movement in Scotland in the late 13th century. Their aim was to free the country from the English, who had invaded in 1296. Wallace led the Scots to victory at Stirling Bridge in 1297, but his army was heavily defeated at Falkirk the following year. He travelled in Europe, seeking assistance from the Pope. He returned to resume the fight for independence, but Wallace was betrayed to the English, and captured at Robroyston on the north eastern corner of the city of Glasgow, then sent to London for trial. He was hanged, drawn and quartered for treason, despite his argument that Edward I of England was not his king, and so it could not be treason. His head was set on a spike at London Bridge, and the parts of his body put on display in various towns in Scotland. His resistance was continued by Robert the Bruce, who was crowned king in 1306.
Other references: Elderslie

Wallans (*)
South Lanarkshire
Ruin or site   OS 72   NS 812487?
3 miles south west of Carluke, near A72 and River Clyde, near Overton.
Site of a castle, once on an island and used as a refuge by William Wallace.

Walston (*)
South Lanarkshire
Ruin or site   OS 72   NT 060455?
4 miles east of Carnwath, at Walston, 1.5 miles north of Elsrickle, off minor roads north and east of A721.
Site of a fortified house held in the 15th century by the Hepburns, which had passed by 1650 to the Baillies.

Waygateshaw House (**)
South Lanarkshire
Private   OS 72   NS 825484
4.5 miles north west of Lanark, and 2 miles south west of Carluke, on minor roads west of B7056 and east of A73, on east bank of River Clyde, at Waygateshaw.
Waygateshaw House is a 16th century courtyard castle, consisting of a 16th century tower house with 17th century wing. It has a modern block and a 12 ft wall which encloses the fourth side of a small court-yard. The entrance to the yard is through a moulded arched gateway which is guarded by gunloops. Over the entrance gateway stood the dog-like animals and a re-sited sundial, as described by McGibbon and Ross. These have been replaced by a pair of lions. Another pair in the form of a lion and li-oness in an alternative style stand over the later southern arched entrance. These are said to once have been the supporters of a large sundial which stood in the garden.
The tower house is rectan-

Waygateshaw House

211

gular, of three storeys and with a small stair wing. There was probably a parapet above with a garret, though these have gone. It now has a modern roof. The
walls have gunloops, one guarding the entrance to the yard, a second in the
northern wall, and a third guarding the entrance in the re-entrant. There are a
few small windows.

The basement is vaulted and consists of two chambers. In the wing a particularly steep turnpike stair reaches all floors. The hall is vaulted, and, as usual, is
on the first floor. Above this the room has been rebuilt to form a garret, lower
than the original, though the original fireplace has been remodelled to form a
window. The extension of the 17th century is of three storeys and a garret. There
is no vaulting, and an original fireplace on the second floor.

This was a property of the Murrays of Touchadam, though passed to by marriage to Alexander Lockhart in 1539. Stephen Lockhart was indicted in the
murder of Henry Lord Darnley in 1572. The family were forfeited for taking
part in the Pentland Rising of 1666, but later regained the estate. It was sold to
the Weirs in 1720, and then passed to the Steel family. It has been restored in the
1980s, though was burnt to a shell about ten years ago. It is in need of much
repair.

Wellpark House *see* Easter Greenock

Wester Greenock Castle *see* Greenock Castle

Wester Greenock Schaw Castle *see* Easter Greenock

Westhall Tower (**)

South Lanarkshire
Ruin or site   OS 72
NT 048473
*5 miles east of Carnwath,
on minor roads north and
east of the A721 from
Newbigging, 0.5 miles
east of Weston, at West-
hall.*
Only the once vaulted
basement remains of a
16th century L-plan
tower, possibly built by

Westhall Tower

the Grahams who acquired the lands in 1477. It later passed to the Hepburns,
Douglases, and the Lockharts. It was one of a series of nine towers within Dunsyre Parish, two of which apparently stood at Westhall, though the second was
more probably at Weston.

Weston (*)

South Lanarkshire
Ruin or site   OS 72   NT 043476?
5 miles east of Carnwath, on minor roads north and east of the A721 from Newbig-ging, at Weston.
Probable site of a castle, the second of two sites mentioned has having stood at Westhall.

Westshield (***)

South Lanarkshire
Ruin or site   OS 72   NS 946494
5 miles north east of Lanark, on minor roads north of A70, east of A706, west of B7016, just north of Mouse Water, at Westshield.
Westshield is a rectangular 16th century tower, extended by two 17th century gabled wings and a square stair tower in the re-entrant. Additional low wings were added, though later partly removed.

The tower now represents the eastern portion of the main block, extended length wise by one extension, while the other lies at right angles along the east gable creating an L-plan. All have corbiestepped gables, and enlarged moulded windows.

The original keep is built of rubble, and has four storeys and a garret. It may originally have had a parapet and wall walk, though now in keeping with the extensions, the roof extends to the wall head providing eaves. The wall head is decorated by a cornice, and there are a variety of chimney stacks with string coursing. The ground floor consists of three vaulted chambers, and an unvaulted room within the extension to the west. A turnpike stair within the stair wing rises from the entrance at the foot to all floors. The hall occupied the entire first floor of the keep. Bedrooms and private rooms utilised the floors above.

A poor example of a heraldic panel displays the arms of Denholm, the family who built the castle. It passed to the Lockharts of The Lee in the 17th century. The property is becoming ruinous.

White Castle (*)

South Lanarkshire
Ruin or site   OS 72   NT 018417?
4 miles south east of Carnwath, just south of B7016, at White Castle.
Site of a castle.

Windgate House (**)

South Lanarkshire
Ruin or site OS 72   NT 009297?
5 miles south west of Biggar, on minor roads south of A702, at Coulter, near Cow Gill Burn, on southern side of Lamington Hill, at or near Cowgill.
Windgate House is a small ruined bastle house of the 16th century with vaulted basement.

Wintercleugh House (*)

South Lanarkshire
Ruin or site   OS 78   NS 980114
4 miles south east of Elvanfoot, on minor road and track south of A702, near Wintercleugh Burn, 1 mile north east of Wintercleugh, east of Mid Height.
There are scant remains of a small tower house other than the basement. The foot of a turnpike stair remains in one corner, and the structure appears to have been burnt out. It had been abandoned by the 17th century.

Wishaw House (*)

North Lanarkshire
Ruin or site   OS 64   NS 790555?
In Wishaw, north of A721, 0.5 miles north of railway station, at south eastern corner of golf course, estimated site only.
Wishaw House was a mansion of the 18th and 19th centuries which had a building of 1665 at its core. An earlier house stood on the site, and it is possible that portions of this were also incorporated.

It was a property of the Hamiltons.

Woodhead Castle (*)

The Lennox & East Dunbartonshire
Ruin or site   OS 64   NS 606783
3.5 miles north east of Milngavie, south of A891, in the grounds of Lennox Castle Hospital, just west of 'Castle'.
Woodhead is a very ruinous 16th century tower house set on the edge of a precipice. It was built by the Lennoxes of Balcorrach, who were continually feuding with the Kincaid family. Curiously, they became one family, when a Kincaid married the Woodhead heiress, and adopted the name Lennox Kincaid. The Lennox family were descended from an early Earl of Lennox, and the grandson of the couple mentioned had staked a remote, and unsuccessful, claim to the Earldom. To show that he carried the wealth to back up his claim, he built Lennox Castle, a grand mansion next to Woodhead. He left Woodhead as a picturesque ruin. It is now so overgrown that it remains unseen until closely approached. There are few features remaining.

Some Sites to Visit

Many of the ruins described in the text are accessible with care but permission to visit sites on private property should always be sought and privacy respected. The following places are open to the public. Information should be checked with the sites themselves before undertaking any journey and inclusion is not an indication or recommendation that a site should be visited. Common sense should dictate at which sites particular care should be taken, especially with vehicle security and child safety.

Balloch Castle Country Park
Earthworks of castle in picturesque country park.
Park open all year; visitor centre Easter-Oct, daily 10.00-18.00
Explanatory displays. Visitor centre. Gift shop. Tearoom. Picnic areas. BBQ area. WC. Disabled facilities. Car parking.
Tel: 01389 578216

Bothwell Castle
Historic Scotland
Fine ruinous castle.
Open all year: Apr-Sep, daily 9.30-18.30; Oct-Mar, Mon-Wed and Sat 9.30-16.30, Thu 9.30-12.00, closed Fri, Sun 14.00-16.30; last ticket 30 mins before closing; closed 25-26 Dec and 1-2 Jan.
Explanatory boards. Gift shop. WC. Car and coach parking. £.
Tel: 01698 816894   Fax: 0131 668 8888

Cadzow Castle
Historic Scotland
Ruined castle in Chatelherault Country Park. Castle is currently being consolidated by Historic Scotland.
Park open the public except Christmas and New Year – castle view from exterior; visitor centre open Mon-Sat 9.00-17.00, Sun 12.00-17.00.
Chatelherault: Guided tours. Visitor centre. Explanatory displays. Tearoom. Picnic area. WC. Woodland walks. Garden. Disabled access to visitor centre and to some paths. Car and coach parking.
Chatelherault – Tel: 01698 426213   Fax: 01698 421537

Calderglen Country Park *see* Torrance Castle

Cameron House
Hotel
Hotel in a picturesque location on the banks of Loch Lomond.
Hotel & leisure centre – open all year.
96 rooms with ensuite facilities. Restaurants. Leisure facilities, including indoor pools. Marina. 9 hole golf course.
Tel: 01389 755565   Fax: 01389 759522

Cardross Manor House
NTS
Site of manor of Robert the Bruce
Access at all reasonable times.

Castle Semple Country Park
Country Park – Belltrees Peel
Castle Semple Country Park (part of Clyde Muirshiel Regional Park) is based around Castle Semple Loch, and there are woodland walks, sailing, canoeing, windsurfing and rowing. Ruin of church of the Semples are nearby.
Park open at all reasonable times; visitor centre open summer, daily 12.30-dusk; winter, daily 12.30-16.30.
Visitor centre. Cafe. Information centre. Picnic areas. BBQ. Limited disabled access. Car parking. £ (use of loch).
Tel: 01505 842882

Cathcart Castle
Fragmentary ruin in Linn Park.
Access at all reasonable times.
Children's zoo. Woodland walks. Special needs play area.
Tel: 0141 637 1147

Chatelherault *see* Cadzow Castle

Colzium Castle
Ruined castle. The gardens at Colzium include a fine collection of conifers and rare trees in a walled garden. 17th-century ice house and glen walk.
Walled garden open Easter-Sep, daily 12.00-19.00, Oct-Mar, Sat-Sun 12.00-16.00.
Tearoom. Picnic tables. WC. Glen walk. Ruins of castle. Arboretum. Curling pond. Clock theatre. Pitch and putt course. Kilsyth Heritage Museum. Disabled access. Parking. £ (pitch and putt only).
Tel: 01236 823281/0141 304 1800

Corehouse
Private House
Tudor Revival mansion, built in the 1820s for the Cranstouns. Nearby is
ruined Corehouse Castle.
Open for guided tours some days of the year – telephone for details.
Guided tours only. Parking. ££.
Tel: 01555 663126/0131 667 1514

Craignethan Castle
Historic Scotland
Fine ruined castle.
*Open Apr-Sep, daily 9.30-18.30; Oct-Nov, Mon-Wed and Sun, 9.30-16.30, Thu
9.30-12.00, closed Fri, Sun 14.00-16.30; last ticket 30 mins before closing.*
Exhibition and explanatory boards. Gift shop. Tearoom. Car parking. Group
concessions. £.
Tel: 01555 860364   Fax: 0131 668 8888

Crookston Castle
The National Trust for Scotland; managed by Historic Scotland.
Ruined castle.
Access at all reasonable times – collect key from keeper at bottom of path.
Basic torch and footwear recommended – a visit for the fitness fiend!
Tel: Keeper (Mrs McCourt) – 0141 883 9606/Historic Scotland – 0131 668 8800
Fax: Historic Scotland – 0131 668 8888

Culcreuch Castle
Castle/Hotel.
Hotel – open all year and to non-residents.
8 rooms with ensuite facilities. Restaurant and 2 bars. Meetings, functions,
weddings and parties. Gift shop. Self-catering lodges. Country park. Disabled access to function suite, ground-floor bar and WC, as well as ground-
floor bedroom. Parking.
Tel: 01360 860228   Fax: 01360 860556

Dalzell Country Park
Private house in country park
The house is not open to the public but there are woodland walks. There is
also Baron Haugh's Nature Reserve, an RSPB reserve.
Access at all reasonable times.
Disabled access.
Tel: 01698 269696 (RSPB reserve)

Darnley Castle
'The Mill' restaurant.
Restaurant. Parking.
Tel: 0141 876 0458

Dumbarton Castle
Historic Scotland
Spectacular stronghold from early times on north bank of Clyde.
Open all year: Apr-Sep, daily 9.30-18.30; Oct-Mar, Mon-Wed and Sun 9.30-16.30, Thu 9.30-12.00, closed Fri, Sun 14.00-16.30; last ticket 30 mins before closing; closed 25-26 Dec and 1-2 Jan.
Explanatory displays. Gift shop. WC. Car parking. Group concessions. £.
Tel: 01389 732167   Fax: 0131 668 8888

Finlaystone House
Mansion.
Grand mansion and gardens.
House open by appointment only; gardens and grounds open all year 10.30-17.00; visitor centre and refreshments open May-Sep, daily 11.00-16.30.
House: guided tours only. Visitor centre with Clan MacMillan exhibits, doll museum, and Celtic art display. Gift shop. Tearoom. WC. Gardens. Disabled access to ground floor and grounds and WC. Parking. £.
Visitor centre – Tel: 01475 540505   Fax: 01475 540505
Email: info@finlaystone.co.uk   Web: finlaystone.co.uk

Geilston House
The National Trust for Scotland
Gardens including walled garden and wooded glen – house not open.
Garden open Apr-Oct, daily 9.30-17.00.
Limited parking. £.
Tel: 0141 332 7133

Hallbar Tower (Tower of Hallbar)
Vivat Trust
Restored tower house.
Open all year: Sat 14.00-15.00 by appointment only; also four open days a year.
Limited parking. Limited disabled access. Holiday accommodation available.
Tel: 0171 930 8030   Fax: 0171 930 2295   Email: aniela@vivat.demon.co.uk

Hamilton Palace *see* Strathclyde Country Park

Kincaid House Hotel
Hotel
Tel: 0141 776 2226

Mugdock Castle
Ruined castle in country park.
Park open all year: summer 9.00-21.00; winter 9.00-18.00; visitor centre, daily 9.00-
17.00.
Explanatory displays. Visitor centre. Gift shop. Restaurant. Tearoom. Picnic
and BBQ areas. WC. Play areas and walks. Craigend stables and bridle
routes. Disabled access and WC. Tactile map. Car and coach parking.
Tel: 0141 956 6100

Newark Castle
Historic Scotland
Fine castle.
Open Apr-Sep, Mon-Sat 09.30-18.30; last ticket 30 minutes before closing.
Sales area. WC. Car and coach parking. Group concessions. £.
Tel: 01475 741858   Fax: 0131 668 8888

Palacerigg Country Park
Open Apr-Sep, Mon-Sat 09.30-18.30, Sun 14.00-18.30; last ticket 18.00.
Visitor centre with displays including natural history and peat cutting. Cafe.
Picnic area. BBQ. WC. Childrens zoo. Disabled access. Parking.
Tel: 01236 720047

Pollok House
Mansion in country park; managed by The National Trust for Scotland.
Fine mansion and museum in country park, which also has the famous
Burrell Collection.
Open house, shop and restaurant Apr-Oct, daily 10.00-17.00; Nov-Mar, daily 11.00-
16.00; closed 25-26 Dec and 1-2 Jan.
Guided tours. Gift shop. Tearoom. WC. Partial disabled access. Parking.
Tel: 0141 616 6410

Provanhall
The National Trust for Scotland: managed by the City of Glasgow Council. Open all
year by appointment except closed Dec 25/26 and Jan 1/2, and when special events
in progress.
Parking.
Tel: 0141 771 4399

Some Sites to Visit

Shieldhill
Castle/Hotel
Hotel – open all year and to non-residents.
16 rooms with ensuite facilities. Restaurant and bistro. Weddings, conferences, private parties and meetings. Parking.
Tel: 01899 220035   Fax: 01899 221092
Email: enquiries@shieldhill.co.uk   Web: www.shieldhill.co.uk

Strathaven Castle
Ruined castle.
Access at all reasonable times.
Explanatory board. Parking nearby.

Strathclyde Country Park
Site of Hamilton Palace. Orbistan.
Open all year, daily 7.00-22.45; closed Christmas and New Year
Guided tours. Visitor centre. Roman remains of bathhouse. Hamilton motte and mausoleum. Remains of mining village. Sailing. Fishing. Explanatory displays. Restaurant. Tearoom. Picnic areas. BBQ sites. WC. Woodland walks. Amusement park. Disabled access. Car and coach parking.
Tel: 01698 266155

Tollcross
Public park.
Access at all reasonable times.
Tennis. Gardens. International class swimming pool and sports centre.

Torrance Castle (Calderglen Country Park)
Visitor centre house in castle in country park.
Country park open all year; visitor centre open summer, Mon-Fri 10.30-17.00, wknds & public hols 11.30-18.30; winter months daily 11.30-16.00.
Guided tours by arrangement. Explanatory displays. Gift shop. Courtyard cafe. Snack bar. Picnic areas. Ornamental gardens. Wooded gorge and parkland. Children's zoo. Disabled access. Car and coach parking.
Tel: 01355 236644

Wallace's Buildings
Site (reputedly) of the birthplace of William Wallace.
Monument: access at all reasonable times.

Additional Sites

The following list comprises other likely sites. These have either not yet been confirmed as having fortified buildings, or simply require further research before a worthwhile entry can be facilitated. If any reader has further information regarding any of these sites, or other sites presently listed or unlisted, I can be contacted by letter via the publisher, or by e-mail:

gordonwmason@currantbun.com.

Also visit the web site at:

www.castlesontheweb.com/members/wurdsmiff/castles.htm

Site Name	Area
Auchenbowie	The Lennox & East Dunbartonshire
Baillieston	The City of Glasgow
Balvie	The Lennox & East Dunbartonshire
Blairtummock	The City of Glasgow
Blairvadach	The Lennox & East Dunbartonshire
Blantyre Old Place	South Lanarkshire
Blarrachneem	South Lanarkshire
Bothwellhaugh	North Lanarkshire
Camphill	City of Glasgow
Cander	South Lanarkshire
Carnwath Mill	South Lanarkshire
Castlebrocket	South Lanarkshire
Castlehill (Torrance)	The Lennox & East Dunbartonshire
Cormiston Towers	South Lanarkshire
Craigbet	Renfrewshire
Craighead	South Lanarkshire
Cumberhead	South Lanarkshire
Daldowie	The City of Glasgow
Drumchapel	The City of Glasgow
Drumhead	The Lennox and East Dunbartonshire
Dullers	South Lanarkshire
Gladstone	South Lanarkshire
Glengeith	South Lanarkshire
Hall of Kype	South Lanarkshire
Inchterf	The Lennox & East Dunbartonshire
Keppoch	The Lennox & East Dunbartonshire
Kilmardinny	The Lennox & East Dunbartonshire
Kirkhope	South Lanarkshire
Larabank	Renfrewshire
Little Clyde	South Lanarkshire
Middleton	Renfrewshire
Milliken	Renfrewshire
Old Yetts	North Lanarkshire
Parisholm	South Lanarkshire
Penwold House	Renfrewshire
Smithwood	South Lanarkshire
Tweedieside	South Lanarkshire
Waterside	South Lanarkshire
Westraw	South Lanarkshire
Whitefoord	South Lanarkshire

Glossary Of Terms

Arch A self supporting structure, usually rounded, though occasionally curved to a point at the apex. Used to support loads.

Arrow Slots Long vertical slots through a wall allowing use of a bow.

Ashlar Being of regularly sized and dressed block of stone, squared and even faced.

Attic Rooms within the roof space entirely below a gabled roof.

Aumbry Originally almry, a cupboard built within a wall, a recess usually above floor level used to carry sacred vessels for mass then later used domestically.

Bailey A secondary defensible area enclosed by a ditch and palisade, usually containing subsidiary buildings. Usually larger than the associated motte.

Barmkin A small defensive courtyard framed by the buildings of a complex and a linking wall.

Bartizan A projecting corner tower with roof, usually corbelled out and providing a watch room with enhanced views of the approaches.

Basement The lowest storey of a building, occasionally below ground level.

Bastle House A small fortified building, usually with byre or barn on ground floor, and domestic rooms on the floor above. Usually the strongest building of a group within farmstead or similar settlement.

Battlement A fighting area at the wall head, formed by a crenellated parapet and walkway.

Bay Window A projecting window at ground level, with squared or sharp corners.

Boreland Another term for the mains or home farm, supplying provisions for the castle.

Broch An early stone tower, with double wall and single narrow entrance. Had several wooden floors and a fighting platform or roof. Possibly used as a bolt hole when the community was under attack.

Caphouse A small watch chamber at a stair head, often providing access to a parapet walk, occasionally rising from within the parapet.

Caponier A stone shelter traversing a ditch from which covering fire could be given along its base, thus preventing it being crossed.

Caput Anciently the military, administrative and judicial centre of the barony; power base.

Castle A building containing defensive features as part of the architectural design. Range includes simply fortified house to the fortress of a noble family or royalty.

Castellations Battlements and turrets, this term usually applies when these features are added to enhance the appearance of a later unfortified mansion, and the features are purely decorative.

Classical Having features of design associated with Greek and roman buildings, such as pillars and pediments. An architectural style.

Conduit A channel through a wall, usually used as a drain for sinks or garderobes.

Corbiestepped from Scots corbie = crow. Squared stones forming a step sequence crowning a gable.

Corbel A projecting stone step used to support a protruding structure.

Cornice a decorative moulding filling the space below the eaves, or at a ceiling/wall join.

Courtyard Castle Usually built of stone, enclosed by a high wall which may be interrupted or surround the main buildings. In early examples the internal buildings were simple lean-to wooden structures. Later examples were normally large and politically important places.

Crenellated A battlement consisting of crenels and merlons, that is gaps and blocks spaced alternately giving the traditional appearance of a battlement.

Crowstepped See Corbiestepped.

Curtain Wall A high wall drawn around the area of a bailey or courtyard.

Diocese The administrative area supervised by a Bishop.

Donjon A keep representing the central stronghold of a larger courtyard castle.

Doocot A Scots word for dovecote or pigeon house.

E-Plan, T-Plan, L-Plan, X-Plan and Z-Plan Describing the shape of the building when viewed from above, and the letter that resembles.

Eaves The sheltered area below the overhang of a roof.

Enceinte An older term for curtain wall.

Entresol A secondary floor, often only partial, built out below ceiling or vault level to provide sleeping quarters, or a gallery for musicians.

Fosse A ditch.

Gable The end wall of a building, usually with triangular shape at roof level when a sloping roof is used. Associated in Scotland's early architecture with corbiesteps.

Garderobe A toilet usually built into the thickness of the wall, and usually draining to the outside by a chute.

Garret A small building upon the roof of a tower, separated from the wall head by a flat area or wall walk. Usually set within battlements.

Gothic A form of architecture characterised by narrow windows and pointed turrets, high pitched roofs and pointed arches. Lacking classical features.

Gunloop A hole built through a wall to allow the firing of muskets or small cannon, and with some variation such as external splays to allow the aiming of the weapon.

Hall house A long defensive building usually of two storeys with a hall above a basement. Often called a palace, palis or place in Scots.

Harled Roughcast and whitewashed.

Heraldic Panel A stone frame containing a carved stone or wooden representation of the coat of arms of the occupying family.

Keep The main tower or fortified building of a castle, the strongest building and final refuge, the administrative centre.

Machiolation A slot or space between overhanging stone work, usually corbels, allowing liquids or objects to be dropped upon assailants at the base of the wall.

Main Block The primary residence or structure of the castle. Usually contained the private rooms and hall of the resident lord.

Mains The home farm of the castle, see Boreland.

Moat Either dry or water filled, a deep surrounding ditch protecting the approaches to a castle or fortified enclosure.

Motte Corrupted to moat, though meaning the steeply sloped mound within a ditch upon which the main residence was sited in early timber and earth castles.

Motte and Bailey An early defensive system originating in Roman times. Consisting of a large raised area within a ditch, within which a second ditch surrounded a motte. Both areas were normally protected by a timber palisade, or stout defensive fence.

Moulding Ornamental work of continuous cross-section.

Mullion A vertical spar dividing a window.

Mural Within the thickness of a wall.

Newel The centre post of a spiral or turnpike stair.

Ogee Shaped by a double curve, bending in alternate directions. OG, shaped as the interface of these letters.

Oriel A bay window projecting out above ground level.

Palace, Palis, or Place The Scots term denoting a hall house.

Parapet The wall preventing a fall from a sudden drop, as at a wall head, usually in early Scottish architecture forming a defensive feature.

Parish In Scotland, the administrative area of the local church.

Peel Originally a court with palisade, later a small tower of wood and then of stone.

Pit Prison A cell within a wall, usually entered only from above by a hatch.

Portcullis A heavy wooden or iron gate which rose vertically to open, and guided by grooves in the wall.

Postern A secondary or minor gate, allowing a rear or side exit.

Re-entrant The internal aspect of a corner, where two buildings join at right angles.

Rib-Vaulting Where a vaulted ceiling is decorated or strengthened transversely by projecting stone in the form of ribs.

Round A roofless bartizan.

Royal castle Property of the Crown, usually held by a Keeper or Constable. Often administered by a Governor.

Scale and Platt A stair formed by short straight flights with small landings at the corners.

Shot Hole see Gunloop.

Steading (Scots) A small group of buildings forming a farm.

String Coursing A projecting thin line of moulded stone work, decorative in nature, which runs around the external walls.

Talus An outward sloping of the base of the walls, providing a wider more stable base for a structure on softer ground.

Tower House A self contained house with the rooms one on top of another. Usually there was a vaulted basement with the hall above, then private rooms on subsequent floors.

Transom A horizontal spar dividing a window.

Turnpike Stair A spiral stair formed around a central pillar or newel, usually very steep to give advantage to the defending swordsman at a higher level within. The direction of turn of the stair was decided so that the newel prevented a free swing of a sword when facing upstairs.

Turret A small tower attached to a larger building.

Vault A ceiling of stone use to prevent fire rising to the storeys above, and normally arched to bear the weight of the other floors.

Yett Scots word for a strong hinged gate, usually of interwoven iron bars.

Wall-walk A footpath along the top of a wall, usually protected by a parapet.

Watchroom A room at a stair head used as a look-out point for the approaches to the castle, larger than a caphouse.

Bibliography

The research of long disappeared castles usually involves many hours, or even days of searching through old local histories, library work and records departments. The following list comprises those volumes, which are more readily available and provide information on the more commonly documented sites and surviving structures.

The Castles of Scotland, 2nd Edn, Martin Coventry, Goblinshead 1997

Illustrated Maps of Scotland, from Bleau's Atlas Novus of the 17th Century, Jeffrey Stone, Studio Editions London, 1991.

The Queen's Scotland, The Heartland, Nigel Tranter, Hodder & Stoughton, 1971.

The Incomplete History of Castlemilk, Castlemilk Local History Group, pub. Workers Educational Association 1993.

The Fortified House in Scotland, Nigel Tranter, 5 vols James Thin, 1986

A Shorter History of Dunbartonshire, I. M. M. Macphail, Spa Books 1962

The Castellated and Domestic Architecture of Scotland, McGibbon & Ross, 5 vols. James Thin 1990

Scotland's Castles, Chris Tabraham, Historic Scotland 1997

Villages of Glasgow, Aileen Smart, John Donald, Vol. 1 1988, Vol 2 1996

Robert Bruce & The Community of the Realm of Scotland, Geoffrey W. S. Barrow, Edinburgh University Press, 1988

Scotland, A New History, Michael Lynch, Pimlico 1992

The Castles of Scotland, Maurice Lindsay, Constable, 1994

The Encyclopaedia of Scotland, Ed. J. & J. Keay, Collins 1994

Dumbarton Castle, I. M. M. Macphail, John Donald 1979

The History of Rutherglen and East Kilbride, Rev. D. Ure, Glasgow Press 1793

The Annals of the Parish of Lesmahagow, J. B. Greenshields, Caledonian, 1864

Discovering - The River Clyde, I. MacLeod & M. Gilroy, John Donald 1991

The South Clyde Estuary, F. A. Walker, RIAS, 1991

Glasgow's Rivers and Streams, Brotchie, 1914

Drumchapel, D. R. Robertson, John Wylie & Co, 1939

The Story of Bishopbriggs, J. A. Russell, Strathkelvin Dist. Libraries, 1979

A History of Cambuslang, J. A. Wilson, Jackson & Wylie, 1929

Eastwood District, History & Heritage, T. C. Welsh, Eastwood Dist. Libraries, 1989

Castles & Mansions of Renfrewshire, Millar, c.1899

Et al.

Family Index

Index

Index

Index